MODERN BRITISH FARCE

Modern British Farce

A Selective Study of British Farce from Pinero to the Present Day

Leslie Smith
Principal Lecturer in English
Polytechnic of North London

MACMILLAN
PRESS

First published in 1989

Published by
THE MACMILLAN PRESS LTD
Houndmills, Basingstoke, Hampshire RG21 2XS
and London
Companies and representatives
throughout the world

Phototypeset by Input Typesetting Ltd, London SW19 8DR
Printed in Hong Kong

British Library Cataloguing in Publication Data
Smith, Leslie, 1929–
Modern British Farce: a selective study
of British farce from Pinero to the present
day.
1. Farce 2. English drama—19th
century—History and criticism
3. English drama—20th century—
History and criticism
I. Title
822'.0523'09   PR635.F35
ISBN 0–333–44878–2

For Ken Cohen and Charles Tylee.

Contents

Preface

This book provides an introduction to an almost completely neglected area of modern British drama – farce. An obvious symptom of that neglect is the fact that a number of the plays discussed here are out of print: John Chapman's *Dry Rot* and *Simple Spymen*, and Colin Morris's *Reluctant Heroes;* others exist only in Samuel French or equivalent acting editions: Pinero's *Dandy Dick*, Ray Cooney's *Run For Your Wife*, Michael Pertwee's *A Bit between the Teeth*, and *She's Done It Again*. From time to time, a *Selected Plays* edition of a particular dramatist appears when a popular revival, especially if done at the National Theatre, confers a kind of 'classic' status on the writer: such was the case with the appearance of Ben Travers' *Five Plays* (Penguin) hard on the heels of the National's production of *Plunder*, and of Pinero's *Selected Plays* (Eyre Methuen) after successful revivals of *The Second Mrs Tanqueray* at the National, and of *The Magistrate* some years before at the Chichester Festival Theatre. But a proper collected edition, with notes, introduction, and stage-history, of Pinero's farces, or Travers's farces (there are, after all, more than five), or the Whitehall or post-Whitehall farces? Need it be said that one would search in vain for these, though they exist in plenty for many 'serious' contemporary dramatists?

Why? Perhaps it is the persistence of the critical snobbery, referred to in Chapter I, whereby farce is accorded an inferior status – coarse slapstick that is instantly forgettable. Recent writers have, it is true, sought to redress the balance: Katharine Worth, in *Revolutions in Modern English Drama*, has acknowledged farce's importance, and its contribution to more 'serious' drama; Jessica Davis, in her study of farce for the Critical Idiom series (Methuen), has rebutted some of the sillier generalisations; and Peter Davison, in *Contemporary Drama and the Popular Tradition*, has written perceptively of the cross-fertilisation that exists in modern drama between the so-called 'legitimate' theatre, and the 'illegitimate' popular tradition, as represented by music-hall, farce, melodrama and pantomime. But more work is needed in this area. Among individual dramatists, Joe Orton is taken seriously, because of the stylish wit of his language, and the subversive inventiveness he brought to farce; but he is an exceptional figure. Other dramatists – Ayckbourn, Stoppard, Shaffer – rate serious critical attention, but little notice is given specifically to farce in accounts of their work. There is no detailed or sustained discussion of the farces of Pinero, Travers, the Whitehall or post-Whitehall teams in any book on modern British drama, and no account which places their work in a continuing tradition of British farce on which many contemporary 'serious' dramatists have drawn.

Such an account, then, as is offered in this study, is long overdue. The farces in themselves merit analysis and discussion, not least to rebut some of the still current assumptions about farce's alleged 'meaninglessness' or its primitive naïvety. The increasing awareness in drama studies of the play as text for performance, and that what seems banal or inert on the printed page may come gloriously alive in the theatre, should make for a more receptive climate for a book on farce. It is, after all, as Leo Hughes says,

> involved far more directly and intimately in the business of the theatre than any other dramatic form.
>
> (Ch. 1, note 30)

There is also a salutary blow to be struck against the still existing class distinctions of modern drama as they affect farce, by placing the Whitehall and post-Whitehall farces at the centre of this study, and relating them to such earlier farces as those of Pinero and Travers, as well as to later farces produced by contemporary dramatists.

Throughout, a theme of this book is that farce is not as conservative a genre as is sometimes supposed; that, on the contrary, its practitioners have been extremely adept and skilful in experimenting with it and relating it to contemporary life. Farce, despite Shaffer's insistence to the contrary, has not 'been destroyed by the permissive society' (ch. 1, note 42). It has, in fact, taken on a new lease of life.

Though the book is not unmindful of theory, endeavouring to

test out generalisations concerning farce against specific examples, and to come to some conclusions concerning the nature of farce, its emphasis remains practical rather than theoretical: a descriptive analysis of plays which are central to any understanding of farce, and of which any generalisations that are made must take account.

The book is, finally, an introduction, not an exhaustive account. I have chosen to look initially at certain main sequences of farces associated with a particular dramatist or a particular theatre, and have not, therefore, found room for certain excellent pre-1950 farces, such as Brandon Thomas's *Charley's Aunt* or Phillip King's *See How They Run*.

In writing as much for the general reader and theatregoer as for the student and teacher of drama, I hope I may have been able to communicate some of my own enjoyment of the works discussed, and that this introductory study may prompt other critical work in this neglected area.

L.S.

Acknowledgements

I would like to record my gratitude to the following for the help I have received from them: the Faculty of Humanities Research Committee of the Polytechnic of North London for some remission of teaching hours to complete this book; the staffs of the British Library, the Polytechnic of North London library, the library of the British Theatre Association and the Westminster Reference Library.

The author and publishers wish to thank Methuen and Co Ltd, for permission to reproduce the extracts from the *Collected Plays* of Joe Orton.

Chapters 3 and 6 are revised and rewritten versions of articles which appeared in *Modern Drama* (vol. XXVII, no. 3, Sept. 1984) and *Adam International Review* (nos 394–6, 1976). I am indebted to the editors, Jill Levenson and Miron Grindea for permission to use this material.

Finally, I would like gratefully to acknowledge the stimulus, encouragement and help I have derived from friends and students (particularly those on the Modern Drama Studies course at the Polytechnic of North London) with whom I have discussed the plays and playwrights dealt with in this book.

1

The Nature of Farce

Jonathan Culler, in *Structuralist Poetics*, argues that part of the basis on which we make sense of texts is 'by the existence of the genre, which the author can write against . . . (and) which is the context within which his activity takes place'.[1] Genre helps to create the contract between reader or spectator and writer, the frame of acceptance which allows us to experience the work in an appropriate way. One of its functions is to establish the *vraisemblable*, what is permitted to happen in a work of art. For example, stereotypes, unlikely coincidences, frenetic activity are to be expected in the world of farce but are unlikely to occur in a naturalistic drama. At the same time it is important to remember, as Heather Dubrow points out, that

> a writer may deliberately confound our tentative assumptions
> about the genre in which he is writing, or a work that is essen-
> tially in one literary form may include episodes in or allusions
> to many other literary forms as well.[2]

As to the first, Ayckbourn, in *Bedroom Farce*, arouses expectations in his title which are confounded in the actual events of the play, since none of the three bedrooms on stage is ever used for the activities we traditionally expect in farce. As to the second, Act II of Pinero's *Dandy Dick* (the Dean's temptation scene) quotes from and uses elements from the world of melodrama; and one function (not the most important) of 'Truscott of the Yard' in Joe Orton's *Loot* is to parody the genre of detective fiction (particularly the Sherlock Holmes stories of Conan Doyle):

> My methods of deduction can be learned by anyone with a keen
> eye and a quick brain. When I shook your hand I felt a rough-
> ness on one of your wedding rings. A roughness I associate
> with powder burns and salt. The two together spell a gun and

1

sea air. When found on a wedding ring only one solution is possible.

(p. 214)

Dubrow also reminds us that the boundaries between genres are not clearcut:

> A particular work of art may conform to a single clearcut generic pattern and in so doing resemble, as it were, a primary colour. . . . Or it may move between distinguishable but related genres as, say, *The Faerie Queene* does, and hence remind us of intermediate colours like yellow-green.[3]

Hence, of course, the difficulty of generalisation concerning the salient characteristics of any specific genre.

In this account of modern British farce, I have chosen to discuss plays which do unmistakeably display that primary colour. But even here the pattern is by no means always simple and clearcut. Assumptions about the way farces end, or the primacy of action over language in the genre, are very much open to question. Thus wit and elegance of language *can* co-exist with the frenetic activity of farce, and certainly do so in the work of Pinero and Orton. One legitimate way of describing this is as movement between related genres – farce and comedy of manners (and David Hirst, in *Comedy of Manners*, studies Orton's work in this context[4]). I would prefer, however, to combat the often met assumption that the dialogue in farce is totally unmemorable (an assumption that usually goes hand in hand with the idea that the physical action also involves only coarse buffoonery) by putting the emphasis instead on the sophistication of which the genre is capable, both in its action and its language. There is a linguistic resourcefulness and variety of humour available to the farce writer, evident in Ayckbourn, Shaffer, Cooney and Chapman as well as in Pinero and Orton, and taking a number of different forms, of which the elegant repartee of Orton is only one.

For it is true, as Jessica Davis's book on farce well documents, that the genre has, in general, been looked down upon and held in low esteem by critics and writers. John Dryden, in his Preface to *An Evening's Love* (1671) castigated it for grimaces . . . forced humours and unnatural events . . . what is monstrous and chimerical.

Thomas Wilkes, in *A General View of the Stage* (1759), repeated Dryden's criticisms, saying that farce was

fit only to entertain such people as are judges neither of men nor manners.

In our own century, L. J. Potts has labelled it 'comedy with the meaning left out';[5] Allardyce Nicoll refers to its 'gross and improbable characterisation';[6] and Cleanth Brooks and R. B. Heilamn insist that

the situations in farce do not mean anything . . . farce is by its own nature one-dimensional . . . commonplace. Any farce . . . fails, by being fundamentally off-centre, to challenge greatness, or even seriousness.[7]

There have been, it is true, some honourable exceptions to this depressing view of the genre, voiced chiefly by men of the theatre rather than critics. Nahum Tate makes a spirited defence of it in the Preface to *A Duke and No Duke* (1693)

I know not by what Fate it happens (in common Notion) to be the most contemptible sort of Drama.

So did David Garrick, whose writing of and acting in farces gave the genre the kind of support it had often lacked in the past. Garrick would often round off an evening of tragedy in which he had played King Lear or Richard III, with a farcical afterpiece to demonstrate his versatility, rather as Sir Laurence Olivier did in his celebrated double bill of Sophocles' *Oedipus Rex* and Sheridan's *The Critic*. Nearer our own day, the great Russian actor and director, Meyerhold came to regard farce and pantomime as the theatre's life blood:

The idea of the actor's art, based on a worship of mask, gesture and movement, is indissolubly linked with the idea of the farce. The farce is eternal.[8]

But in general farce has not been well thought of, and it is worth considering briefly why this should be so.

There are of course bad farces, as there are bad tragedies, bad comedies, bad plays of all kinds. And that inveterate theatre-goer of the 90s who became one of our greatest dramatists, G. B. Shaw, complains sharply of the stale plot devices of conventional late 19th-century farce:

> We have had it again and again under various titles: Act I, John Smith's home; Act II, the rowdy restaurant or casino at which John Smith, in the course of his clandestine spree, meets all the members of his household, including the schoolboy and the parlourmaid; Act III, his house the next morning, with the inevitable aftermath of the complications of the night before; who that has any theatrical experience, does not know it by heart?[9]

Shaw, in his impatience with the genre, is here inclined to underestimate the extent to which even conventional or stale plot devices can be freshly and imaginatively handled; and indeed, his own *You Never Can Tell* is a case in point. But, in any event, hard cases do not make good law, and Shaw's attack is directed at the hard cases. There are, however, as Jessica Davis, in her study of the genre, points out, two factors which may have worked against farce, and contributed to its being undervalued.[10] In the first place, it was a latecomer to dramatic terminology, and unsanctioned by classical authority. When the term does come into critical use in the Renaissance and Augustan periods, there is a frequent attempt to equate it with 'low life', on an extension of the supposedly Aristotelian principle of distinguishing between tragedy and comedy on the basis of the social level of the characters. Fielding begins the Prologue to his play *Lottery* (1732):

> Comedy delights to punish fools,
> And while at nobler game she boldly flies,
> Farce challenges the vulgar as her prize.

Thus the idea of characters of a low social status, and a general coarseness of language and manners attached itself, quite unjustifiably, to farce. A second factor that may have worked against farce was that it was often used as a comic 'filler' to an evening's programme. The name is actually derived from the Latin, 'farcire', to stuff, and the word 'farce' or its modernised form, remains in both French and English as a rather old-fashioned term for a stuffing for meat and other food – as in forcemeat. A related point is that farce always found a ready home in other dramatic forms. It was often one ingredient in a play, and served as a foil to a serious theme, or to a different kind of comedy: as happens, variously, with Mak's sheep-stealing, in the Towneley *Secunda Pastorum*, the Politick Would-be sub-plot of *Volpone*, the madhouse sub-plot of *The Changeling*. It is in the nature of foils to be seen as subservient. And it may be that in distinguishing it from comedy, too much emphasis came to be placed on 'the more exaggerated characterisations, the cruder coincidences, and the grosser pieces of joking,' as belonging to farce, leaving 'the more sophisticated elements of plot, character and theme' as belonging to comedy.[11]

Thus a kind of inferior status becomes accepted for farce; and something of that inferior status creeps into various attempts to define the nature of the genre. Jessica Davis, quoting the *Oxford English Dictionary's* definition, 'a dramatic work, (usually short) which has for its sole object to excite laughter' supplements it with reference to 'broad, physical, visual comedy, whose effects are pre-eminently theatrical and intended solely to entertain; comedy which is slapstick if you like, in a more or less coherently funny narrative'.[12] *The Oxford Companion to Theatre* declares that 'the word farce is applied to a full-length play dealing with some absurd situation hinging generally on extra-marital relations; hence the term, bedroom farce'.[13] The *Encyclopaedia Britannica's* definition of farce is that it is 'a form of the comic in dramatic art, the object of which is to excite laughter by ridiculous situations and incidents, rather than . . . by the delineation of the play of character upon character, which is that of comedy'.[14] And J. M. Brown, in the *Saturday Review of Literature*, writes,

Farceurs belong to a race apart. They have as little in common with comedians as comedians have with tragedians. The sky is the limit so far as they are concerned. No holds are barred. Every trick or stunt is legitimate if only they can get away with it. And why not? The sole point and justification of a farce is that it be funny. It is a comedy written with a slapstick rather than a pen. Its business is to make us accept the impossible as possible, the deranged as normal, and silliness as a happy substitute for sense.[15]

These attempted definitions and descriptions are acceptable and useful in certain respects, but all generalisations require qualification, and in some respects what is quoted here can be actively misleading. Thus a recurrent feature of the definitions is the assumption that the 'sole object' of farce 'is to excite laughter'; the *sole* point of a farce is that it be funny . . . and make us 'accept silliness as a substitute for sense' (my emphasis). Such statements seem designed to warn us off the idea that farce has any serious significance, or that what prompts laughter is in itself worth examining. Yet, as Jessica Davis reminds us, there is an essential human predicament embodied in farce;

> Comedy is drawn from the most human of strivings: our continual impulse to rebel against convention and morality and our continued efforts to master our own bodies and our physical environment. Most often, the joke entails the failure of the attempt, but it is a failure which must also touch the audience, since the joke is on us all as members of the human race.[16]

Man's spirit is trapped within and must express itself through man's body. Small wonder, then, that there are connections between Farce and Theatre of the Absurd. Norman Shapiro, in his Introduction to a translation of four Feydeau farces, writes of the common ground shared by Feydeau and Ionesco; of how both dramatists project

> the aimlessness and unpredictability of man's fate in a haphazard (or at least inexplicable) universe, in which things – mainly base – will happen to him for no obvious or compelling reason.[17]

The cabin-scene in the Marx Brothers film, *A Night at the Opera*, in which more and more people and objects come crowding into a ship's cabin, could thus be related to Ionesco's *Le Nouveau Locataire*, in which the tenant is finally buried under the unending stream of furniture. Ionesco, indeed, in a response to a question on literary influences, declared that the three biggest influences on his work had been Groucho, Chico and Harpo Marx.[18] There are connections also between farce and tragedy, and Rhymer perhaps wrote more perceptively than he realised in *Tragedies of the Last Age* (1677) when he labelled the tragedy of *Othello*, 'none other than a bloody farce without salt or savour'. Farcical situations are, indeed, often tragic situations back to front, or tragic situations viewed in a bizarre light. Walter Kerr invites us to imagine how an audience would react if, in Sophocles' *Oedipus at Colonus*, the blinded Oedipus, expelled from Thebes for marrying his mother and killing his father, had met another man precisely like himself, a second man who'd married his mother and killed his father.[19] Immediately the situation would become laughable, material for farce rather than tragedy. A relevant modern example of this occurs in Joe Orton's *What the Butler Saw*. Orton admitted to being influenced by Strindberg;[20] and both the business of the strait-jackets in this play, and the tormented marital relationship of Dr Prentice and his perpetually sex-starved wife, owes much, I would suggest, to Strindberg's *The Father*. But Orton, by multiplying the straitjackets in Act II, and adding some lunatic touches to the Prentices' marriage – Mrs Prentice is allowed to attend a 'coven' of lesbians because Mr Prentice counts as a woman, applies the surrealist and anarchic techniques of farce to material, which, in Strindberg, is treated as 'straight'. Material that is painful, intolerable, tragic in real life can be used by the farce-writer for his own humorous purposes. The scene in Act II of Alan Ayckbourne's *Absurd Person Singular* where Eva Jackson successively tries, with ever increasing incompetence, to kill herself, by jumping from a window, taking an overdose, putting her head in the gas-oven, hanging herself, swallowing paint-stripper, while life goes bumbling on around her, oblivious of what she is trying to do, is a classic example of the dramatist using the most painful material, not with heartless frivolity, but to make a comment, or achieve a cathartic release through laughter.

I referred above to the concealed assumption in many definitions of farce that the laughter farce arouses is unworthy of analysis; that it is a crude response to coarse buffoonery. On the contrary, it is as important to consider why we laugh at a good farce, as to examine why we are moved by a great tragedy. What often fuels that laughter is the capacity farce has for acting out and giving expression to our wilder and more anarchic imaginings and impulses. 'The victories of farce register vital revolts against reason's heavily regulative hand', writes Morton Gurewitch.[21]

Freud, in *Jokes and their Relationship to the Unconscious* (1904), pointed out how the fantasies of humour bypass taboos, permit more primitive underlying impulses to express themselves in ways which the conscious mind would forbid. 'Like dreams,' says Eric Bentley, 'farces show the disguised fulfilment of repressed wishes.'[22] There is a release of inhibitions, a holiday from conventional morality; the carnival spirit is triumphant and outrage is permissible. Harpo Marx puts Eric Bentley's point in more graphic terms:

> People all have inhibitions and hate them. We just ignore them. Every man wants to chase a pretty girl if he sees one. He doesn't, I do. Most people at some time want to throw things round recklessly. They don't, but we do. We're sort of a safety valve through which people can blow off steam.[23]

But if merriment and pleasure, the release of inhibitions, is one side of the coin, unease and disquiet is the other side of the coin. If the pleasure of joking, as Jessica Davis points out, is 'partly festive', it is also 'partly aggressive (and) such a combination of elements, festive and aggressive, has been shown to characterise the fertility rituals which lie at the roots of dramatic comedy'.[24] In the Roman Saturnalia, the Medieval Feast of Fools, authority is mocked, roles reversed; there is a very real aggressiveness at work. 'Without aggression,' writes Eric Bentley, 'farce cannot function'.[25] And he takes an example from one of Chaplin's films, partly because Chaplin, unlike W. C. Fields, is generally regarded as a less aggressive farceur than others. Not so, says Bentley; admittedly

> he *seemed* less violent because he put the violence in the other characters . . . but the Tramp of Chaplin is not exclusively masochistic. He is also a sadist. One remembers what happened in *The Kid* when Charlie finds himself literally holding the baby. By all means he is going to become a charming and sentimental foster-father, but as he sits there with his feet in the gutter he notices an open drain, and he has almost thrown the baby down it before sentiment comes again into its own. It is by touches like that – and never by sentiment alone – that Chaplin has shown himself a great comic.[26]

Groucho Marx is another good example. Groucho writes of the difference between the amateur and the professional comedian. An amateur thinks it's funny if you dress a man up as an old lady, put him in a wheel chair, and give the wheel chair a push that sends it spinning down a slope towards a stone wall. But, to make it funny for a professional, asserts Groucho, 'it's got to be a real old lady'.[27] There is a core of ruthlessness, a demonic energy, in the best farce, that that observation points to accurately enough. Jessica Davis would seem to get her emphasis somewhat wrong, when, in examining 'what kind of joking is characteristic of farce', she characterises it as joking that 'invites laughter by the violation of social taboos (but) avoids giving offence . . . adhering to a balanced structure in which the characters and values under attack are ultimately restored to their conventional positions'. The aggression, she goes on to suggest, has to be 'both sufficiently precise to be psychologically valid and yet sufficiently delimited to qualify as play'.[28] Such a neat balancing act between the festive and aggressive impulses, tidy though it be, suggests a final cancelling out and neutralising effect which seems to go contrary to the true spirit of farce. One cannot really imagine a W. C. Fields, a Groucho Marx, a Feydeau, a Joe Orton, saying to themselves, 'I've gone too far . . . I must delimit my aggression . . . I must restore the status quo, in order to avoid giving offence.' It is true, as a matter of observation, that many, though by no means all, farces end with a return to normality. But is it much more than a token restoration of order, a precarious patched-up truce in the perennial fight against the forces of disorder? Isn't what often remains more vividly in the imagination, the darker or wilder events that have preceded it? I would suggest that the best farce leaves us with the troubling thought – what if disorder is the norm, anarchy and chaos do prevail, and the Lord of Misrule has taken over, not just for a festive two hours of make-believe, but indefinitely?

If we turn now to what the definitions have to say concerning the techniques and subject-matter of farce, it will be to note Jessica Davis's reference to 'broad, physical visual comedy, whose effects are pre-eminently theatrical', the OED's reference to 'some absurd situation, hinging generally on extra-marital relations', the *Encyclopaedia Britannica's* 'ridiculous situations', and J. M. Brown's assertion that (farce's) 'business is to make us accept the impossible as possible, the deranged as normal'. Jessica Davis's statement is misleading if we go on to assume, as she seems to, that 'verbal and literary artifice is overwhelmed by physical action in farce.'[29] Pinero, Orton, Ayckbourn, Stoppard all offer testimony to the contrary. And there is often a verbal agility in the dialogue and repartee of a good farce that corresponds to the physical agility sometimes required by the actors. The theatricality of farce is, however, quite rightly stressed, a point Leo Hughes also makes when he insists that farce is 'involved far more directly and intimately in the business of the theatre than any other dramatic form . . . it cannot profitably be thought of apart from the theatre in which it was produced'.[30]

This involvement may take the form of a close association between the farce-writer or writers and a team of actors performing in a particular theatre. Pinero's farces were associated with the Royal Court in the 1880s; Ben Travers with the team of Tom Walls, Ralph Lynn and Robertson Hare at the Aldwych in the 1920s; Michael Pertwee, John Chapman and Colin Morris with Brian Rix's Whitehall team in the 1960s. The involvement is also, of course, demonstrated in the peculiar importance attaching in farce to stage business; to timing, movement and gesture, to the use of stage space. On gesture, Peter Shaffer has said, with reference to his own farce, *Black Comedy*, that 'it's almost all gesture. You could almost put plate glass between the audience and the stage and still something comic would emerge from the acted play'.[31] This is certainly true of the major piece of comic choreography in Act II in which most of the room's furniture has to be returned to a neighbouring room during a black-out without the owners of the furniture or various guests being made aware of the fact. The near catastrophes that result can be savoured by an audience, though invisible to the actors, because of the reversed light/darkness convention Shaffer establishes from a moment early in Act I when there is a power failure and the lights come on rather than switch off. Movement in farce, moreover, is often stylising or patterned movement, as the following stage directions suggest:

HAROLD, CLEO and BRINDSLEY . . . *cross their legs in unison.*
(Shaffer's *Black Comedy*, p. 36)

Salome seizes (the Dean's) *hands, Sheba his coat tails and turn him round violently*, (and when joy has turned to dismay) *Sheba sits aghast on the table, Salome distractedly falls on the floor.*
(Pinero's *Dandy Dick*, p. 73)

In Stoppard's *Dirty Linen*, every time Maddie Gotobed bends over to reveal a glimpse of cleavage or buttocks the action 'freezes' and a light flashes, creating the effect of a press-photographer filming a pin-up pose. Pieces of stage business, difficult to visualise in reading farce, come alive with hilarious effect in performance, as for example, Ronnie's Laocoonian struggle to help Hook on with his overcoat in Ben Travers *Thark*, Dr. Prentice's continual offerings of cut flowers to his wife in Orton's *What the Butler Saw*, the business of the disembodied arm offering plates and dishes from behind a curtain in Pinero's *The Magistrate*. The skills called for in the actor in farce are clearly considerable; and it is a matter of more than timing, verbal and physical agility. Nothing kills farce more surely than any kind of rib-nudging determination to be funny on the part of the actor. A straight face and the utmost seriousness is essential. 'Nobody', said Ben Travers in tribute to Ralph Lynn, 'ever appreciated as well as Lynn how intensely serious is the job of being funny.'[32] Finally, clothes, costume, dressing and undressing, and props of all kinds assume key importance in farce. The straits to which Posket's midnight adventures have reduced him in *The Magistrate* are signalled by the unfortunate red necktie he has to don in Act III. The cocktail cabinet in Cooney and Hilton's *One For the Pot*, the do-it-yourself dressing table in Ayckbourn's *Bedroom Farce*, the discarded knickers of Stoppard's *Dirty Linen* – all have important parts to play in the action. A French theatre critic and contemporary of Feydeau's, Sarcey, even went so far as to say, 'In a play by Feydeau no character comes into a room and puts his hat on a chair without my telling myself, Aha! you can bet that hat wasn't put there for nothing!'[33] In farce, objects often seem to acquire a life of their own, and the intractable impediments of the physical world offer an obstacle course to the characters. The cabin scene in the Marx Brothers' *A Night at the Opera*, to which I have already referred, provides a classic example.

The definitions also referred to absurd and ridiculous situations, and to the farce-writer's ability to make us accept the impossible as possible. The starting point in farce may be normality; but that normality is pushed further and further towards absurdity, anarchy, even nightmare. Once a hostage to fortune is given, accident and mischance multiply. The accelerating momentum of the plot, what Bergson refers to as the 'snowball effect',[34] which engulfs all the characters, is a typical feature of good farce, bringing with it a sense of danger. 'Danger', writes Bentley, 'is omnipresent. One touch, we feel, and we shall be sent spinning in space.'[35] Ionesco, noting a resemblance between his own work and Feydeau's, found the likeness 'not in the subject-matter, but in the rhythm. In the organisation of a play like *A Flea in her Ear* (*La Puce à L'Oreille*), for example, there is a kind of acceleration of movement, a progression, a kind of madness. In it one might discover the essence of theatre, or at least the essence of the comic. . . . For, if Feydeau pleases, it is not for his ideas (he has none), nor for the stories of his characters (they are silly); it is this madness, this seemingly regulated mechanism, that, however, comes apart through its very progression and acceleration'.[36] But it comes apart, let us note, only under the watchful eye, and controlling brain of the dramatist. As Feydeau put it, 'When I am arranging all that madness that unleashes the spectators glee, I am not amused by it. I keep the cool calm poise of the chemist measuring out his medicine.'[37] If we are to be carried along on farce's journey into anarchy, we must be persuaded by the logic of each successive step along the way, even if the final result seems supremely illogical. The masters of farce have all been masters of technique, able to structure absurdity, work the successive discoveries, reversals, coincidences, and repetitions of farce into an intricate and completely satisfying pattern. Farce, as Booth puts it, is 'the disciplined expression of anarchy, the logical presentation of a crazy world'.[38] Shaffer's early stage-direction in *Black Comedy*, precisely delineates that controlling sense of design, that 'disciplined expression of anarchy' which his farce so successfully demonstrates:

> *The Boy's look is cool; narrow, contained and sexy. Throughout the evening, as things slide into disaster for him, his crisp, detached shape degenerates progressively into sweat and rumple, just as the elegance of the room gives way relentlessly to its usual near-slum appearance. For the place as for its owner, the evening is a progress through disintegration.*
>
> (p. 5)

Black Comedy provides one example; Pinero's *The Magistrate*, provides another – in particular Act II, in the successive confusions and revelations at the Hôtel des Princes, where all the characters who should not under any circumstance meet, do meet under appropriately compromising conditions: here we have that sense of the 'logical presentation of a crazy world' which is the peculiar province of farce.

There is, finally, something peculiarly satisfying about formal control exercised to promote anarchic confusion, the extraordinary mixture of madness, with the most rigorous logic. And the recognition of this lies behind such tributes as John Russell Taylor's to Feydeau, 'the craft becomes art . . . a triumph of pure style'.[39] or Beatrice Dusanne's even greater compliment to the same dramatist: 'There are moments when the progression of an act of Feydeau offers the same secure feeling of satisfaction in surprise as the workings of a Bach fugue.'[40] Given the meticulous sense of pattern, it is not surprising that nothing can be altered, as producers of Feydeau have discovered to their cost. Jacques Charon says,

> Once I left out a couple of instructions which I thought were unimportant. A few scenes later the whole play toppled, the plot came askew. Not only every word of dialogue by Feydeau but every gesture is carefully thought out by the author.[41]

There is one issue, not touched on in the definitions listed at the beginning of this chapter, that is of particular relevance to a study of farce which begins with a late Victorian practitioner, and ends with such contemporary practitioners as Orton, Ayckbourn and Stoppard: that is the question of whether a society more settled in its views of law, order and morality than our own provides a climate of opinion more favourable to farce. Farce's cathartic release, it has been argued, is less necessary in a 'liberated' society, whatever the term 'liberated' means. Thus, Peter Shaffer alleges that 'farce has been destroyed by the permissive society'.[42] And his opinion is echoed by a critic, R. W. Corrigan, introducing a selection of classical farces:

> As more liberal sexual attitudes develop, farce has tended to move to other realms. . . . Talking to some of my students about the subject of farce, I discovered that they did not find the bedroom variety very funny. Sex, they said, was increasingly a take it or leave it matter for most of their generation, and they were neither outraged nor titillated by it when it was represented in the theatre. They even went on to admit that they had actually acted out most of their sexual fantasies – at

least all of those which with even a modicum of taste could ever be presented on the stage. Money, business, bureaucratic power and the system – these, they insisted, were the widely held values of our time and hence the more appropriate subject matter for farce.[43]

Farce, more than Corrigan's students allow for, has always mocked 'the system' and though the bedroom variety that Feydeau made popular in the late 19th century, and which comes down to us through Ben Travers, the Whitehall farces, and *No Sex Please, We're British*, does centre on wives and mistresses, infidelity and cuckolding, sexual themes have often co-existed with political or social themes, from Aristophanes' *Lysistrata* to Joe Orton's *Loot*. But the assumption underlying Shaffer's comment, and Corrigan's, is, certainly, that farce functions best in a repressive or convention-ridden society such as, say, late Victorian or Edwardian England, where its fantasies and fun can act as a safety-valve, a pleasurable release of feelings in the audience that can't be acted on in their everyday lives. Eric Bentley pictures himself and us, at the performance of a farce, 'seated in dark security (enjoying) . . . the adventure of adultery, ingeniously exaggerated to the n'th degree without incurring the responsibilities or suffering the guilt, without even the hint of an affront to the wife at our side'. And he also asserts, 'where there is no established virtue, there can be no sense of outrage . . . the marriage joke exists only for a culture that knows itself committed to marriage'.[44] So Bentley's argument, though it stops short of Shaffer and Corrigan's conclusions, seems to point in the same direction: the permissive society has weakened farce. With marriage, morals, 'established virtue' under attack, so would run the argument, the compensatory liberation provided by farce is less necessary. Yet farce, far from being weakened, seems positively to have been strengthened of recent years; and it is necessary to question some of the assumptions behind Corrigan and Shaffer's assertions. To start with, I think that to some degree a term like 'the permissive society' is a journalistic invention, touching on superficial changes in public behaviour, in modes of dress, or ways of talking, but not always indicating anything deeper. A stock complaint of the 60s and 70s took the form of the speaker lamenting the fact that while all his buddies, if he could believe them, were living it up, 'having it off' with a variety of desirable people, he was always left out. Where the action was, was never where he actually happened to be. Liberation for the speaker was more apparent than actual. On the other hand, one can point to a number of external factors in our society during the last two decades that have encouraged a freer, less convention-ridden approach to sexual behaviour. There have been changes in legislation – the Divorce Reform Act of 1969, which broadened the grounds for divorce, the Sexual Offences Act of 1967 which no longer made homosexual behaviour between consenting adults in private a criminal offence, the Theatres Act of 1968, abolishing the precensorship of plays by the Lord Chamberlain. Feminist and gay rights movements have worked towards better social understanding; counselling and psychiatric help for emotional and sexual problems have been more readily available. All these offer some evidence of more liberated attitudes. But, given that these exist, do they really remove the *raison d'être* of farce? I would say not, mainly because I think Corrigan's argument is based on a false premise. The appeal of farce is at one level universal, not tied to a particular set of historical circumstances. All civilised society depends on a system of checks and balances. All sexual behaviour is subject to a variety of constraints, however 'permissive' the age. If, as Desmond Morris asserts, man is the sexiest of the apes, he is also a rational being, with social, family and public responsibilities. The conflict between the rational and the animal, between civilised restraint and primitive impulse, between id and ego, authority and licence may take different forms in different ages, but it is a permanent feature of human nature, and one which most farces exploit for their own humorous or subversive purposes. It is, of course, true that the holiday from normal behaviour, the outrage on morality, depends on our having some reminder of conventional standards of behaviour against which to measure the departure from convention. There is much value in including in farce some authority figure, be he magistrate, policeman, government inspector, pillar of the church, and/or a meekly conventional average citizen who worships at authority's shrine, sometimes with disastrous consequences for himself (Mr McLeavy in *Loot*, Harold Twine in *Rookery Nook*.) Rebellion needs a context, something to rebel against: the Marx Brothers need that pillar of respectability, Margaret Dumont, to rampage around; D'Arcy and Freddy in Ben Travers's *Plunder* need Scotland Yard to pit their wits

against; Feydeau's erring husbands need the structure of bourgeois marriage to give spice to their adventures.

But the authority principle does not disappear in a more liberated society. It may, however, take different forms. Where licence
is pushed to an extreme, as in Joe Orton's work, the authority
figures, Inspector Truscott, Dr. Rance, may appear correspondingly grotesque, mirror-images of the anarchic forces they seek to
control. But let us not forget that Inspector Truscott owes a good
deal to the real life figure of Detective Sergeant Challenor, who
was suspended from the police force in 1965 after a police enquiry
found that in his zeal to secure convictions, he had planted
evidence on law-abiding citizens. As Orton said, when receiving
the *Evening Standard* award for *Loot* as the Best Play of 1966:
'Everyone else thinks the play is a fantasy. Of course the police
know that it's true.'[45]

I would suggest, in conclusion, that, given there is some
evidence of more liberal attitudes in manners and morals, this, far
from lessening the farce-writer's opportunities, in fact increases
them. Challenges of a new and refreshing kind are offered to the
forces of convention. More assumptions are called in question.
The battle between order and anarchy, authority and licence can
be joined on a variety of fronts, some of them quite novel. The
tangled web of a Pinero, or a Ben Travers farce is spun usually
out of a relatively innocent peccadillo – a flirtation, an out of hours
drink or two, the placing of a bet on a racehorse by a rural Dean.
More representative figures of modern farce are Joe Orton's Dr
Prentice, accused of being a 'transvestite, fetishist, bisexual
murderer (with) . . . deviation overlap' (*What the Butler Saw*,
p. 428) or Tom Stoppard's Maddie Gotobed who has cut 'a sexual
swathe' through 119 members of Parliament, and is 'going through
the ranks like a lawn-mower in knickers' (*Dirty Linen*, p. 20).

2
A. W. Pinero and the Court Farces

W. D. Dunkel, in his critical biography of Pinero in 1941, writes of how Pinero won fame and fortune in the period 1885 to 1891, with a dozen plays, many of them farces, and then revealingly he goes on to say,

> but had he quit in 1891, at the age of 36, there would have been no justification to write a book about him. . . . For to this point in his career, he had not written for posterity; he was only a remarkably successful writer for the commercial theatre.[1]

Dunkel's observation reflects accurately enough the opinion of Pinero's contemporaries: thus a critic, reviewing *Dandy Dick* after the first night in 1887, praised it highly, but went on to reflect,

> the pity of it is, that it is bound to be so ephemeral; for it is as certain as anything can be that your *Magistrates* and *Schoolmistresses* and *Dandy Dicks* will never be heard of again when their first popularity is exhausted. They are for the moment and the moment only. Plays like *The Squire* (a tragedy) may live and tell another age about Pinero and his style; but a *Dandy Dick* will be unrecognisable.[2]

Time has a way of making many critical judgements seem inept, and these seem particularly so today. Ironically enough, the serious 'society dramas' such as *The Second Mrs Tanqueray*, *The Notorious Mrs Ebbsmith* and *The Profligate*, in which Pinero tried to water down Ibsen for English tastes, are today largely neglected and unperformed (though there was a notable revival of *The Second Mrs Tanqueray* at the National Theatre in 1981); but the trio of farces he wrote for the Royal Court Theatre under the management

17

of John Clayton and Arthur Cecil, *The Magistrate* in 1885, *The Schoolmistress* in 1886 and *Dandy Dick* in 1887 tell a different story. They have remained popular and performable in a number of revivals, and have not dated as the serious dramas have. Alastair Sim achieved notable successes in them, appearing as the Dean in *Dandy Dick* at Chichester and in the West End in 1973, and as Posket in *The Magistrate* at Chichester in 1969. More recently, 1986 has seen successful revivals of *Dandy Dick*, with Anthony Quayle as the Dean, at the Richmond Theatre, and of *The Magistrate*, with Nigel Hawthorne as Posket, at the National. Concerning the latter, it is interesting to note that, in one critic's mind, Sim's performance as Posket is still the benchmark against which to judge subsequent performances. Praising Nigel Hawthorne's interpretation, the critic of the *Financial Times* none the less found himself recalling

a strain of surreal panic forever associated in my mind with Alastair Sim in the main role. Nigel Hawthorne does not have the aura of celestial despair . . . (Awaiting the return of the ladies from jail in Act III, Hawthorne) poses in the window like a shadow with back ache. I recall Alastair Sim all but sliding into the wallpaper, back to the audience, searching for a crack in the wall; Mr Hawthorne wants to regain domestic poise, not obliterate his very existence.[3]

The Schoolmistress is less often performed, though it received a BBC Television production in 1981, and would stand up every bit as well as the other two farces to stage revival. Perhaps a reason for its comparative neglect is that it has, until recently, been out of print.

If Pinero's serious dramas are on the whole deservedly forgotten, and it is his farces that live, while the reverse of this was predicted in his lifetime, can the reason for the reverse be, as Michael Billington suggests, that 'he was a much greater technician than he was thinker or philosopher'?[4] Not entirely so, since the judgement presupposes a lack of serious content for farce and implies that one may measure seriousness by some kind of extractable 'message', or overt concern with social or political problems, When Pinero essayed this, the results were shallow and predictable. No: Pinero put his shrewdest insights and sharpest social comments into his farces. And it is the techniques and stagecraft of these farces that carry those insights to us today. Form and content are inseparable, whereas in the serious dramas there is a tendency for them to separate out, and a certain curdling affect to occur.

If farce, as Leo Hughes suggests, is 'involved far more directly and intimately in the business of the theatre itself than any other dramatic form',[5] Pinero certainly learnt that business. Stage-struck from boyhood, he went as often as he could to the Sadlers Wells Theatre in Islington, and to the Prince of Wales Theatre in Tottenham Street, where the plays of Tom Robertson were first performed. He was later to pay affectionate tribute both to the dramatist and the theatre in *Trelawney of the Wells*. From the age of 10 to 15, Pinero worked as a solicitor's clerk, but in his late teens began to write plays and send the manuscripts around to actor-managers of the day, one of whom wrote back, 'Dear Sir, your stuff is of no earthly use to me. For God's sake fetch it away as soon as possible.'[6] His biographer quotes him as saying that he wanted to write about people of wealth and leisure because such people had sufficient money to do interesting things such as getting into trouble with the law. The observation is, perhaps, significant in relation to the brushes with the law that befall the Dean in *Dandy Dick* and Mr Posket in *The Magistrate*. When Pinero's father died, Pinero was 19; he obtained his first job in the theatre by going up to Edinburgh, and persuading Mr and Mrs Wyndham to take him into their much talked about company at the Theatre Royal as a 'general utility', which meant that he took a variety of small walk-on parts or parts with a line or two of dialogue. The company broke up when the Theatre Royal burnt down, and Pinero moved to Liverpool where he got a part as a 'walking gentleman' in a play written by Wilkie Collins. Collins met him, liked him, and recommended him for a part in a subsequent play to R. C. Carton, actor-manager at the Globe Theatre. Pinero was now 21. Henry Irving, who was producing and acting at the Lyceum in 1876, saw Pinero in Carton's production, liked the young actor's work, and invited him to join his company at the Lyceum. He stayed with the company five years, and was esteemed for his seriousness, his professionalism, and his meticulous attention to detail. He began to get his own plays performed, studying the craft of the well-made plays of Scribe and Sardou with care. He started with curtain-raisers, graduated to full-length plays, and often directed them himself and played in them. In 1883, he married an actress, Myra Holme. By 1885, the year in which the first of the Court farces, *The Magistrate*, was completed, he had served an invaluable ten year apprenticeship as an actor; he had established himself as a dramatist; and he had acquired the reputation of being a very strict director of his own work. 'His way was the only way' writes Dunkel, and he required 'the repetition of some minor piece of stage business until it was done to his satisfaction'.[7] Hesketh Pearson paints the same picture:

> He was mad on details, telling actors exactly how to move, what gestures to make, precisely where and when to stand or sit, how to stress words.[8]

Furthermore, Pinero took great care to get the detail of his backgrounds correct: a performance of *Dandy Dick* was given for persons connected with the turf – racehorse owners, trainers, jockeys – and all agreed that the farce avoided any technical mistakes. With his background of theatre experience in his early years, Pinero had learnt his craft; he could, as Dunkel puts it, motivate 'the turns in his plot sequence with unerring skill. For he understood stage business, the timing of motion and sound, and above all, the reactions of an audience to the physical properties on the stage itself'.[9]

Pinero's farces at the Court Theatre between 1885 and 1887 were not of course an isolated and unique phenomenon. He had written farces before, in the shape of curtain-raisers, and one full-length farce, *In Chancery* in 1884, and he was to write others, although M. R. Booth is of the opinion that the later examples (*The Cabinet Minister* 1890 and *The Amazons*, 1893), are better described as satiric comedies. The best of his work in farce, was, however, for the Royal Court in the 1880s, and in this study, I shall be particularly concerned with *The Magistrate*, *The Schoolmistress* and *Dandy Dick*.

Initially, though, it is necessary to place the farces in a wider context. The examples of Labiche, Sardou and Feydeau in France had led to the establishment in the late Victorian theatre of the three-act farce, usually on a theme of sexual misadventure, befalling a middle-class wife and/or husband, involved in a series of compromising situations from which it seems impossible they will ever extricate themselves. W. S. Gilbert's 1873 version of Labiche's *Le chapeau de Paille d'Italie* – entitled *The Wedding March*, began the vogue. There was a spate of translations and adaptations; and the name of Charles Wyndham at the Criterion

Theatre became particularly associated with anglicised French farce. Examples of these anglicised French farces before Pinero's work was performed were such plays as *Pink Dominoes* (based on *Les Dominoes Roses*) performed at the Criterion Theatre in 1887, and Boucicault's *Forbidden Fruit* in 1880. Both plays have a second act set in a well-known pleasure ground by the Thames, Cremore Gardens, a place of assignation and intrigue whither all parties come; both have a comic waiter; both conform to what Bergson called the 'snowball' principle: that is to say, the train of events, once set in motion, grows in size and speed to envelop every bystander – a levelling device which reveals to the audience the equal culpability of all. The structure of each play is of the kind satirised by G. B. Shaw in the passage quoted in Chapter I (p. 3):

Act I, John Smith's home; Act II, the rowdy restaurant or casino at which John Smith, in the course of his clandestine spree, meets all the members of his household, including the schoolboy and the parlour-maid; Act III, his house the next morning, with the inevitable aftermath of the complications of the night before.

Such farces were, of course, in general, less anarchic and subversive than the French farces of Feydeau and Labiche. They went less far; their purpose, suggests Booth, was

to amuse in a jolly and properly moral way, to cast a friendly avuncular eye on the minor vicissitudes of home and family.[10]

It is characteristic that the erring husband at the end of *Forbidden Fruit* is made to say,

I have tried the taste of forbidden fruit (he has had a night out in the pleasure gardens with Zulu, the female cartridge – one of the acrobats at Cremore). I don't like it. A fast life looks charming to those who see it as spectators look at a play, but you have introduced me behind the scenes, and I prefer the illusion to reality.[11]

Shaw seems to have felt that the English attempt to domesticate French farce in Victorian England was doomed to failure, and writes sadly of the homeliness of our English attempts to volatise ourselves sufficiently to breathe that fantastic atmosphere of moral irresponsibility in which alone the hero of farcical comedy, like Pierrot or Harlequin, can realise himself fully.[12]

A consideration of Pinero's best farces suggests that this is very far from being the case.

That *The Magistrate* owes something to the anglicised French farces of its day is evident enough. The structure of the farce conforms closely enough to the stereotype satirised by Shaw. The convergence of all, or almost all, of the parties on the private dining room at the Hôtel des Princes in Act II (the French name is itself significant) shows Pinero skilfully anglicising a staple ingredient of French farce, and exploiting for his own purposes the principle Feydeau built upon, that all the characters who stand most to lose by being brought together in compromising circumstances, must be so brought together to maximum embarrassment and confusion. Common also to Pinero and French farce is the use of what Bergson identified as the 'snowball' principle, referred to above. John Russell Taylor, putting it slightly differently, writes of Pinero's skill in establishing, 'a chain reaction, starting from one outré situation', and asserts, his 'great strength . . . lies in arranging things so that, given the initial premise, everything seems naturally to follow on from it'.[13] The comment is accurate enough, but it also sums up well enough one of the structural principles of a Feydeau or Labiche farce. But, a critic might argue, the superficial links with French farce only serve to throw into relief the basic differences. Shaw refers to 'homeliness', Booth to 'casting a friendly avuncular eye on the minor vicissitudes of home and family'. This is damning with faint praise indeed. Is the relative innocence of Pinero's farces in fact debilitating? Should there not be in the best farce that aggressiveness that Bentley insists upon (ch. I, p. 9), and also a degree of subversive anarchy, and even nightmare, that is absent in his work?

Certainly, the darker shadows that can be cast by farce are not very directly in evidence in *The Magistrate*. Where an element of the sinister or the morbid appears, its very extravagance highlights the absurdity of the situation. Such is the effect of the dark threats uttered by the besotted parlour maid to the boy she fancies, whose attentions are elsewhere:

Cast your eye over this before you sleep tonight. Part of a story in *Bow Bells* called 'Jilted', or 'Could blood atone'. Wrap it in your handkerchief . . . it came round the butter.

(p. 8)

Similarly, Horace Vale's gloomy imaginings (in the incongruously 'bon viveur' surroundings of the Hôtel des Princes), concerning dying of a broken heart, are too comic to cast a shadow:

My people have eight shelves in the catacombs at Kensal Green. . . . My shelf is four from the bottom.

(p. 28)

Moreover, the indiscretions and moral lapses involved in this play appear, to a modern audience, as very minor peccadillos indeed. It would be difficult to imagine a more innocent farce. Agatha Posket, widowed at 35, knocks five years off her real age when she remarries, with the result that her 19-year-old son is regarded as only 14. The incongruity of a supposed 14-year-old in an Eton collar flirting, gambling, drinking, telling blue jokes and keeping a room in a West End hotel – this is highly comic, and, within the conventions of Victorian society, offers, certainly, an image of impropriety that the original audience might have found shocking. Today, the incongruity remains amusing but there is hardly an element of shock. What other sins are committed in *The Magistrate?* Agatha's second husband, Aeneas Posket, the magistrate, tells a lie, and goes out for a night on the town, ostensibly to rescue his stepson from the dubious pleasures of the Hôtel des Princes, (whither Agatha has also gone to plead with an old family friend, Colonel Lukyn, to preserve her secret). The police raid the hotel, but only because they are not keeping to the licensing hours. (And, in the upshot, it is not even an offence that is committed; Bullamy gets the defendants off on a technicality, since, as he puts it, the law 'allows a man who rents a little apartment at an inn to eat and drink with his friends all night long'). The guilty ones are discovered, but not in bed together, merely hiding in the dark, under tables and behind curtains. The only physical contact in the scene occurs when Posket is pinched by his wife as they both hide under the table. The magistrate evades arrest by precipitous flight, and, in court the following morning, confronted by his wife and sister-in-law in the dock, is so carried away by his own efforts to preserve a respectable facade that he sentences them to a week in jail.

There is little here, then, that could be interpreted as very wicked or immoral behaviour. However, it is important to remember that when convention and propriety rule as strictly as they did in Victorian England, small deviations from the norm can be just as disruptive and creative of anarchy as the wilder deviations from the norm in contemporary farce. Mr Posket's misadventures assume a genuinely nightmarish quality as he is inexorably propelled towards the moment when he has to deliver judgement on his wife and sister-in-law. It is also worth remembering the explanation offered by William Archer for the reputation of English farces for extravagant naughtiness despite the innocence of the texts. Martin Meisel, in *Shaw and the Nineteenth Century Theatre*, quotes him thus:

Writing about F. C. Burnand's adaptation of French farce . . . he declares, 'The Bowdlerising process is carried on by means of a sort of cipher to which everyone has the key. When Mr Burnand introduces us to a variety actress or a female acrobat, we all know what was the lady's profession in the original French, and that elastic and convenient term 'flirtation' covers a multitude of sins and covers them in a very gauzy fashion.[14]

This is true up to a point. I believe, though, that Pinero sometimes plays amusingly on the apparent disproportion between the fierceness of the outrage expressed and the mildness of the conduct that has provoked it. An example of this occurs at the end of *The Magistrate*, when Mr Posket, endeavouring to keep his own end up in the matrimonial battle of words, says,

No wife of mine sups unknown to me, with dissolute military men; we will have a judicial separation, Mrs Posket.

(p. 70)

A member of the audience's response to this moment could well be a divided one: with one part of his or her mind amused at the ironic disporportion between solemn outrage and trivial offence; with another taking pleasure at 'reading the code' and substituting a more suitable form of sensual pleasure for the relatively innocent one of dining with the dissolute military man.

Shaw's complaints concerning the predictability and the homeliness of British farce apply even less to Pinero when we consider how skilfully he exploits what for Eric Bentley is a feature of key importance in farce: the element of role-playing, of keeping up appearances, such that the social mask worn, and the real face of the natural man beneath it, are constantly at odds:

In farce, unmasking occurs all along. . . . Bring on stage a farcical comic like Harpo Marx and all appearances are in jeopardy. For him all coverings exist to be stripped, all breakables to be broken. . . . Farce promotes and exploits the widest possible contrast between tone and content, surface and substance.[15]

Bentley acknowledges that unmasking can be as much a feature of comedy as of farce, but 'unmasking in comedy will characteristically be the unmasking of a single character in a climactic scene, like that of Tartuffe'.[16] His point is that in farce the element of unmasking occurs more frequently; there is always the threat that the social mask may slip, that there may be a failure to keep up appearances. This threat is present throughout *The Magistrate*. Aeneas Posket is a more rounded character than we often find in farce, idiosyncratic, unconventional and believable. From the beginning, the magistrate's mask sits rather uncomfortably on his face: he has such a reputation for benevolence on the bench that he has to be reprimanded for inflicting such light penalties; he pays most of the fines he imposes; and he employs ex-lags in his household. One can see why Hamilton Fyfe characterised Pinero's farce as 'based upon incongruity, (arousing) merriment by appealing to that sense of the unfitness of things which lies so near the root of humour'.[17] Mask and face then, are built into this incongruity; Posket the natural man, kindly, benevolent, capable of being led astray; and Posket the official man, the magistrate, custodian of morals and legality.

Pinero is particularly successful in scenes where mask and face are in conflict, where the man and the magistrate are at odds. One such scene occurs at the end of Act I, where Posket fights a losing battle with his conscience and better judgement, and is finally persuaded by Cis to disobey his wife and visit the Hôtel des Princes. The initial vacillation, the growing stubbornness and resolve, prompted by Cis, who takes the lead in organising him and prompting him in the necessary white lies – these successive stages of Posket's decline into 'man about town' are subtly and amusingly plotted. What emerges at the comic climax of the scene is the contrast, very typical of farce, between the effective role-players, the accomplished tricksters (of whom Cis is one), who can confidently bluff their way out of tight corners, and those, like Posket, the 'innocent abroad', who are miserably incompetent at doing so. Thus, when Cis prompts Posket on what to say to the manservant in giving him a small bribe (say, 'Wyke, you want a new umbrella – buy a very good one. Your mistress has a latch-key, so go to bed') the statements come out in Posket's mouth in a hopelessly garbled form:

Go to bed – buy a very good one. Your mistress has a latch-key – so – so you want a new umbrella.

(p. 24)

By contrast again, Posket's wife, Agatha, is much cooler in emerg-encies and, like her son, able to bluff effectively. When caught out by her husband inventing a serious illness of a lady friend to 'cover' her secret meeting with Colonel Lukyn, she merely observes, concerning the friend's letter that Posket has scanned in vain for evidence of illness,

No, but can't you read between the lines, Aeneas? That is the letter of a woman who is not at all well.

(p. 18)

Posket's return to his magistrate's court after the disastrous night out offers the crowning example in the play of the man and the magistrate ludicrously at odds with each other. He tries to resume his customary role as guardian of the law, but keeps relapsing into the role that the night's events have cast him in, that of fugitive from the law. The split personality resulting is ironically focused in the contrast between Posket's attempted magistrate-like demeanour and his unkempt and dishevelled appearance, pointed up by the hastily acquired gaudy necktie, and the strip of plaster on the bridge of his nose. The contrast between mask and face is acted out comically when Posket debates with himself whether to agree to Colonel Lukyn's request for an urgent interview before the court sits:

WORMINGTON. Such a course would be most unusual. . . .
POSKET. But I am a man as well as a magistrate. Advise me,
Wormington, advise me
WORMINGTON (*considering*). Well – you can apply to yourself
for permission to grant Colonel Lukyn's request.
POSKET (*hastily scribbling on Lukyn's card*). I do – I do – and after
much conflicting argument I consent to see Colonel Lukyn
here, immediately.

(p. 56)

And, when Lukyn comes in equally dishevelled, and also with a
plaster on the bridge of his nose, the comic mirror-images he and
Posket present of each other express, as only the language of
theatre can, the farcical, but also serious, point of the scene. As
Shakespeare's Lear has it, 'See how yon justice rails upon yon
simple thief. Hark, in thine ear: change places, and handy-dandy,
which is the justice, which is the thief?'
The dramatic irony of the ensuing scene hinges on the fact that,
the more Lukyn endeavours to warn him indirectly that it is his
own wife who is going to appear in the dock before him, the more
determined Posket is to resume his conventional role. Indeed, as
he warms to his task, he becomes more than usually magistrate-
like, and the audience savours, with a kind of horrid pleasure, the
irony of watching him bent, Oedipus-like, on his own undoing.
Thus, of the prisoner's husband (himself!) he says,

let it be my harrowing task to open the eyes of this foolish
doting man to the treachery, the perfidy which nestles upon his
very hearth rug.

(p. 59)

And when Lukyn, beside himself with exasperation, says,
'confound you, Posket – listen!' Posket loftily replies,

I am listening, sir, to the voice of Mrs Posket – that newly
made wife still blushing from the embarrassment of her second
marriage, and that voice says, 'strike for the sanctity of hearth
and home, for the credit of the wives of England – no mercy!'

(p. 59)

The climax, as Posket falls through the thin ice on which he has been skating, occurs off-stage, as we hear a shriek from the two women, a cry from Posket, and hubbub in the court. Posket staggers back on stage, having finally recognised and understood the true situation, but too late, having sentenced his 'nearest and dearest' to 'seven days, without the option of a fine'. The final touch of humour lies in the unaccustomed and uncharacteristic severity of the sentence. That severity, however, is an appropriate product of Posket's own guilt, and his over-strenuous attempts to compensate for it.

Posket, then is the main example of mask and face in conflict, of natural man tripping up the respectable citizen with duties and responsibilities. But aspects of this conflict appear also in other characters, notably in scenes where the natural man's appetites come into conflict with the social decorum of Victorian society. Characteristically for the period, this conflict centres not on sex, but on food; and it contributes notably to the humour of the scene at the Hôtel des Princes in Act II, whither, unknown to one another, most of the main characters come. Thus Charlotte, during Agatha's interview with Colonel Lukyn, becomes obsessively hungry, and tormented by the food so near at hand yet seemingly unobtainable. Horace Vale, who has had to hide on an unsafe balcony in the pouring rain to allow the ladies their private conversation with his friend, is similarly racked by hunger; while Colonel Lukyn, for his part, is torn between a real concern for his friend's plight (fearing that the balcony will give way beneath his weight), and his social duty to pay attention to Agatha's story concerning the deception she has practised on her husband. The resulting comedy of cross-purposes is handled by Pinero with skill and subtlety:

LUKYN. I'm afraid you've come to tell me Posket is ill?
AGATHA (*surprised*). I – no – my husband is at home
   There is a sharp gust of wind heard with the rain. Lukyn starts.
LUKYN. Lord forgive me! I've killed him
AGATHA (*with horror*). Colonel Lukyn!
LUKYN (*confused*). Madam!
AGATHA. Indeed, Mr Posket is at home.
LUKYN (*glancing at window?*). Is he? I wish we all were . . .
AGATHA (*tenderly*). You were at my little boy's christening?
LUKYN (*with his thoughts elsewhere*). Yes – yes – certainly.
AGATHA. You remember what a fine little fellow he was.

LUKYN (*thoughtfully*). Not a pound over nine stone.

AGATHA. Colonel Lukyn!

LUKYN (*recovering himself*). I beg your pardon, yes – I was at the christening of your boy . . . I remember the child very well. Has he still got that absurd mug?

AGATHA. Colonel Lukyn!

LUKYN. Madam?

AGATHA. My child is, and always was – perfect

LUKYN. You misunderstand me! I was his godfather, I gave him a silver cup.

AGATHA. Oh, do excuse me (*puts handkerchief to her eyes*). How did I become acquainted with such a vulgar expression. I don't know where I pick up my slang. It must be through loitering at shop windows.

LUKYN rises

Oh, oh, oh!

LUKYN. Pray compose yourself. I'll leave you for a moment.

Goes to window. L. and up C.

AGATHA. (*across table to Charlotte*). How shall I begin, Charley?

CHARLOTTE. Make a bold plunge do! The odour of cooking, here, to a hungry woman, is maddening

VALE softly opens window and comes into the recess, the curtains concealing him from those on stage.

VALE (*pulling curtain slightly aside*). This is too bad of Lukyn! I'm wet to the skin and frightfully hungry! Who the deuce are these women?

(pp. 31–3)

As the scene progresses, Pinero's mastery of stage-business is admirably demonstrated. The sound effects and noises off make their contribution: the sound of the pouring rain and the wind key us up to expect the worst for Horace Vale standing on the balcony; bursts of song and laughter from Cis and Posket threaten to reveal their presence to the ladies; Vale's mournful asides behind the curtain concerning his disappearing dinner make their contribution. There is the skilful use of stage space, with Vale supposedly on a dangerous balcony, and then hiding behind a curtain so that Lukyn thinks he's plunged to his doom; and Lukyn inside but preoccupied with what's going on outside; then there is the business of the disembodied arm (Vale's) stretching forth with plates, dishes and lemons, Pinero making us wait with comic suspense for the moment when the women see the ghostly arm and scream with terror. Clothes and costume details are very important also in this play. In an age which in any case attached particular importance to the conventions of costume, the right dress for the occasion, we would expect the farce writer to be alert to the humorous possibilities of deviations from the norm. We have already seen how Posket's 'fall from grace' is signalled in Act III by his gaudy neck-tie, dishevelled clothes and nose-plaster. In a different way, in Act I, Cis's Eton collar, suggesting the 14 year old, emphasises the disparity between the expected behaviour of a boy of that age, and Cis's actual 'man of the world' stance. Conversely, his appearance at the end of the act, fashionably dressed as a young man about town, underlines the paradox and irony of the situation. Here, in Act II, the small detail of Vale picking up the wrong hat, (Lukyn's) when he goes out to stand in the rain on the balcony, and finding that it is a size too large for him, lends comic point to the ensuing scene when he returns and indignantly calls Lukyn to account for his plight. The image of a dripping and despondent Vale standing in an over-large hat renders his protests comically ineffectual. And even his reconciliation with Charlotte gets an effective laugh when she nestles romantically up to him, only to find him too damp to get to close quarters with. Pinero is also a master of climax, and his ability to build each act to a satisfying and dramatically convincing climax is amply demonstrated in this scene: Lukyn's growing difficulties with the two women, then with Vale; Charlotte's and Agatha's growing dismay at the series of unexpected encounters – with a ghostly arm, with the man it belongs to, with strangers under the table, and with the police, leading to their commital to Posket's own court; and the Act's final tableau, expressed in the stage-direction which really clinches the climax:

> *Agatha sinks into chair R.C., Charlotte at her feet, Lukyn overcome*
> *falls on Vale's shoulders down L.*
>
> CURTAIN
>
> (p. 49)

While the tableau was a familiar convention of the Victorian theatre, Pinero uses it here and for other scene endings in the play with skill and comic inventiveness. He also makes use of a similar kind of stylised choreography in such scenes as the letter reading scene in Act I. Here Cis, Charlotte and Agatha receive and open their letters in choric unison:

> With a simultaneous movement they take out letters, throw envelopes on floor and all lean back and read their letter.

(p. 17)

The letters are clearly an artificial plot-device, essential to the tangle of subsequent complications. But, far from endeavouring to hide the artifice, Pinero draws attention to it, takes delight in it, and parallels it in the movements of his actors. Comparable elements of artifice and stylisation are to be observed in two other aspects of Pinero's art. One is the use among the minor characters of types who are dominated by a rigid mental set of attitudes. Bergson's theory of humour depended very much on the idea of rigidity: 'any mechanical "inelasticity" which leads a man to behave in an automatic way . . . makes us laugh quite quickly. . . . The comic is that side of a person which reveals his likeness to a thing'.[18] This kind of rigidity occurs when certain of Pinero's characters become fixed in a particular way of speaking or acting, or carry over their hobby or trade into their private life. Thus the greatest compliment Posket's fellow-magistrate, Bullamy, can pay concerning his choice of a wife is, 'I never committed a more stylish elegant creature', (p. 11) and Vale carries his interest in horse-racing into the most inappropriate contexts, saying of his fiancée, 'Oh lovely! A most magnificent set of teeth. . . . She rides eight stone fifteen' (p. 28). There is also an air of studied artifice in the way Pinero deliberately re-establishes in Act III the familiar atmosphere of household routine characteristic of Act I, thus underpinning the return to hearth and home and to relative normality. The chambermaid's darkly jealous asides, Bullamy's consumption of jujubes, the visit of Beatie the music teacher, all echo the opening of Act I. And when Agatha and Charlotte, released from jail, appear for a showdown with Posket, there is once again the sense of Pinero playfully calling attention to the artifice of the moment. If, in farce, fate and mischance lead the characters a merry dance, the playwright will choreograph that dance with style and wit:

> AGATHA and CHARLOTTE enter. POPHAM goes out. The two

ladies are pale, red-eyed, and agitated. They carry their hats or bonnets, which are much crushed.

AGATHA   )
CHARLOTTE) _– falling on to BULLAMY's shoulders_). O-o-h-h!

BULLAMY (_down C._). My dear ladies!

AGATHA. Preserver!

CHARLOTTE. Friend!

AGATHA. How is my boy?

BULLAMY. Never better.

AGATHA (_fiercely_). And the man who condemned his wife and sister-in-law to the miseries of a jail.

BULLAMY (_looking about, not seeing POSKET_). Ahem! Posket – oh – he

AGATHA (_quickly_). Is he well enough to be told what that wife thinks of him.

BULLAMY. It might cause a relapse!

AGATHA. It is my duty to risk that.

CHARLOTTE _has raised the covers of the dishes on the table._

CHARLOTTE (_with an hysterical cry_). Food!

AGATHA. Ah!

AGATHA _sits R. and CHARLOTTE L. of table; they both begin to devour teacake voraciously. POSKET, conquering his feelings, comes down R.C._

POSKET (_with an attempt at dignity_). Agatha Posket.

AGATHA (_rising, with her mouth full, and a piece of teacake in her hand_). Sir!

CHARLOTTE _takes the tray and everything on it from the table and crosses with it to door R. Simultaneously BULLAMY crosses at back to door L._

BULLAMY (_at door_). There's going to be an explanation.

CHARLOTTE (_at door_). There's going to be an explanation.

BULLAMY   ) _(together, aside)._ There's going to be an
CHARLOTTE) ¯ explanation.

CHARLOTTE _and BELLAMY go out, quietly closing the doors behind them._

POSKET. How dare you look me in the face, Madam

AGATHA. How dare you look at anybody in any position, Sir?

(p. 69)

Here stylisation of action, movement and language creates a sense of events accelerating towards the denouement; it allows the audience to enjoy in a detached way the untangling of a complicated web of deception; and, by playfully creating a series of unrealistic effects, Pinero discourages any too literal-minded questioning of the premise on which the whole farce is built – Agatha Posket's concealment of her own and her son's age, which she is about to admit. The quarrel and the explanation follow. Cis announces his engagement to Beatie; Agatha forbids it, Posket over-rules her, and one final tableau completes the play:

AGATHA *sinks into the chair as the CURTAIN falls.*

(p. 73)

In sum, *The Magistrate* is a fine example of a farce in which mask and face are in conflict, in which a context of grave decorum and respectability is first established and then set at naught, and in which Pinero's mastery of construction and of stage business create what Booth has described as essential to the world of farce: 'the disciplined expression of anarchy, the logical presentation of a crazy world'.[19]

In Pinero's second Court farce, *The Schoolmistress* (1886), his mastery of farcical techniques is again in evidence. As in *The Magistrate*, humour results from characters trapped in particular modes of behaviour and speech. Rear-Admiral Rankling's naval preoccupations and his nautical language intrude absurdly into a speech congratulating a newly-married couple:

RANKLING. Not only am I the commander – the father – of a ship – of a daughter. . . . I am also the husband of a heavily plated cruiser – er – um – h'm – of a dear lady.

(p. 50)

Mr Gogg, the fireman, carries his propensity for telling amusing anecdotes into the middle of the fire rescue operation in Act II; and Dinah's husband, Reginald, regularly falls into jealous rages directed at any man who talks to or notices his wife. As in *The Magistrate*, Pinero expertly sets up a place of assignation for Act II in which all the parties who should on no account meet, do meet – although with the interesting difference that in this case the place of assignation is itself a fraud: a double role is assigned not only to the principal character of the schoolmistress, but to her educational establishment; thus, Volumnia College for the

Daughters of Gentlemen is made to double, in Act II, through Vere Queckett's deception, as bachelor lodgings suitable for an ill-assorted mixed party of ladies and gentlemen. And, as in *The Magistrate*, we have a dinner that goes wrong: the feast that was to be, as Lazenby suggests,

> a symbol of revolt against all the conventions (Dinah's against parental authority, the other girls against Miss Dyott's, Vere's against his wife's, the male guests against their soberer roles) turns out to be a grave disappointment: the lark pudding is 'architecturally disproportionate' to the number of guests, and the oysters are suspected of being 'inland oysters' (it has been 'a long time since they had fortnight at the seaside')[20]

There is also a great deal of comedy, as in the previous play, resulting from characters desperately trying to keep face, cover up, or bluff their way through various deceptions: some are splendidly adept at it, others miserably inadequate. In the former category we have the Principal of the Ladies College, Miss Dyott, alias Constance Delaporte, the actress who plays Queen Honorine in a new comic opera:

> MISS DYOTT. Oh, deceiver!
> QUECKETT. You talk of deception! What about the three o'clock train from Paddington.
> MISS DYOTT. It was the whole truth – there was one.
> QUECKETT. But you didn't travel on it! What about the clergy-man's wife at Hereford.
> MISS DYOTT. Go there – you will find several!
> QUECKETT. But you're not staying with them . . .
>
> (p. 68)

Queckett performs with much less panache under pressure, as when, rashly claiming Miss Dyott's pupils as his nieces, he is cross-examined by the irascible Rear-Admiral, who is well up on family history:

> QUECKETT. . . . these are my sister Isabel's girls.
> RANKLING. Why all your sister Isabel's children were boys.
> QUECKETT. Were boys, yes.
> RANKLING. (*irritably*) *Are* boys, sir.

QUECKETT. Are *men*, now. H'm! I should have said these are
my sister Janet's children.
RANKLING. Oh! I've never heard of your sister Janet.
QUECKETT. No – quiet retiring woman, Janet.
RANKLING. Well then, whom did Janet marry?
QUECKETT. Whom *didn't* Janet marry! I mean, whom *did* Janet
marry? Why, Finch Griffin of the Berkshire Royals.
RANKLING. Dear me, we're going to meet Major Griffin and
his wife on Christmas Day at the Trotwells

(p. 44)

And, as in *The Magistrate* so here, Pinero's stage directions show
his realisation of the effectiveness at certain moments of a carefully
stylised choreography of stage action. Thus, '*the heads of the three
girls . . . appear one above the other, spying*' (p. 28); or, '*Peggy and
Queckett, by a simultaneous movement, rush to the two doors and close
them*' (p. 33); or, '*Reginald rushes to Dinah and embraces her frantically.
There is a general cry of relief as Mallory embraces Peggy and Gwendoline
throws her arms around Saunders*' (p. 61). We also see Pinero making
use in *The Schoolmistress*, as later in *Dandy Dick*, of elements from
the world of melodrama, and creating comic incongruity because
of the disproportion between portentous language or 'heavy' stage
business, and the ridiculous situation involved. Yet there is an
appropriateness in his use of such elements, in that the farce
world, like that of melodrama, involves its characters in progressively more desperate situations. Thus, in *The Schoolmistress*, we
have the night wanderings of Act III, the disturbed soliloquies of
the characters as they come and go, and the repetition of a
particular rhetorical question: 'Will the day never break?' (Gwendoline, p. 56); 'Are we never going to have any more daylight?'
(Rankling, p. 60); 'Oh, will it never be daylight? Does the milkman
never come to Portland Place?' (Miss Dyott, p. 82). There is the
duel with umbrellas that nearly takes place between Queckett and
the Rear-Admiral in Act III (p. 65). And there is, at the beginning
of the play, Tyler the porter, pursuing his passion for fireworks
with all the obsessive addiction a drunkard in a Victorian melodrama would have for the bottle:

TYLER. Fireworks is my only disserpation. There ain't much
danger unless anybody lunges at me . . .

JANE (*palpitating*). Oh don't Tyler! How can you 'ave such a
'ankering?
TYLER . . . It's their 'orrible uncertainty I crave after!

(p. 20)

The central event of *The Schoolmistress* is a mishap of a more
spectacular kind than occurs in *The Magistrate* – the conflagration
that consumes Volumnia College, resulting, needless to say, from
Tyler's carefully planted fireworks hobby. The conflagration is a
kind of image for and extension of the conflagration that also
consumes the private lives of the characters – there too fires burn
and smokescreens conceal. The connection is made explicit in the
splendid climax of Act II, in which Miss Dyott, like a Valkyrie in
Wagner's *Ring*, appears on the fire-escape amid the flames, '*in the
gorgeous dress of an opera-bouffe Queen, with a flaxen wig, much disar-
rayed, and a crown on one side*' (p. 55). But the fire is also an essential
ingredient in the plot (as it will also be in *Dandy Dick*), in that it
necessitates the removal of the characters to Rear-Admiral Rankling's house, where what Pinero designates the 'Nightmare' of Act
III occurs.

The role-playing in this farce is also of a more adventurous kind,
and the ironic incongruity set up between mask and face of a
correspondingly more striking nature. Miss Dyott, as Principal of
a Ladies College, is a figure, apparently, of extreme respectability;
her double life, however, involves her in the opposite role of
actress, and an actress, moreover, not of the serious stage, but one
involved, disreputably in Victorian eyes, in singing and dancing in
public, as she is forced ultimately to acknowledge:

MISS DYOTT. It is true . . . that last night, while you and my
pupils were dilating, I was singing – ay, and at one important
juncture, dancing.
QUECKETT (*with horror*). No, no – not dancing!
MISS DYOTT. Madly, desperately, hysterically dancing!

(p. 68)

There is also, from the beginning of the play, a promising variety
of deceptions that augur well for later complications and misadventures: not only Miss Dyott's double life, but her secret marriage
to the Hon. Vere Queckett; the further secret marriage of one
of her pupils, Dinah, the Rear-Admiral's daughter, to Reginald

Paulover; and, finally, Queckett's pretence, in his wife's absence, that the ladies College is really bachelor lodgings suitable for a louche dinner party.

Pinero's conception is also adventurous in two other respects. Miss Dyott's variety role is undertaken to support the bankrupt aristocrat she has married, and there is a challenge here to the stereotype male role as the breadwinner, active in the big world outside the home, with the wife as the passive, housebound, domestic drudge. Pinero's play refreshingly – and boldly – reverses the customary relation of the sexes. Here, Queckett is housebound, and incompetently in charge of the domestic arrangements (he squanders the housekeeping money and servants' wages on the dinner party, and neglects to pay the fire insurance premiums). Meanwhile his wife brings home the money from her public success as an actress. Nor is her case an isolated one. The women in this play take the initiative and ultimately call the tune. Thus it is Peggy, the pupil marked out to be a governess, who successfully leads a rebellion against convention in Act III. When Mallory says of Reginald, 'Our host has forbidden him the house', Peggy forthrightly summons her troops: 'Girls, shall we open the front door, or shall we remain the mere slaves of etiquette?' (p. 58). It is she who finds and uses the keys of the Rear-Admiral's house to release Dinah (though she inadvertently in fact releases Queckett). And she deliberately overturns masculine prerogative in doing these things: 'I take the responsibility for this. I am a girl' (p. 60). and, most conclusively of all, Pinero gives both the senior married women of the play, Mrs Rankling and Miss Dyott, a scene in which they compare notes as to their respective husbands, and find them sadly wanting:

MISS DYOTT. . . . Let me open your eyes as mine are opened. We have engaged to love and to honour two men.
MRS RANKLING. I have done nothing of the kind.
MISS DYOTT. I mean one each.
MRS RANKLING. Oh, excuse me.
MISS DYOTT. Now, looking at him microscopically – is there much to love and to honour in Admiral Rankling?
MRS RANKLING. He is a genial after-dinner speaker.
MISS DYOTT. Hah!
MRS RANKLING. It is true he is rather austere.
MISS DYOTT. An austere sailor! All bows abroad and stern at

home. Well then – knowing what occurred last night – is there anything to love and to honour in Mr Queckett?

MRS RANKLING. Nothing whatever.

MISS DYOTT (*annoyed*). And yet he is undoubtedly the superior of Admiral Rankling. Very well then, do as I mean to do – put your foot down. If Heaven has gifted you with a large one, so much the better.

(p. 63)

There ensue scenes of satisfying dramatic irony, in which the two women turn the tables on their husbands, rebel against the masculine assumptions as to their appropriate roles, and put them firmly in their places.

The farce is, finally, original in the way Pinero allows Miss Dyott's role-playing to reach its logical but extreme conclusion. There is no return to the status quo or to respectability at the end of the play. Miss Dyott brazens it out, defies public opinion, embraces her new career, and rejects the old one. And she makes the audience her willing accomplices, as Pinero gracefully and deftly breaks the illusion at the end of the play, reminding us that the schoolmistress who is playing the actress is herself the actress of the company, playing both those roles:

MISS DYOTT. Tyler has rendered me a signal service. He has demolished Volumnia College. From the ashes of that establishment rises the Phoenix of my new career. Miss Dyott is extinct – Miss Delaporte is alive, and, during the evening, kicking. I hope none will regret the change – I shall not, for one, while the generous public allow me to remain a favourite.

(p. 72)

A recurrent feature of the farce world is that its entanglements are usually set in train through some fatal step taken in the wrong direction by the victims, who give a hostage to fortune and are threatened with disaster as a result. In Pinero's third farce for the Court, *Dandy Dick*, 1887, the Dean's daughters, Salome and Sheba, have done so by incurring debts with their dressmaker (in order to be finely attired for a regimental ball to which they have been invited by their admirers, Major Tarver and Mr Darbey). These debts their father is both unwilling and unable to pay. For his part, the Dean has given his own hostage to fortune by offering

£1000 which he has not got to repair the church's spire if seven other donors will do likewise. The absence of money and the necessity of finding some is, then, the mainspring of the farce. The means of acquiring some relate to the Deanery's proximity to a racecourse; and to the Dean's ill-judged invitation to his widowed sister, Georgiana Tidman (once known as the 'Daisy of the Turf') to stay with him.

Pinero's first Act is a model of exposition, not only in laying the groundwork for the later complications and misadventures, but also in establishing the right mood and expectations. The opening conversation between the Dean's daughters hits off exactly the right note of conspiratorial plotting, a kind of opening gambit in the game of guilty secrets that is to develop. There is a comic 'appropriate inappropriateness' in the names, Salome and Sheba. Appropriate as it may be for a Dean to give his daughters biblical names, these particular names are of Old Testament temptresses! The relationship of the two girls to each other is subtly suggested – companions in conspiracy, but also sexual rivals, Salome the older and more serious, Sheba, younger but more precocious and high-spirited; so too is their relationship to their father, in which they appear half-way between obedient, well-behaved children and rebellious women of the world. But though the relationships strike true, Pinero keeps us at a distance, establishes the mood of a high-spirited overture, and the expectancy of a merry dance to follow. He does this in large part by the appropriate stylisation which he imposes on the characters and their movements, and on the whole stage picture. Thus he conceives of the two girls as a duo: they act in unison, work together, set each other off. Pinero in his stage directions suggests exactly the effects he wants: 'The girls clutch each other's hands' (p. 3); 'they throw themselves into each other's arms' (p. 2); 'they both walk about excitedly' (p. 1). The sense of high-spirited role-playing in the two girls is also strong. When their suitors, Major Tarvey and Mr Darbey, are announced, they arrange to 'run away and then come in unconsciously'; and when they do so, they enter in a studied grouping: 'Salome has her arm round her sister's waist and looks up to her with a sweet trusting smile. They start in confusion' (p. 5). This is in character, but it also supports and extends the sense of an amusing game that is about to be played for our enjoyment. The two military men are themselves conceived very much as type-characters, almost in fact a double act, in which one acts as a foil to the other: Major Tarver, middle-aged, Darbey a *'mere boy'*; Tarver *'alternately in a state of great excitement and depression'*, Darbey *'pompous and patronising'* (p. 4). And there is Georgiana Tidman. The Dean has constructed a romantic and sentimental picture of the sister he has not seen for many years as a 'sad, broken creature, a weary fragment, a wave-tossed derelict . . . a chastened widow' (p. 13). And Pinero adeptly underlines the mood of family piety by the touching tableau indicated in the stage direction as the Dean begins his tale:

> With his head bent he walks to a chair, and holds out his hands to the girls who go to him and kneel at his feet.'

> (p. 12)

But the fantasy is quickly exploded by the reality as the vigorous, assertive figure of Georgiana Tidman strides in a moment later. The contrast between what we expect and what we get is highly comic. The humour that Bergson identified that resulted from rigidity, 'when someone becomes fixed in a particular way of speaking which is used for the most unsuitable subjects', (see discussion of *The Magistrate*) is again well exemplified in the person of Georgiana, with her horsey vocabulary and turf metaphors:

> It's nearly twenty years since you and I munched our corn together. . . . It's kind of you to give me a dry stable and a clean litter. . . . I shan't be sorry to get my nosebag on.

> (p. 15)

The language is funny in itself, but funnier within the studious calm and sobriety of the Deanery, and in its dismaying effect on the Dean who is quite unable to deal with the alarming presence of his sister. The characterisation depends to a degree on the stereotype of the horsey woman, bossy and assertive, but there is a core of truth to it, and Hamilton Fyfe records how, in the 1930 production, Marie Lohr 'indicated very ingeniously the gradual increase of womanly charm over horsiness and masculinity as her affection for Sir Tristram grew.'[21] Sir Tristram, Georgiana's partner in horsebreeding and a former college friend of the Dean's, is the last visitor to the Deanery in Act I. As the Act progresses, the smell of the stables increasingly invades the Deanery, and Pinero gradually makes us aware of a certain fearful fascination that gambling on the horses begins to exercise not only on the daughters (who persuade Georgiana at the end of the Act to place a bet on Dandy Dick) but also on the Dean. Here, as with Posket in *The Magistrate*, is a man settled into his official role, but tempted by the natural man beneath. We see in Act I a self-esteem and concern with his dignity that positively invite catastrophe; and we are also made aware through Sir Tristram's memories of the Dean's student days of his earlier passion for gambling. The groundwork is now laid for the complications of Act II.

It is in this Act that the real conflict between mask and face develops. But the prelude to this conflict is the stultifying banality and boredom of an after-dinner 'at home' in the Deanery, against which the excitement of subsequent events is to stand out. Pinero uses the 'double act' of Darbey and Tarver to great effect here, as they offer to entertain the company with music, but comically use the occasion to put each other down:

TARVER (*to himself*). He always presumes with his confounded
    fiddle when I'm going to entertain. He knows that his fiddle's
    never hoarse and that I am, sometimes.
DARBEY (*to himself*). Tarver always tries to cut me out with his
    elderly chest C. he ought to put it on the retired list.
TARVER. I'll sing him off his legs tonight. I'm in lovely voice.
    (*He walks into the library and is heard trying his voice, singing,
    'Come into the garden, Maud.'*)
DARBEY (*to himself*). He needn't bother himself. While he was
    dozing in the carriage, I threw his music out of the window.
                                                                    (p. 27)

Pinero points up the stiff unnaturalness of the 'At Home' in the stylised grouping and asides of the assembled company, as Darbey plays the violin and Sheba accompanies him. Each of the listeners is comically preoccupied with his or her own problems, each pays no attention to the music:

THE DEAN (*mumbling to himself*. A thousand pounds to the
    Restoration Fund and all those bills to settle – oh dear! oh
    dear! What shall I do?
SALOME (*to herself*). I hope my ball dress will drive all the other
    woman mad!
TARVER (*to himself – glaring at DARBEY*). I feel I should like to
    garrote him with his bass string.

GEORGIANA (*frowning at her betting-book*). I think I shall hedge a bit over the Crumbleigh Stakes.

DARBEY (*as he plays, glancing at TARVER*). I wonder how old Tarver's chest C likes a holiday.

SHEBA (*as she plays*). We must get Pa to bed early. Dear Papa's always so dreadfully in the way.

GEORGIANA (*looking round*). No – there's nothing like it in any other country. A regular, pure, simple English Evening at Home!

(p. 28)

This evening, however, will be far from simple. First comes Blore, the servant, with a copy of *The Times; 'the music stops abruptly. All the ladies glare at Blore and hush him down'* (p. 29). But the Dean has specially requested the paper, and discovers from it, to his dismay, that his rash offer to pay £1000 towards repairing the spire if seven others do likewise has been taken up. There quickly follows a second catastrophe: a fire in the neighbouring Swan Inn, where Dandy Dick is stabled. The result, to the Dean's further dismay, is that Dandy Dick has to be stabled in the Deanery. The scene is now set for the Dean's temptation and fall. Left alone, he soliloquises:

What dreadful wave threatens to engulf the Deanery! A horse of sporting tendencies contaminating my stables, his equally vicious owner nestling in the nursery – and my own widowed sister, in all probability, smoking a cigarette at her bedroom window with her feet on the window ledge! (*Listening*) What's that? (*He peers through the window curtains.*) I thought I heard footsteps in the garden. I can see nothing – only the old spire standing out against the threatening sky. (*Leaving the window shudderingly.*) The Spire! My principal creditor! My principal creditor, the most conspicuous object in the city!

(p. 38)

There is a nicely judged rhetoric here; the speech is verbose in the manner of Victorian sermonising and therefore appropriate to the Dean; but its highly coloured, melodramatic flavour seems also comically excessive in relation to the harmless horse and its owner, and suggestive, in a sub-textual way, of the fatal fascination that racing and gambling have for the Dean. The farce world being one in which mischance and mistiming always have their part to play in enmeshing the victim, the Dean is then beset by a series of coincidences: Blore happens to find on the Dean's desk the sum of £50 – exactly the amount Georgiana has urged him to put on Dandy Dick; and the odds happen to be ten to one, so that a win would do much to offset the expense of repairing the spire:

> THE DEAN. What made you tempt me with these at such a moment?
> BLORE. Tempt you, sir! The window was hopen and I feared they might blow away.
> THE DEAN (*catching him by the coat collar*). Man, what were you doing at St Marvell's Races last summer?
> BLORE (*with a cry, falling on his knees*). Oh, sir! Oh, sir! I knew that high-spirited lady would bring grief and sorrow to the peaceful, 'appy Deanery! Oh, sir, I *'ave* done a little on my hown account from time to time on the 'ill, halso hon commission for the kitchen!
> THE DEAN. I knew it – I knew it! . . . Oh, Edward Blore, Edward Blore, what weak creatures we are!
> BLORE. We are, sir – we are – 'specially when we've got a tip, sir. Think of the temptation of a tip, sir.
> THE DEAN. I do, Blore – I do.
>
> (p. 39)

In these exchanges, the Dean is like a moth fluttering nearer and nearer to a flame. The very extremity of his recoil from Blore suggests that he sees in him a mirror-image of himself. Finally, temptation can be resisted no longer, and the Dean, 'with hysterical eagerness' lays his bet:

> Fifty! There's the money. (*Impulsively he crams the notes into* BLORE's *hand and then recoils in horror.*) Oh! (*sinks into a chair with a groan.*)
>
> (p. 39)

Elements from the world of melodrama are very effectively used in the ensuing scene. Tempest and storm rage outside as the Dean wrestles with his conscience, for all the world like some clerical King Lear – 'Rain, thunder. How it assimilates with the tempest of my mind!' (p. 40). Trying to calm himself by reading, he snatches from the shelf a book that turns out to be (consistent with the other coincidences in the scene) *The Horse and its Ailments*, by John Cox MRCVS, a book the Dean had used to doctor his old mare at Oxford. Since Dandy Dick is suffering from a chill, the Dean, with the best of motives, determines to administer a bolus to the horse, and instructs Blore accordingly:

THE DEAN. Blore, I feel it would be a humane act to administer to the poor ignorant animal in my stable a simple bolus as a precaution against chill. I rely upon your aid and discretion in ministering to any guest in the Deanery.

BLORE (*in a whisper*). I see, sir – you ain't going to lose half a chance for tomorrow, sir – you're a knowin' one, sir, as the sayin' goes!

THE DEAN (*shrinking from BLORE with a groan*). Oh! (*He places the medicine chest on the table and takes up the book. Handing the book to BLORE with his finger on a page*). Fetch these humble but necessary articles from the kitchen – quick. I'll mix the bolus here. (*BLORE goes out quickly.*) It is exactly seven-and-twenty years since I last approached a horse medically. (*He takes off his coat and lays it on a chair, then rolls his shirt-sleeves up above his elbows and puts on his glasses.*) I trust that this bolus will not give the animal an unfair advantage over his competitors. I don't desire that! I don't desire that! (*BLORE re-enters carrying a tray, on which are a small flour barrel and rolling-pin, a white china basin, a carafe of water, a napkin and the book. THE DEAN recoils, then guiltily takes the tray from BLORE and puts it on the table.*) Thank you.

BLORE (*holding on to the window-curtain and watching THE DEAN*). His eyes is awful; I don't seem to know the 'appy Deanery when I see such proceedings a' goin' on at the dead of night. (*There is a heavy roll of thunder – THE DEAN mixes a pudding and stirs it with the rolling-pin.*)

(pp. 40–1)

The stage-directions in this extract again recall the world of melodrama, and appropriately enough cue in a further turn of the plot as Blore, to further his own chances with a different horse, decides to mix strychnine in with the bolus, which he does to further accompaniments of thunder. Out of one climax, then, the Dean's first succumbing to temptation, Pinero builds another, the mixing of the bolus, and a third, Blore's counter-plot. By the time the Dean has donned Sir Tristram's coat and sealskin cap (thus completing the transformation from unworldly cleric to shrewd man of the world), experienced ominously *'a dreadful sinking of the heart'*, extinguished the lamp, and exited to do the deed, as *'the thunder rolls'*, the scene has been wrought up to a pitch which would hardly be inappropriate for the murder of Duncan in *Macbeth*. Perhaps indeed a comic allusion is intended, for other details reinforce the idea: the lighted candle that Sir Tristram carries after the Dean's exit, the nightmare that wakes Georgiana up, and the gate-bell ringing violently at the end of the act. The result is effectively farcical because of the disproportion between the auditory and visual signals we receive and the acts they are designed to comment on. The trap having been suitably baited, Pinero now springs it on the hapless victim. With a nice stroke of dramatic irony, Sir Tristram's groom, Hatcham, brings news that 'Topping the constable's collared . . . the villain that set fire to The Swan – in the hact of administering a dose to the 'orse'. And only Blore – and the audience – know the true identity of the prisoner. 'They've got the Dean!' is Blore's aside as the curtain falls (p. 47).

Ben Travers was to claim that he learnt from Pinero 'the general formula for farce: Act II – the sympathetic and guileless hero is landed into the thick of some grievous dilemma or adversity. Act I – he gets into it, Act III – he gets out of it'.[22] Thus far, then *Dandy Dick* follows that general formula. But before the Dean 'gets out of it' further complications ensue in Act III. At the first sight we have of the Dean in Scene I, he is peering over the wicket-gate of his temporary cell in the country police station, enveloped in a fur cap with ear flaps down. He looks for all the world like the horse he has medicined. And, as in the equivalent scene in *The Magistrate*, the conflict between mask and face is a particularly acute and comic one. As with Posket, so here, as the situation grows worse, so the Dean's efforts to resume the style appropriate to his office redouble. His language becomes more verbose and stilted than ever. So grandiloquent is he in fact, that Hannah is scandalised into thinking that the long words betoken some dreadful crime:

HANNAH (*on her knees, clasping her hands*). Tell me what you've done, Master dear; give it a name, for the love of goodness.

THE DEAN. My poor Hannah, I fear I have placed myself in an equivocal position.

HANNAH (*with a shriek of despair*). Ah!

THE DEAN. You appear to misapprehend the precise degree of criminality which attaches to me, Mrs Topping. In the eyes of that majestic, but imperfect instrument, the law, I am an innocent, if not an injured man.

HANNAH. Ah, stick to that, sir! Stick to it, if you think it's likely to serve your wicked ends!

(pp. 53–4)

But he is brought down to a more basic level by the pangs of hunger, and Hannah's offer of some of the joint she has cooked for her husband. Tempted by the natural man's bodily needs, he succumbs, only to be 'caught in the act' by the irate and jealous Noah Topping. If this were French farce, the discovery would not involve eating another man's lunch, but bedding another man's wife. The humour of the situation as Pinero handles it is that the act generates exactly the same degree of moral indignation as would be appropriate for the sexual offence. Noah talks of 'the 'ome you 'ave ruined and laid waste' (p. 48). He commandeers the baking tin as 'evidence against my profligate wife' (p. 61); and he will add to the other charges against the Dean, the charges of 'allynating the affections of my wife' and 'the embezzling o' my midday meal, prepared by her 'ands' (p. 58). The connection between food and sex is made quite explicit when, at the end of the play, Noah's final complaint against the Dean is that 'the man was a unknown lover of my nooly made wife', to which Georgiana replies in a cool put-down worthy of Joe Orton: 'You mustn't bring your domestic affairs here; this is a subject for your own fireside of an evening' (p. 78). In *Dandy Dick* then, as in *The Magistrate*, there is a double pleasure in such moments: amusement at the ironic disproportion between the offence and the reaction it provokes, but pleasure also in an English variation on a French theme, whereby sex is translated into food and we are to some degree encouraged to translate it back again.

The Dean now compounds his initial indiscretion by taking part in a plan to escape from his imprisonment. There is a contrast here to Posket's behaviour in *The Magistrate*. Conflict between mask and face was a very real one in Posket's case, and Posket was essentially the innocent victim. In the case of the Reverend Augustin Judd, interesting elements of irony and ambiguity begin to appear. For the more involved in misadventure the Dean gets, the more he begins to savour the 'wickedness' of his behaviour, though he continues to wear his clerical mask. The pleasure of playing the double role of respected cleric and man on the run is particularly evident when, at the very moment of pocketing the key to the handcuffs, the Dean takes the opportunity of saying 'a few parting words in the home I have apparently wrecked':

> THE DEAN. In setting out upon a journey, the termination of which is problematical, I desire to attest that this erring constable is the husband of a wife from whom it is impossible to withold respect, if not admiration.
> NOAH. You 'ear 'im!
> THE DEAN. As for my wretched self, the confession of my weaknesses must be reserved for another time – another place (*To Georgiana*) To you whose privilege it is to shelter in the sanctity of the Deanery, I give this earnest admonition. Within an hour from this terrible moment, let the fire be lighted in the drawing room – let the missing man's warm bed be waiting for the master – a change of linen prepared. Withold your judgements. Wait.
>
> (p. 65)

A high moral tone here co-exists with shrewd hints to his sister on making ready for the fugitive after his escape. Moral rectitude continues comically to co-exist with knavery to the end. Prepared to jump jail himself, but thwarted by the change of horses, the Dean none-the-less reproves those who rescue him willy nilly: 'Do I understand that I have been forcibly and illegally rescued? . . . . Who has committed such a reprehensible act) (pp. 69–70). Forced finally to confess that he has backed a horse, but learning that Blore has put the money on the wrong one, he reads him a moral lesson: 'I could have pardoned everything but this last act of disobedience. You are unworthy of the Deanery. Leave it for some ordinary household (p. 77). And when Blore counter-attacks with a bit of polite blackmail, the Dean finds another piece of moral camouflage, for which Blore gives him the hint:

BLORE. Suppose grief drove me to my cups?
THE DEAN. I must save you from intemperance at any cost.
Remain in my service – a sad, sober, and, above all, a silent
man!

(p. 77)

There is a tongue-in-cheek quality about these exchanges which
pleases, rather as in cinema such Ealing comedies as *Kind Hearts
and Coronets* and *The Ladykillers* pleased: a reputable and moral
front is preserved to cover disreputable behaviour. If hypocrisy
was a prevalent vice of Victorian England, here it is delicately and
effectively mocked.

As the play ends, Pinero resolves the complicated intrigues with
skill, wit and playful artifice. As in *The Magistrate*, we are returned
to the secure world of the opening scene, in this case the morning-
room of the Deanery. There is the same deliberate choreographing
of stage movement and grouping, as, for example, in the stylised
pantomime of joy and dismay as the daughters first happily greet
their returned father, (*SALOME seizes his hands, SHEBA his coat-
tails and turn him round violently*), and then react with shock when
they learn he's discovered their extravagance with the dressmaker,
(*SHEBA sits aghast on the table – SALOME distractedly falls on the
floor.*) (p. 73). There is the same sense, after the 'disciplined
anarchy' of the previous events, of a merry dance in which the
partners may at last come together; and Pinero takes advantage
of the obligatory proposal scene in which the military men offer
themselves to Salome and Sheba, to mock affectionately the
conventions of popular romance:

SHEBA. Oh, Mr Darbey, I have never thought of marriage
seriously.
DARBEY. People never do till they *are* married.
SHEBA. But think, only think of my age.
DARBEY. Pardon me, Sheba – but what is your age?
SHEBA. Oh, it is so very little – it is not worth mentioning.
Cannot we remain friends and occasionally correspond?
DARBEY. Well, of course – if you insist –
SHEBA. No, no, I see that is impracticable. It must be wed or
part. All I ask is time – time to ponder over such a question,
time to know myself better.
DARBEY. Certainly, how long?

SHEBA. Give me two or three minutes. Hush!

(pp. 67–8)

It is a scene to which Oscar Wilde may well have been indebted eight years later, in *The Importance of Being Earnest*. And Pinero's final touch is to have Georgiana break the illusion of the fourth wall, and address the audience directly, to point a moral, and solicit applause:

> SIR TRISTRAM. Why, Judd, there's no harm in laughter, for those who laugh or those who are laughed at.
> GEORGIANA. Provided always – first, that it is Folly that is laughed at and not Virtue; secondly, that it is our friends who laugh at us (*to the audience*), as we hope that all will, for our pains.
> ### CURTAIN
> (p. 80)

Thus gracefully are we returned from the invented world of the farce to our own real world.

3

Ben Travers and the Aldwych Farces

The Aldwych farces of the 1920s and 1930s provide a classic example of a fruitful collaboration between a playwright – Ben Travers – and a team of actors, headed by Ralph Lynn, Robertson Hare and Tom Walls, who managed and directed the company. My discussion of these farces will focus on three in particular, *Rookery Nook* (1926), *Thark* (1927) and *Plunder* (1928), as representative of Travers's work at its best and most characteristic, and on the three leading members of the company already referred to, who seemed especially to stimulate the dramatist's inventive flair.

The collaboration came about because Walls leased the Aldwych Theatre in 1923 as a base for a very successful farce by Will Evans, called *Tons of Money*, in which Ralph Lynn and Yvonne Arnaud scored notable hits; it was followed by a second farce, *It Pays to Advertise*, which did poor business. As a result, Walls looked around for a play to take its place. Hearing of Ben Travers's *A Cuckoo in the Nest* from Lawrence Grossmith, an actor who had acquired the stage rights of the play, but now wanted to dispose of it, he arranged a meeting with the playwright, and from this sprang eight years of fruitful co-operation between the company and the man who was to become their 'house dramatist'.

Initially, however, Ben Travers had considerable reservations about teaming up with Tom Walls and Ralph Lynn. He prided himself on the core of reality in his farces, on, as he puts it

> making the characters recognisable types of human beings. The funniness must be in the situation and circumstances in which these human beings find themselves, and these are only funny because the characters are so recognisably human.[1]

And he was many years later to criticise the National Theatre's

1976 production of *Plunder* for its 'lapses into extraneous funniness' (p. 165). But he associated Walls and Lynn with the broader caricatures of music-hall:

> Tom Walls. I had seen him sometimes, an unfunny and over-red-nosed comedian playing small parts in musical shows. The father-in-law who was the leading support character in the *Cuckoo* called for a straight comedy actor. . . . The idea of Tom Walls red-nosing and reeling his way through it dismayed me.
>
> Ralph Lynn, I had seen only once, and that in a very silly music-hall sketch. (Lynn specialised in monocled, 'silly ass' types, celebrated in music-hall songs like *Gilbert the Filbert* or *Reckless Reggie of the Regents Palace*). Wouldn't this mean that the conscientious young husband of my farce would be caricatured and nincompooped into fatuous unreality?
>
> (p. 88)

Ruefully, he later recognised how wrong he was: 'The glorious restrained study that Tom made of the befuddled Major Bone surprised me as much as it gratified me. . . . (And as for Ralph Lynn), 'I was about to join forces with the greatest farce actor of our time' (p. 88).

The problems Ben Travers became aware of were of a different kind. They were partly due to Tom Walls's cavalier and dictatorial actor-manager ways. Thus, Walls would ignore the third act of the play he was directing and acting in until the last week of rehearsals. In the case of *A Cuckoo in the Nest*, this led to a most distressing ordeal for Travers: by the time the first and second acts had been revised and rewritten as rehearsals proceeded (Travers being a very professional collaborator and always willing to adapt his material to the team), the original third act had become totally inappropriate; and Travers had completely to rewrite the third act to an extremely tight deadline, while suffering himself from whooping-cough. Walls would also leave the learning of his own role to a dangerously late stage, with the result as Travers recounts, that he would sometimes dry; and more often than should have been the case, need the assistance of a prompt. It seems also that during the London run, Walls 'would constantly prolong the interval between acts while he entertained desirable guests in his dressing room' (p. 111), and he frequently didn't appear when he was billed to appear. Ralph Lynn, by contrast, was impeccably professional and serious about his work:

> (Ralph) was never satisfied so long as there was a single line in any of his scenes which wasn't right. All through the run of a farce he would worry and experiment until he got the thing to his liking. In those moments, there were none of the waggeries and wisecracks of his leisure hours; we were concentrating on the solemn problems of creating laughter. Nobody ever appreciated so well as Ralph how intensely serious is the job of being funny.
>
> (p. 94)

But Lynn also had a gift for 'making it new', which sometimes took the form of improvising a new and brilliantly effective piece of business; something which Travers admired in his work:

> Often in the course of our long years together, I looked into his dressing room after a show and said: 'That was a lovely bit of business tonight in the second act. Don't forget to keep it in.' And he asked blankly, 'Why, what did I do?'
>
> (p. 91)

Less productive of the playwright's admiration were Lynn's occasional verbal 'adlibbings':

> At rehearsals of the *Cuckoo*. . . . I listened to Ralph's interpolations with aversion. Some, admittedly, were good; but I felt uneasy about taking the nominal responsibility for a line like this: when, having written a false name in the visitors' book, his entry is inspected by the puritanical landlady, 'You don't write very clear,' 'No, I've just had some very thick soup.' I gently protested, but Ralph said he'd like to try it, and it always got a big laugh. And, after all, it's exactly the sort of thing Ralph himself would have said in the circumstances.
>
> (p. 91)

It would seem, however, that as the relationship of playwright and actor matured, Travers became expert at giving Lynn opportunities for pieces of comic business (some of which I refer to below), while Lynn restrained his tendency to improve upon the playwright's text; although, in such a working relationship, a degree of cross-fertilisation must have existed, and one cannot finally determine today whether a particular piece of comic business, or even a particular gag, now enshrined in the text, originated with Travers or with Lynn.

A further challenge that Travers had to meet in his writing for the company was the necessity to preserve a due balance between the roles of Tom Walls and Ralph Lynn. He found himself under the necessity of producing scripts that were in effect aimed at creating a 'double act', as for such contemporary television acts as Morecambe and Wise or The Two Ronnies. By 1926, when *Rookery Nook* was produced, Lynn and Walls were regarded as co-stars, comedians of equal standing; and the first result of this was that they had become, and were always to remain,

> extremely sensitive and aware, not only about their own individual material so much, but about each other's. I had not merely to write farces containing two leading male characters of equal importance, but to organise my scripts so that in their scenes together, if one were given a line calculated to raise a laugh, the next laugh had to go to the other. Or if, unavoidably, A got two laughs in succession, B must forthwith be allowed to bring the score level. It was an intriguing exercise, and proved very beneficial to the farces. Tom and Ralph soon learned to rely on me to observe the fifty-fifty rule, but at the outset they kept a pretty sharp look-out about it. The only time I was interrupted in my reading of *Rookery Nook* was when, at one point, I had given Ralph what sounded like three to nil, and my drawing-room rang with Tom's quick challenge: 'Hi-hi – what's all this?'
>
> (p. 95)

Lynn and Walls may sound unduly small-minded or self-regarding in this account, but they were in fact showing an instinctive awareness of their farcical potential as a double act. Walter Kerr, suggesting that 'comedy insists not upon the uniqueness of the hero's qualities but upon their commonness,' draws attention to the importance of working in tandem in comedy:

> More often than not comedians come two by two from the ark, one tall and one short, one fat and one thin. A comedy team is

more easily arrived at than a comedy star working solo, because the double image instantly suggests the prevalence of what is deplorable in the human condition. Oliver Hardy is not the only incompetent in the world, Stan Laurel is his proud equal. Even when one member of the team is little more than a 'straight man', rapidly setting up loaded questions for his zanier companion to answer witlessly, he is sorely missed when he is gone.[2]

Not the least of Ben Travers's skills as a farce writer was his ability, once prompted by Walls and Lynn, to utilise their contrasting and complementary skills. The parts he created for Tom Walls – Clive Popkiss, the fancy-free cousin of Gerald in *Rookery Nook*, who gets the spare girl in the end, Hector Benbow, the sporty baronet in *Thark*, and Freddy the professional jewel thief in *Plunder*, draw to a considerable degree on Walls the man. His off-stage characteristics were those of a sportsman, a hard drinker, a gambler, a ladies man, a bossy, extravagant and racy man about town – a combination, if you will, of Clive, Hector and Freddy. The parts he created for Lynn, Gerald Popkiss for *Rookery Nook*, Ronny Gamble in *Thark*, D'Arcy Tuck in *Plunder*, build on the silly ass, monocled idiot persona, which was largely a stage creation of Lynn's, predating the association with Travers. Travers also built notably on the physical skills and unerring sense of timing that Lynn the actor possessed. *Thark*, for example, is particularly rich in pieces of comic business that arise out of the Ralph Lynn/Ronny Gamble character: the comic mime with the whisky on his entry in Act I; the laocoonian struggle that develops later in the act as Ronny incompetently tries to help Hook off with his overcoat; and the business in Act II with the flowers, in which they drop out of the wrapping, leaving him presenting the empty paper to Kitty.

But Travers's real achievement lay in the way he made of these separate creations in each play, a double act in which each partner acted as foil to the other. We can see this at work in *Thark* in the opening exchanges between Sir Hector Benbow (Walls) and his nephew Ronny Gamble (Lynn). It is interesting to note, incidentally, that with each new farce, Walls alternated between playing someone of his own age and real life appearance, and an elderly character part. 'He preferred the former,' writes Ben Travers, 'but he was incomparably funnier and easier to cater for as gentlemen

of riper years; and in *Thark* he was at his best'.[3] In the extract that
follows, Ronny's dropping of conversational bricks depends for
its funniness on Benbow's gruff, irritated rejoinders:

BENBOW. I've had some very awkward news, my boy. Your
aunt's coming back home tonight.
RONNY. What? And Kitty?
BENBOW: No. Just your aunt – that's enough ain't it?
RONNY. I say, why is auntie coming home? Has she heard
something about you?
BENBOW. What d'yer mean? There is nothing to hear about
me.
RONNY. I know. That's why I asked in that surprised way.
....
BENBOW. There's nothing to hear, I tell you.
RONNY. I know – that's just what I say. And very glad I am
of it.
BENBOW. Glad of what?
RONNY. Glad that she heard nothing – because she can't have,
because there's nothing to hear.
BENBOW. I can think of nothing that could have brought her
home.
RONNY. Well naturally, I can think of nothing. . . . But now
auntie's home, Kitty will be left all alone in Bath.
BENBOW. That's all right, she's old enough to look after herself.
RONNY. I know, and that's just when girls begin to get looked
after. You know, uncle, Bath's a very dangerous place. . . .
Full of Beaux – you know – Beau Somethings.
BENBOW. Not now. Only old people with gout.
RONNY. Oh, I see bow legs.
BENBOW . . . They only go there to drink water.
RONNY. Oh, really? I'm surprised you've ever heard of the
place.

(pp. 17–19)

The dialogue has some of the flavour of a cross-talk act, with
Benbow as 'straight man' and Ronny as 'joker'. Ronny keeps
up a disrespectful, slightly mocking running commentary egging
Benbow on, and sometimes tripping him up. Benbow is slow,
ponderous, rather self-satisfied, Ronny quick and funny, in a
zany, rather harebrained way. It was, no doubt the skill with

which Travers used the two men as foils to each other that explains why, in the haunted room sequence at the end of the play, as Travers recounts it, 'the incident of Tom and Ralph as joint occupants of a small double bed produced a longer and louder sequence of laughs than any other scene between the two in the history of Aldwych farces,'[4]

In *Plunder*, where Tom Walls played the part of a professional jewel thief, Freddy Malone, and Ralph Lynn his reluctant accomplice, D'Arcy Tuck, Ben Travers felt that he had accomplished the difficult task of making his central characters robbers and (accidental) murderers, while keeping them laughable and sympathetic, by exploiting the contrast in the personalities of Ralph and Tom. The contrast is particularly effective at the end of Act II, Scene I. In the extract that follows, Freddy's grim-faced professional anxiety and concern serves initially to highlight D'Arcy's alarmingly amateur recklessness, his tendency to regard robbery as a merry jape, without potentially serious consequences. But as the true situation dawns on him, the smile freezes on his face:

FREDDY. Now look here, D'Arcy. If you think you'll have any regrets, now's your time to chuck it.

D'ARCY. Chuck it? I'm going through with it, for her sake. She might think it's wrong, but I know it's right. I'm in it up to the – shins.

FREDDY. Good boy . . . you can have one more drink if you like.

D'ARCY. No. I don't want drinks. I've got no fear.

FREDDY. Haven't you? Then get some. That's where everyone falls down sooner or later at this game. They think it's easy.

D'ARCY. What? But you said this would be easy?

FREDDY. That's just why you've got to be afraid. Afraid of the tiniest slip. One footprint might do it – one finger mark.

D'ARCY. I'll wear gloves. They always wear gloves.

FREDDY. Some people think the police are easily fooled. *Are* they?

D'ARCY. Well, you've fooled them before now.

FREDDY. Never. What I've done is never to let 'em suspect. I've got a very high opinion of Scotland Yard.

D'ARCY. Scotland Yard? But no one from Scotland Yard will come here?

FREDDY. Of course, they'll come tomorrow.

D'ARCY. Why?

FREDDY. Why? We're not going to scrump apples. Do you know what we could get for this?

D'ARCY. *No*.

FREDDY. Ten years.

D'ARCY. Ten! I didn't think it would be so much as that. You didn't make this very clear to me.

(pp. 44–5)

Later in the play, when both men are cross-examined by Scotland Yard, the humour of the scene depends on the precisely anti-thetical nature of the two interviews: Freddy is cool and imperturbable under pressure; D'Arcy is nervous, accident-prone, scatter-brained, yet effectively blocks all attempts to incriminate him with a lunatic logic that is all his own:

SIBLEY. I can prove you ran downstairs, out of the house and straight to the garage. Now, definitely, did you or did you not?

D'ARCY. I did not (*pause*). Unless –

SIBLEY. Unless what?

D'ARCY. Unless you mean when I did.

SIBLEY. In any case why were you down in the hall so soon?

D'ARCY. So soon as what?

SIBLEY. Well, so soon as you *were*?

D'ARCY. But that's ridiculous – I mean, if I *was* there as soon as I was there – I mean – naturally – there I was.

(pp. 74–5)

The pairing of Walls and Lynn, then, was central to Travers's farces. but, as Walter Kerr says, developing his argument about duality in comedy,

there is a tendency for the team to increase and multiply, so that we continue to expect comedy as we go to see the Three Stooges, or the Four Marx Brothers, or the Five Little Foys. Seriousness produces no such gatherings of the clan.[5]

Specifically, in the Aldwych team, there was Robertson Hare. Ben Travers had not written the Harold Twine role of the henpecked husband in *Rookery Nook* with Hare in mind. But he played it, and, as Travers writes,

> the fact that he played it initiated and practically dictated a new feature in Aldwych policy. The farces thereafter generally had to contain a situation in which he stood between an inexorable Walls, and a plausible but no less ruinous Lynn, to be fleeced of his fair repute, of his cash, and of his trousers.
>
> (p. 97)

And Travers goes on to suggest that Hare's shortness of stature, his baldness, and the clerical intonation of his voice helped establish him as the familiar 'earnest little citizen' who is a born victim.

To an extent, then, from *Rookery Nook* onwards, the Walls-Lynn double act became a triple act. In *Thark*, Robertson Hare appeared as Hook, 'a middle-aged and rather careworn manservant, with a manner which is the result of years of bullying'; and in *Plunder*, he played Oswald, the middle-aged mother's boy, who tries gormlessly to woo Freddy's accomplice, Prudence, and the constant butt of D'Arcy's jibes. But his most effective incarnation in the plays here discussed remains that of Harold Twine, the most respectable, inhibited and mild-mannered of men; trailing after his formidable wife, '*looking like a rabbit at a stoat's tea party*', and constantly involved by Gerald and Clive in a series of compromising situations, as in the following extract, where he unwillingly agrees to help conceal the presence of a girl in the house:

GERALD. . . . As man to man – swear not to say a word.
TWINE. Oh, but it's awful.
CLIVE. It isn't.
GERALD. It isn't. Come round early tomorrow and I'll tell you all. Till then, swear!
CLIVE. Go on. Swear, blast you!
TWINE. Oh!
GERALD. You're always in the vocative. Swear!
CLIVE. Hurry up! Swear!
TWINE. Oh, botheration!
CLIVE. Not that kind of swear, you fool! Promise.
TWINE. Well, I daren't tell Gertrude that that girl's here.
GERALD. Daren't? That's all right. That's a swear. And come round in the morning early.

TWINE. But the harm will be done by then.
GERALD. Harm? There's no harm I tell you.
CLIVE. Of course not, you evil-minded little man . . .
GERTRUDE (*appearing at kitchen door down L*). Harold!
TWINE. Yes, dear.

....

GERALD (*seizing TWINE as he is following*). Remember Twine,
   you've sworn.
TWINE. Oh, misery me!

....

GERTRUDE (*heard off*). Harold!
CLIVE. Don't hang about. Go on.
GERALD. Go on. Get out.
                    (*TWINE exits up R.C. leaving door open*)
                                                        (pp. 46–50)

To complete the team, two other principals were also important:
Mary Brough, for whom Travers created a series of roles that
played variations on the theme of the bossy, physically formidable,
rather vulgar middle-aged lady, interfering in other people's lives
(Mrs Leverett, the 'daily' in *Rookery Nook*, Mrs Hewlett, the ex-
housekeeper trying to do the heroine out of her inheritance in
Plunder, and Mrs Frush, the nouveau-riche tenant of *Thark*); and
Winifred Shotter, who appeared first as Rhoda Marley in *Rookery
Nook*, and went on to play the roles Travers created to supply the
love interest in subsequent farces (Kitty Stratton in *Thark*, Joan
Hewlett in *Plunder*). Thus the plays were, as G. S. Fraser
comments, shaped around a cast composed of,

the horsy, cunning Tom Walls; the silly ass Ralph Lynn, always
dropping his monocle; the bald, clerkish, bespectacled
Robertson Hare always liable at some point in the play to have
his trousers removed for perfectly logical reasons; the slim,
pretty Winifred Shotter, equally liable to dash across the stage
in her underclothes; and Mary Brough, the gruff, suspicious
landlady.[6]

Much of the audience's pleasure in the Aldwych farces must
have derived from the familiarity of this team. Macqueen Pope
writes of the Aldwych first nights that

(they) were like great family parties, for Tom Walls got a team
together whom the audience felt were their personal friends.
They always had to speak off-stage before entering to give the
applause which they received a chance to die down and not
hold the play up too much.[7]

Even Walls's propensity to dry was, it seems, expected and
enjoyed by the audience. He 'would . . . wink at the audience,
and say to the stage manager in the prompt corner, 'Now then,
Bobbie, what is it', and Bobbie Dunn would tell him, to the intense
delight of the audience, who loved this little human and intimate
touch.'[8] Also part of the ritual was the fact that Travers would trip
up when he came on to take a call: 'He was expected to, and if
he did not then Tom would arrange it himself and trip him.'[9]

The audience for the Aldwych farces would get in each play a
combination of familiarity with newness, of the known with the
unknown. Thus, they would bring to each successive reincar-
nation of the victimised Robertson Hare character, their knowledge
of previous victimisations, assuredly a bonus for any dramatist.
As a newspaper review of the film adaptation of *Turkey Time* puts it:

> 'The old Aldwych situation', murmurs a member of the audi-
> ence, as Mr Robertson Hare, the collecting box of the carol-
> singers in his hand and apprehension shining from his spec-
> tacles, and pathetically depressing the corners of his mouth, is
> led firmly to the middle of the screen by those two relentless
> gaolers, Mr Tom Walls and Mr Ralph Lynn. There was no
> plaintiveness, no irritation in the murmur; rather was it a tribute
> to the wizardry of the Aldwych company in accomplishing the
> extremely difficult feat of repeating itself without becoming
> wearisome. A serious student of the Aldwych farces would be
> able to pick out parallel after parallel from other plays for the
> string of preposterous incidents which go to make up the plot
> of *Turkey Time*.[10]

The combination of sameness with difference is, however, best
studied in the parts Travers wrote for Ralph Lynn. The parts are
sufficiently unlike to prevent the audience feeling that the author
is repeating himself in a stale, unprofitable way, yet sufficiently
like to provide a reassuring element of recognition. In *Rookery
Nook*, the 'Britishness' of Gerald Popkiss is well to the fore in

the confrontations with the comic foreigner, the bullet-headed Prussian, Putz. British ignorance of foreign languages, British understatment, the British tendency to regard all foreigners as a joke – all are deployed with some effect to deflate Putz's bluster and braggadacio. In *Thark*, the romantic side of the Ralph Lynn character is more in evidence, though constantly undercut by the misadventures that befall him. There is a touch of the Noel Coward, Evelyn Waugh world of the 'bright young things' of the Twenties, in the relationship of Kitty and Ronny Gamble. And as in, say, *Private Lives*, Travers suggests a genuine affection underlying the persiflage, the facetiousness, and the farcical misunderstandings. In *Plunder*, Travers sets himself two quite new problems with the Ralph Lynn character, D'Arcy Tuck, which he overcomes deftly and skilfully. Firstly, D'Arcy cannot be too much of a fortune-hunter; otherwise the necessary contrast with Freddy would not be there; we would not believe in the romance between him and Joan, and the play would be tilted towards a grim, satirical view of the world, foreign to Travers's farcical purpose. But, equally, he must be just sufficiently interested in the property, and the cheating of Joan by Mrs Hewlett, to join forces with Freddy. So Travers created in D'Arcy the figure of an amiable drone, rather naively delighted that his fiancée has property and money, but not cynically on the make. Love and property are comically mixed up in his mind, but the disarming frankness with which he reveals this does not suggest a calculating man:

JOAN. Well, are you pleased with the place?

D'ARCY. Can this be possible? It all belongs to you.

JOAN. Of course. And it's going to belong to you, too.

D'ARCY. I love to hear you say that. But, Joan, remember, I loved you before I ever knew you had this house and property and money. I suppose there's some money, isn't there?

JOAN. Oh, yes. I don't know how much yet, but there's bound to be heaps.

D'ARCY. Yes, there's got to be. I mean with a place this size, it stands to reason. But I love you quite apart from this.

JOAN. This is nothing. This is only the library.

D'ARCY. I don't care. I should love you just as much in any other of the rooms – drawing-room, dining-room, bathroom – I'm the same all over the house.

(p. 12)

When Freddy reveals that he's a professional jewel-thief, and invites D'Arcy to come in with him, Travers has D'Arcy just sufficiently reluctant, and finally tipped over the edge by honest indignation at the trick played on his fiancée. Browning's lines in *Bishop Bloughram's Apology* well suggest our own response to D'Arcy and the course he subsequently takes in the play:

> Our interest's on the dangerous edge of things,
> The honest thief, the tender murderer,
> The superstitious atheist . . .
> We watch while these in equilibrium keep
> The giddy line midway.[11]

The comic figure of the half-hearted thief, conventionally horrified, underneath rather fascinated by the idea of crime, threatened with disaster, yet winning through, not despite his silliness but because of it, reminds us that Travers, though he uses stereotypes, does not do so exclusively, and can on occasion show a subtlety of observation that is reminiscent of the farce-writer he acknowledges as his master, Pinero.

What, however, all the Ralph Lynn characters have in common is their splendid conversational accident-proneness, the unfailing regularity with which the Lynn character slips on verbal banana-skins, ties himself in verbal knots. Bentley's reference to danger being 'omnipresent' in farce relates here to the tension created as an audience watches Lynn skating on thin ice, and waits for the ice to crack. when, against all the odds, the Lynn character manages to salvage the situation, the tension is released in laughter. A representative example comes from *Thark*. Here, Ronny is endeavouring to reassure Kitty of his devotion, while uneasily aware that he's agreed to cover up for his uncle, by taking the latter's girl friend out to dinner. The extract provides what Ben Travers has described as a distinctive and inimitable feature of Lynn's technique (though he could equally well have described it as a distinctive feature of the scripts he wrote for him):

> the throw-away line. He made deliberate, unfunny, definite and convincing declaration; then, unable to contain his self-satisfaction, he ruined the whole effect by some ill-considered afterthought.

> (p. 91)

RONNY. . . . You know, darling how much I want to be with you. If I'd known you were coming, wild horses wouldn't have dragged me from you. Unless, of course, there'd been a lot of them.

KITTY. I'm sure of it, Ronny, so don't worry any more about it. . . . I'm quite happy as long as I know that you really love me.

D'ARCY. Really love you! Darling, don't say that. Of course I do. Why if anyone came up to me – It wouldn't matter how big he was (*Bus, gestures a very small man, then quickly changes to a tall one*) – and said, 'Ronny' – or 'Ronald', if he didn't know me very well – 'You don't love her', I – I – I wouldn't believe him, – honestly!

....

KITTY. Well, one moment Ronny. We *will* meet for supper?

RONNY (*bringing her down stage*). Meet for supper, darling! Of course we will, darling. (*Returning*) Oh, supper with you – in some shady – night-club – with nothing between us but the table and knives and forks of course, and flowers on the table, and waiters – waiters on the floor; with you by my side – by my front – good-bye! (*Kisses her, Crosses up stage*) Till that – (*Trying to go. At door he misses the handle of the door absent-mindedly picks up tall brass vase and puts it down again.*)

KITTY. (*Holding him up again.*) But, Ronny, where are we going to meet? And when?

RONNY (*Bringing her back again*). Meet – and when? Lucky you called me back again. Meet – and when? Leave it entirely to me. As soon as I'm free, I'll phone you.

KITTY. Yes, but where shall I be?

RONNY. Darling, I don't care where you go. Wherever you go, I'll phone you. Darling you do trust me, don't you?

(pp. 33–6)

As *The Times* reviewer, albeit writing of Lynn's performance in a different piece (*Turkey Time*), puts it:

Mr Lynn goes through his trick of dropping verbal bricks and retrieving them an inch from the ground with that assurance which stamps the slip-fielder with twenty years of experience in first-class cricket behind him.[12]

Part also of the appeal of the Ralph Lynn 'persona' created by Ben Travers lies in another characteristic common to Gerald Popkiss, Ronny Gamble, and D'Arcy Tuck: a vein of schoolboy humour that went appropriately with the 'silly ass', Bertie Wooster aspect of the man. It consists in a kind of innocent cheekiness, an ability to call names and make impertinent remarks, but remarks which are devoid of real malice, and usually attempts by the Ralph Lynn character to 'keep his end up'. Thus, in *Rookery Nook*, we have Gerald calling the daily help 'Mrs Flannelfoot' (p. 8), Robertson Hare, 'you swine of a Twine' (p. 116), and the ferocious Putz alternately 'Putty, old thing', and 'you damn great stiff' (p. 92). In *Thark*, the insults are directed mainly at Lionel, a possible rival of Ronny's in his pursuit of Kitty, and at the sinister butler, Jones, alias Death. In response to Lionel's, 'I shall be here for some time,' we have Ronny's, 'Oh, that's fine. I hope we shall see – nothing of you' (p. 53); and, in response to one of Jones's sinister noises (in this instance a hiss), we have Ronny's, 'Don't worry about him. He probably used to be in the siphon business' (p. 104). In *Plunder*, D'Arcy's choicest insults are reserved for Mrs Hewlett and her son Oswald, 'your nasty son, Nozzle' (p. 23), 'an awful sort of thing like an egg' (p. 16). Mary Brough, who played Mrs Hewlett, was a large lady, and D'Arcy does not let us forget it. Thus, when Mrs Hewlett says, 'You'll have to go a long way to get around me', his response is, 'You're quite right. I'd have to take a taxi' (p. 35).

Thus far, in illustrating the particularly close collaboration between Ben Travers and the Aldwych team for whom he was writing, I have touched on some features of the farces which are of perennial appeal: the skilful and satisfying way they build on the contrasting yet complementary skills of Lynn, Hare and Walls; the combination of familiarity with strangeness, whereby Travers, working within the framework provided by the team and the distinctive farce world he created for them, yet managed to 'make it new' with each successive farce. But a little more needs to be said about the distinctiveness of that farce world.

It is a world which has some resemblance in its humour and character types to the kind of world depicted in the comic post-cards of Donald McGill – postcards which were popular in the inter-war years, and of which George Orwell has written affection-ately and appreciatively in 'The Art of Donald McGill'. The stereo-type figures of this world, as Orwell describes them, were the henpecked husband, the nagging wife or tyrannous mother-in-law, the Edwardian 'knut' or 'masher', in evening dress and opera hat, the lecherous hard drinking man-about-town (sometimes identified with the 'masher', sometimes distinguished from him), the newly married couple on their honeymoon, the comic foreigner, and the comic charlady. The humour of the captions encompassed punning ('Do you keep stationery, miss?' 'Sometimes I wriggle a little'); sexual innuendo ('I like seeing experienced girls home'. 'But I'm not experienced'. 'You're not home yet'); vulgar jokes about big behinds, big bosoms, or the physical functions of the body. Such figures and such humour are the staple of the Ben Travers farces. Lynn, Hare and Walls incarnate figures such as the 'masher', the hen-pecked husband, the lecherous man-about-town. Mary Brough's Mrs Leverett, Ethel Coleridge's Gertrude Twine, and Griffith Humphrey's Putz in *Rookery Nook* offer examples, respectively, of the comic charlady, the nagging wife, and the comic foreigner. Mary Brough's Mrs Frush in *Thark* and her Mrs Hewlett in *Plunder* provide bossy mother/mother-in-law figures. Puns are plentiful, for example:

GERALD. You've been married for years. Get a bodice.
TWINE. All right. A bust one.
GERALD (*in horror*). Certainly not – a sound one.

(*Rookery Nook*, p. 85)

And there are touches of vulgarity, as in the after-dinner scene which opens Act III of *Thark;*

BENBOW (*sitting behind table near Ronny – as the storm is heard outside*). Wind's up.
RONNY (*sitting R. of table – with challenge*). What's that?
BENBOW. All right – I was only referring to the elements.

(p. 82)

It is a world which, as Orwell suggests, is essentially

the music-hall world where marriage is a dirty joke or a comic disaster, where the rent is always behind . . . where the lawyer is always a crook and the Scotsman always a miser, where the newly weds make fools of themselves on the hideous beds of seaside lodging houses and the drunken red-nosed husbands roll home at four in the morning to meet the linen-nightgowned wives who wait for them behind the front door, poker in hand.[13]

Ben Travers's farces are more 'up-market' than this description would suggest, but the music-hall element that Orwell sees as source for Donald McGill's postcards is also present in the farces. Travers may initially have regarded Walls's and Lynn's music-hall background as liable to lead them into caricature; but that was based on a misunderstanding of their artistry, and, I would also suggest, an apprentice dramatist's initial and slightly over-solemn insistence on the 'realism' of *Rookery Nook*. Travers was later to write, in his autobiography, of his admiration for such music-hall figures as Harry Tate, George Robey, Max Miller, Billy Bennett, and the Crazy Gang. Max Miller's sporty vulgarity was not far removed from the Tom Walls persona, as embodied in roles like Sir Hector Benbow or Freddy Malone; among George Robey's most admired sketches were those of the German Professor of Music – a comic Prussian with a lot of mixed-up German English, a possible ancestor of Putz in *Rookery Nook* – as Admiral Juddy, with his 'ferocious Chinese oaths' in the same play, is a blood relation of Major Bloodnock, 'late of the third disgusting Fusiliers', in the *Goon Show*. The 'silly ass' figure of Ralph Lynn survives too in contemporary lower-class versions in the Ron and Eth sketches in *Take It From Here*, or in Eccles of the *Goon Show*. Also the use of 'catchphrases' in *Rookery Nook*, where Mrs Leverett's 'the other bedrooms is elsewhere', and 'earlier than that I cannot be' become running gags returned to throughout the farce, is a familiar music-hall feature.

From another point of view, however, Travers was right to see his work as separate from the music-hall; for, though the cross-fertilisation exists, farce has its own discipline, and any full length play must in itself have a coherence and a structure that could not be found in a series of music-hall turns. Travers admits that, when he first tried his hand at farce,

I was under the delusion still shared by many people that farce was the easiest sort of play to write. I was soon to find out and to continue finding out, that no form of stage entertainment is more difficult successfully to write, to produce or to act.

(p. 63)

The man who taught him most concerning the craftsmanship and techniques involved was Pinero, whom he describes as his 'patron saint'. Sent in 1905 to Malacca as a reluctant clerk to the family firm of wholesale grocers, Joseph Travers and Sons, Ltd., he found, in the small public library there, a set of the plays of Pinero:

> I fell upon them with the rapturous excitement of Ben Gunn lighting upon the treasures of Captain Flint. Work? Business? With such reading on hand, who could be guilty of so unworthy a consideration as trying to do business? Especially in Malacca. . . . They were not merely plays to read. Each one of them was a guide-book to the technique of stage-craft. I studied them as such, counting and noting the number of speeches and the method of plot and character development. I discovered for myself the real secret of Pinero's mastery, namely his attention in every sense to the importance of climax.[14]

And indeed, particularly in *Rookery Nook* and *Thark*, Travers demonstrates his ability to quicken the tempo, complicate the situation, build a climax within what he calls the 'general formula for farce: Act II – the sympathetic and guileless hero is landed into the thick of some grievous dilemma or adversity. Act I – he gets into it. Act III – he gets out of it' (p. 63). In *Plunder*, where there is a steadier narrative line, leading up to and down from the central robbery and death, the Pinero influence is felt more in the conception of D'Arcy Tuck as the innocent accomplice, tempted by Freddy's plans, succumbing to the temptation, and frighteningly compromised in so doing.

Where Travers's craftsmanship and sense of structure are also displayed, is in the opportunity his scripts give for a variety of physical routines, for the establishment of particular mannerisms, gestures and pieces of business associated with a particular character. When such routines are repeated, not mechanically, but as natural responses to a developing situation, they gather a momentum of laughter which gives richness and texture to what on the printed page may seem rather thin. In the same way, a running joke or catch-phrase may attract laughter out of all proportion to its impact in isolation. Obviously one cannot recapture precisely the original routines of the Aldwych team, but a good modern production provides convincing testimony of the opportunities. An excellent example was Mark Kingston's direction of *Rookery Nook*, at the Shaftesbury Theatre, London, in 1986. In this production, Derek Smith's Harold Twine externalised in every nervous twitch how deeply hen-pecked a husband he was; whether peering over the brim of his straw hat and nervously nibbling at it, or bobbing up and down from his seat and taking two steps forward and three steps back, or being physically propelled about the stage by Clive and Ralph, he showed at every turn how the victim in farce is often reduced to the level of automaton or puppet. Peggy Mount's Mrs Leverett exploited, as Mary Brough must have in the original production, her large physical presence. A nudge from her to Harold or Clive in Act I effectively collapsed the recipient; in Act II, her ungainly clumping up and down the stairs, as Mrs Twine now exhorted her on, now called her back, neatly expressed the essence of her role – one of nosy intrusiveness into other people's lives, coupled with subservience to her employer. In Act III, the tension between Mrs Leverett, the watchdog intent on exposing scandal, and Harold Twine, paralysed with fear that his own complicity will be uncovered, was finely caught by each in turn shadowing the other round the stage, the audience savouring the cat-and-mouse game, and laughing when discovery was made. Neither for this passage (pp. 112–14) nor for the previous one (p. 66) are precise stage-directions offered for such routines. But something like them (and different productions could create different routines) is implicit in the writing and entirely true to the spirit of it. Such routines and business, when inventively handled as here, do not imprison characters in a stereotypical framework, but give them added life. In some cases, it is true, the physical mannerisms *were* the character – as in the case of the ferocious Prussian Putz (Lionel Jeffries) with his uniform, jackboots, whip, and snarling dog, or the old sea-dog Admiral Juddy (Geoffrey Sumner), bending at the knees as if about to go into a hornpipe dance, a mannerism picked up and mocked by Clive and Gerald (Ian Ogilvy and Tom Courtenay). But in other cases, text and business lit each other up in ironic and unexpected ways. Nicola McAuliffe's Mrs Twine, for example, signalled a sexuality suppressed beneath her ultra-respectable manner, with her fashionable outfits and her squeal of delight when Juddy pinched her bottom. Tom Courtenay, far from playing Gerald as a monocled, Ralph Lynn look-alike, brought to the role a gentle bewilderment, a puzzled concern, which made his verbal and physical misadventures all the funnier.

To note, then, the possibilities latent in the text, is the more important in Travers's case, since that text lacks the surface wit and elegance of Pinero's.

There is another interesting contrast between Travers and Pinero. In Travers's work there is none of the sense we have in farces like *The Magistrate* or *Dandy Dick*, of the wheel coming full circle, of the safe return in Act III to complete respectability and normality. True, the situation does resolve itself: Gerald and Clara are reconciled in *Rookery Nook*, Ronny gets the girl in *Thark*, Freddy and D'Arcy are cleared of suspicion in *Plunder*. But, significantly, the stifling forces of convention are put to rout at the end of *Rookery Nook*, as Mrs Twine and Mrs Leverett are forced 'over and backwards' by the enraged Putz; and the bag containing Mrs Twine's underclothes is tossed into the air. *Thark* ends with an even more striking stage image of anarchy that is frightening as well as farcical:

> . . . *lightning flashes* . . . *the wind is howling furiously, blowing the curtains across the room – an enormous clap of thunder is heard, blankets and quilt are blown nearly off the bed* . . . *the force of the storm blows the brass candlesticks from the mantelpiece R., also the huge picture falls from above the fireplace – which makes Benbow turn quickly and point the gun that way. Ronny jumps out of bed and starts to beat the gong. Mrs. Frush, Lady Benbow and Kitty rush into the room followed by Jones and Hook, who stand at the door – a huge branch of tree has fallen through the window – they are all scared.*
>
> (pp. 129–30)

And in *Plunder*, with the element of danger built more consistently into the plot (it had the distinction, writes Travers, 'of being the first farce in which the action involved a death', p. 104) the play ends more disturbingly still, with the thieves getting away with their robbery and manslaughter, and one of them, D'Arcy, calmly reading a lesson in morality to Oswald: 'Be honest. It pays in the end' (p. 92). Truly, if Travers looks back to Pinero, he points forward to the Joe Orton of *Loot*, and to the cool effrontery of Nurse Fay's concluding line in that play: 'People would talk. We must keep up appearances' (p. 275).

4

Brian Rix and the Whitehall Farces

Brian Rix greatly admired the Aldwych team idea of playwright, director and actors working together on a series of farces. It was his ambition to carry on that tradition in a West End theatre with his own company. He succeeded admirably, and indeed surpassed the Aldwych Theatre record of ten and a half years for one farce team in one theatre, in consecutive plays. His work there, however, was slow to win critical respect; indeed, throughout the sixteen years of the Whitehall farces, only a few critics, among them Harold Hobson, Ronald Bryden, J. W. Lambert and Alan Dent, could be found to take the farces and the company's work on them seriously. More typical were such dismissive comments as, for *Simple Spymen*, 'keeps simple audiences chuckling comfortably',[1] for *Dry Rot*, 'doubtless intended for an audience of donkeys',[2] for *Chase Me, Comrade!* 'a truly repulsive piece'.[3] Yet a careful study of the Whitehall farces confirms Ronald Bryden's admirably combative defence of them:

> there they are: the most robust survivors of a great tradition, the most successful British theatrical enterprises of our time. Curious that no one can be found to speak up wholeheartedly for them – no one, that is, outside the enthusiastic millions who have packed every British theatre where they have played. It's particularly curious considering the current intellectual agitation for a theatre of the masses, a true working-class drama. Everything, apparently, for which Joan Littlewood had struggled – the boisterous, extrovert playing, the integrated teamwork, the Cockney irreverence of an unselfconscious, unacademic audience bent purely on pleasure – exists, patently and profitably, at the Whitehall. Yet how many devout pilgrims to Stratford East have hazarded the shorter journey to Trafalgar Square to

worship at the effortless shrine of the thing itself? How many Arts Council grants have sustained Mr Rix's company? How many *Evening Standard* awards went to *Dry Rot*? How many theses have been written on the art of Colin Morris, John Chapman or Ray Cooney? The time has come, surely, to fill the gap.[4]

On leaving the RAF in 1948, Brian Rix had formed his own company, Rix Theatrical Productions, and arranged a number of tours in seaside and provincial towns. The company put on such standard repertory pieces as *An Inspector Calls*, *Deep Are The Roots*, and *The Hasty Heart*. Then, one day in 1949, Rix, interested in putting on an army play, and knowing that Colin Morris had already written one called *Desert Rats*, asked to read his latest, *Reluctant Heroes*. He discovered that it was a farce about army life, and was sufficiently impressed by its potential to try it out as a high season production at Bridlington. The result was that

it played to more business than *See How They Run* – and in those days that was equivalent to saying the Archbishop of Canterbury commanded a bigger flock than the Pope.[5]

Rix determined to try to bring it in to London.

The opportunity came in 1950. Rix knew that *Worm's Eye View* at the Whitehall was currently nearing the end of its run, and he invited its presenter, H. J. Barlow, to see *Reluctant Heroes* during its run in Birmingham, with a view to its replacing *Worm's eye View*. Barlow was agreeable, but the Whitehall management had meanwhile chosen a different play to take its place, *The Dish Ran Away*. Fortunately for Rix, *The Dish Ran Away* opened to the 'worst notices imaginable'. The management had second thoughts, and Rix was given his opportunity. His company moved into the Whitehall, opening on 11 September 1950, and began the sixteen-year period of the Whitehall farces.

Colin Morris's *Reluctant Heroes* relies on what Jessica Davis calls the requirements for the simplest kind of farce:

little more than a suitable victim, a practical joker, and a good idea for a prank. . . . As K. M. Lea observes in her study *Italian Popular Comedy*, one clown merely says to the other, Let's do the old man', or 'Let's do him again', and the farce moves forward. At this level, farce is very little removed from ordinary circus clowning, in which unconnected episodes are motivated solely by the availability of a defenceless or gullible victim, without any particular purpose being served by his humiliation.[6]

In the case of *Reluctant Heroes*, there are three defenceless and often gullible victims, the three National Servicemen, Tone, Gregory and Morgan, called up by the 'Minister of Labour' who, as the play reminds us, was in 1950 Shinwell, in the Attlee administration of the day. The recruits are subjected, in time-honoured fashion, to a variety of humiliations by the loud-mouthed authority figure, Sergeant Bell (disrespectfully known as 'Tinkerbell'). As might be expected, there is a great deal of that aggressive joking which is one characteristic of farce. Each rigidly authoritarian and bureaucratic army routine to which the awkward newcomers are submitted – kit issue, inoculations, drill, form-filling, morning inspection – becomes the occasion for insult, scorn and both physical and psychological bullying:

SERGEANT. For inspection, port arms! (*TONE does the drill fairly smartly*) Left 'and against the left breast pocket! (*TONE's hand is too low*) If that's your left breast you must be in the wrong Army. (*Takes hold of rifle and TONE glances at it apprehensively*) Don't look – you know! Cleaned yer rifle, eh? If I was ter sow some sweet peas in the breech, they'd take root. Scoop the muck off it and report ter me before dinner. (*Dusts his hands in an exaggerated manner as he hurls it back*). Ugh! (*Crosses and inspects GREGORY*). What is it about you that makes me feel sick every time I look at yer? What 'ave yer got tucked up there? (*Points to waste*). A basket of kittens? (*Crosses R. of GREGORY*). What a mess, what a mess!

GREGORY (*annoyed*). It's best Ah can do with stuff issued to me.

SERGEANT. The stuff's all right, son, it's what your shape does to it. (*Crosses to GREGORY's R.*) We can't blame the Army for everythink. Tell me son, 'ow much do they pay you a day?

GREGORY (*with contempt*). Four shillin'.

SERGEANT (*imitating him*). Four shillin'! They should 'ave charged you a premium. (*Crosses behind him, views his back*). When I looked at you from the front I thought I'd never seen a more 'orrible sight. Well (*looking up and down his back*) – I 'ave. (*Crosses to TONE and speaking from his R.*) Get an 'aircut tonight! An' another one termorrer.

(p. 46)

If the humour of this is fairly primitive, there is considerable opportunity in *Reluctant Heroes* for comic routines involving on the physical skills and timing of the actors. The climax of Act II offers one example, with the men having to strip off in the presence, unknown to the Sergeant, of the WRAC officer, Gloria Dennis, who is hiding under a bed. Other examples, cited by Beverly Baxter, in his review of the production, as constituting 'two of the funniest episodes in the London theatre',[7] are the kit issue in Act I, with the recruits struggling into highly uncomfortable and ill-fitting army clothes, and the vaccination of the men in the same act by a ghoulish medical orderly, from which the following extract is taken:

ORDERLY. Keep still, unless you want to be vaccinated on the chest.
TONE. If this is vaccination, give me tattooing.
ORDERLY. I must get the bacillus well introduced to the host. There's nothing like a good scab to give me confidence it's taken. (*Puts a plaster over the scratch then moves on to GREGORY who visibly shrinks*). (*Weighing him*) Are you haemophilic?
GREGORY. No – Congregational.
ORDERLY. What I mean is: Are you a bleeder?
GREGORY. Not 'arf!
ORDERLY. You look to me as if you might be haemophilic. One prick with the haemophilic . . . (*Scratches him*)
GREGORY (*More afraid than feeling anything*). Hey, hey!
ORDERLY. Keep still, I don't want to pierce an artery. If I did and you were a haemophilic you'd be lying in a sea of blood. That's it. I expect to see a beautiful scab there within seven days.

(p. 37)

But, as a necessary counterpoise to the aggressive and hostile joking maintained throughout *Reluctant Heroes*, there is an element of festive humour and joyousness associated with sex; the involvement of the recruits with the WRAC officer, and her two attractive Privates, Pat Thompson and Penelope Raymond, provides relief from the bullying humour of the sergeant. So too does the gorm-less amiability of the cheerful North Country recruit, Gregory, the part which Brian Rix made his own, and which, interestingly enough, was offered to George Formby in the film version (though Formby declined it). There is, too, some variety among the authority figures offered by the farce. Though authority is chiefly incar-nated in Sergeant Bell, we have also the ferocious PT instructor, (and Bell's rival) Sergeant 'Aggis' McKenzie, and, at the other extreme, the bumbling 'silly ass' figure of Captain Percy, (played at the Whitehall by the author, Colin Morris) radiating an opti-mistic faith in his recruits which is constantly undercut by their incompetence.

Morris, in his curtain speech on the first night of the original production, thanked everyone for 'enjoying his elongated music-hall sketch of army life',[8] and the critics took their cue from this. Ivor Brown, in a representative review, recorded his appreciation of the 'clowning . . . rough fun (and) good old music-hall gags and goings on' but called its three Acts

> three separate sketches rather than three acts of a play; there is
> fun with a stentorian sergeant and his assorted victims, there is
> fun with undressing and girls under beds, fun with mimic
> warfare and high explosives. All is audible, visible and as easily
> comprehended as a kick in the pants.[9]

But qualification is needed here. The plot on which the 'lazzi', or pieces of comic business, are threaded is, it is true, of the slightest. But there is an element of reversal, which gives some structure to the farce. Sergeant Bell does not get it all his own way, and there is a satisfying dramatic irony in seeing 'the biter bit'. From the appearance of the women in Act II, this reversal is pre-figured, in that Bell, completely secure in the male world of the army, is socially uneasy with the women, as in his stumbling address of welcome to them:

> On behalf of the regiment, I'd like to hexpress our deep regret
> that your first visit to male quarters should be to this 'ut . . .
> er . . . hut. Owing to its size we 'ave to use it has a lecture
> 'ut . . . hot . . . hut! . . . from time ter time. Now while you're
> heah I want you to feel at hease. Hif anythin' 'appens ter cause
> you any worry just let me know. Now, provided you feel confi-

dent being' left alone 'ere for a couple of seconds, I'll go outside and wait for Captain Percy.

(p. 49)

Then, in Act III, it is the Sergeant who is physically assaulted during the manoeuvres by Sergeant McKenzie, and then trussed and immobilised by his men; while McKenzie, in his turn, is intimidated by a ferocious Gregory, who suddenly becomes imbued with true fighting spirit, and has his brief moment of glory covering one of his tormentors with his Bren gun. It is also the Sergeant whose cigarette match accidentally triggers off the thunderflash explosions that end the play on an appropriately anarchic note, and also, and again appropriately, leave Bell grovelling about on his knees, no longer the ferocious bogey-man of Act I.

Finally, it is worth noting Brian Rix's explanation for the appeal of *Reluctant Heroes:*

> It . . . had that indefinable quality of identification. EVERYONE who had ever been called to attention by a bawling NCO recognised something of their own lives – and as most of the male population (and much of the female too) had served in the war or been called up for National Service – we had a ready-made audience of millions.[10]

The element of the music-hall sketch is readily apparent in *Reluctant Heroes*, but, perhaps, without that basis in reality it would not have succeeded. It is a basis in reality partly dependent, as Rix suggests, on the shared experience of actors and audience at the time of the play's first production in 1950, with a war recently concluded and National Service in full operation – though one should add that there is a perennial appeal in the subject of the civilian 'press-ganged' into the military and the collision between different modes of life (as witness the continuing appeal of such television series as *Dad's Army*). But such shared experience would not trigger off a response without Colin Morris's skill in fleshing out the stereotypes of raw recruits, ferocious NCO's and ineffectual officer.

Dry Rot, the farce that succeeded *Reluctant Heroes*, was written, like its predecessor, by a member of Rix's company, in this case John Chapman, who, according to Rix, had 'appeared in so many bad farces he felt his own couldn't be much worse' (p. 121). Rix

read the play, and agreed to stage it on condition that Chapman
re-wrote it to include a better opportunity for Rix himself to play
a prominent part. This Chapman did, and the play was put on.
As a review in *The Stage* puts it, the plot

> concerns the machinations of several questionable characters
> intent on switching two racehorses, who use for this purpose a
> country inn run by an exasperated ex-army Colonel and his
> family.
>
> (quoted Rix, p. 128)

The questionable characters were in fact Alfred Tubbe, the crooked
bookmaker, played first by John Slater, then by Leo Franklyn, his
runner and partner-in-crime, Fred Phipps, played by Brian Rix,
and Flash Harry, another con-man, played by Basil Lord. The play
was directed by Wallace Douglas, who remained as Rix's director,
with one or two exceptions, for subsequent Whitehall and post-
Whitehall farces. It enjoyed immediate success, and ran for some
three-and-a-half years, from August 1954 to March 1958, not quite
equalling the long run of *Reluctant Heroes*, but running it close.

Despite its audience appeal, however, *Dry Rot* is much less
inventively ingenious in its development of the basic situation
than the farce which Chapman subsequently wrote, and which
followed on from *Dry Rot* at the Whitehall, *Simple Spymen*. *Simple
Spymen* was to make skilful and sophisticated use of what Leo
Hughes has called the 'ideal thread' on which to string the beads
of comic business, or 'lazzi' which are 'the real stuff of farce' –
namely, the chase.[11] The problem with *Dry Rot* is that the kind of
chase around which the farcical intrigue centres is of its nature
untheatrical, and must take place off-stage: this is the horse race,
with a fake jockey riding the favourite to victory. The rendering
of this led to problems both in the writing and in the performance
(see below). Moreover, in order to set up various pieces of comic
business involving Fred, Alf and Flash Harry kidnapping and
doping a substitute racehorse under the noses of the Colonel, his
wife and daughter, Chapman has to construct an elaborate and
heavy-handed scenario straight out of a Victorian melodrama,
complete with sliding panel, secret passageway, and a ruined
convent in the hotel grounds, within whose walls is a barn, with
trapdoors leading down to a cellar! Small wonder that *The Stage*
review referred to the 'preposterous plot'! Curiously, when a film

was subsequently made of the stage success, the director, far from recognising that the freedom of the camera to open out the action could help overcome these weaknesses, contented himself initially with, as Rix puts it, 'a filmed version of the stage play' (p. 147), though in the final stages the director realised his mistake and asked Chapman to write a chase sequence which was duly supplied.

What *Dry Rot* does offer is a first attempt by Chapman to create a double act, reminiscent of a music-hall turn, which he was to develop with greater assurance for Brian Rix and Leo Franklyn in *Simple Spymen*. This involved Alf and Fred, with Alf as the accomplished trickster, knowing and manipulative, and Fred as the stooge and incompetent accomplice, inclined to put his foot in it. There are some distant echoes here of the Ralph Lynn/Tom Walls partnership in crime that Ben Travers created in *Plunder*. And John Slater and Brian Rix evidently made the most of the opportunities their material offered them:

> John Slater . . . projects his nonsense with immense gusto and attack. His timing of lines, which are often woefully slender in their humorous content, and his rich gamut of facial expression, are used at all times in the vigorous and effective service of the preposterous plot. . . . As his partner in perfidy, Brian Rix, that frozen-faced moon-calf whose Broad-Acred gormlessness never fails to register, is again very funny and far superior to his material.
>
> (*The Stage*, quoted Rix, pp. 128–9)

Chapman also shows, in the climax to Act II of *Dry Rot*, a fine command of accelerating pace, and an ability to orchestrate effectively the progressive paranoia of the authority figures (Wagstaff and Sergeant Fire) as they tangle now with each other, now with the criminals; while Fred and Alf, for their part, duck out of the cross-examination with a series of zany wise-cracks:

> (*WAGSTAFF opens the door and is confronted with an enormous policewoman, SERGEANT FIRE by name, with a voice of thunder.*)
> FIRE. Understand you rang for help?
> WAGSTAFF. I rang the police.
> FIRE. I am the police – Sergeant Fire reporting.
> WAGSTAFF. It's absurd.

FIRE. Shush! What's the matter with all these people? (Everyone is still on the floor) Are they dead?

WAGSTAFF. Certainly not.

FIRE. Get up. Now make your statement.

WAGSTAFF. The house is surrounded by crooks, but why the devil they've sent you I can't imagine.

FIRE. Shush! (*Spraying all and sundry.*)

WAGSTAFF. Don't shush at me. I was a Colonel in the Army.

FIRE. I was a Brigadier in the ATS. Sit down!

WAGSTAFF. Now look here, Miss – miss –

FIRE. Fire!

WAGSTAFF. Fire!

(*BETH fires the gun straight through the French windows. The COLONEL and the SERGEANT throw their arms round each other and the OTHERS dive on to the floor.*)

WAGSTAFF. Idiot – (*Takes gun from BETH.*)

FIRE. Give me that. (*Takes gun from COLONEL.*)

....

FIRE (*to ALF and FRED*). Come here, what are you doing?

ALF. Getting ready to go to bed.

FIRE (*to FRED*). And you?

FRED. I'm assisting him. I'm his Welsh dresser.

....

FIRE (*to ALF.*) What were you doing in the garden?

ALF. Sowing.

WAGSTAFF. At three in the morning?

ALF. They're early seeds.

FIRE (*to FRED*). And you?

FRED. Weeding.

WAGSTAFF. Why weren't you in bed?

FRED. Well, I don't weed in bed!

WAGSTAFF)
) You're lying.
FIRE   )

FRED)
) Shush!
ALF)

But *Dry Rot* offers all too few examples of such skilful clowning. Act III, it is true, includes one extended piece of comic business in which Brian Rix, as Fred, is taught to ride a horse, using the sofa as a mount, and Alf's braces as reins. But the race itself is, necessarily, a sad anti-climax. Indeed, so lukewarm was the reception on the press night of this scene – in which two of the con-men sit listening to the broadcast of the race – that a hasty 'council of war' was called involving cast and author, and Chapman came up with the suggestion that the scene could be made to work better if a 'tea scene' was introduced:

> If Alf (the bookmaker) and Flash (his runner) were made to be polite over tea when they've just lost everything, it could prolong their agony.

(p. 131)

Brian Rix responded with suggestions for various pieces of comic business involving spilled tea and the precarious passing from hand to hand of cream cakes, sugar bowls and cups; and the result, when built in to the next performance, apparently satisfied Rix that a satisfying comic climax had now been achieved. Such examples of last-minute improvisation and collaboration between playwright and company are not uncommon and could certainly be found in Travers's work with the Aldwych company. Nor would the resulting 'tea business' have been unfunny in the hands of such skilled performers as John Slater, Basil Lord and Charles Cameron (the Colonel). The fact remains, however, that the business in this case is quite extraneous to the farcical situation, and was grafted on to conceal the weakness of the script.

Chapman's second farce for the Whitehall, *Simple Spymen*, which opened on 19 March 1958, and was to run for three years, was a considerable improvement on his first, though it attracted the usual dismissive reviews from a number of critics. *The Stage* review called it, 'an incoherent and utterly implausible collection of farcical clichés,' though the reviewer admitted,

> certain memories linger. Three men identically disguised as stage Turks rush wildly through the customary complement of doors. The Yorkshire busker is smoked out of a recess above the fireplace. Trousers fall and people sit on knitting needles. There are shots from the garden which set all the characters crawling. . . . A rehearsal of a vocal quartet is frustrated when an automatic piano-player persists in performing 'yip-i-addy'.[12]

Kenneth Tynan, in *The Observer*, declared that it had

no plausibility, and no wit. . . . The play, a chaos of slapdash, makes Ben Travers sound like Marivaux; if its standards were nationally enforced, the Crazy Gang would be heard only on the Third Programme.[13]

Contrary opinions were, however, expressed by J. W. Lambert for the *Sunday Times*, and Alan Dent for the *News Chronicle*, both of them noting the contrast between the delighted audience response, and the po-faced reaction of certain dramatic critics and other "superior" first-nighters, who sat, in Lambert's words, 'grim and aloof' (like) Easter Island statues. . . . I record with some embarrassment that this farce, unmistakably vulgar-ho-ho seemed to me extremely funny'.[14]

Properly to appreciate the pleasures of *Simple Spymen*, it is useful to recall the observations of J. M. Brown, quoted in Chapter I, that,

Farceurs belong to a race apart . . . The sky is the limit so far as they are concerned. No holds are barred. Every trick or stunt is legitimate – if only they get away with it . . . (Farce's) business is to make us accept the impossible as possible, the deranged as normal, and silliness as a happy substitute for sense.

Brian Rix in fact explains the appeal of *Simple Spymen* in somewhat similar terms:

The audience loved the slapstick, for it was probably the most knock-about farce I have ever done, and old Leo (Franklyn) gave his funniest performance ever.

(p. 168)

There are many farce writers who take great care to keep their plot worlds in close and continuous connection with the real world, as Feydeau, Pinero and such contemporary venturers into farce as Shaffer, Ayckbourn and Stoppard do. There it is only gradually that the manic misadventures, coincidences and absurdities of farce at its purest take over. But there are also those who, admittedly taking greater risks, plunge us with very little preliminary ado, into a surreal world where anarchy rules and 'no holds are barred'.

Here co-exist, with differing degrees of structural coherence, the farces of Orton and Dario Fo, the films of the Marx Brothers, the Goon Show, and such zanier Whitehall farces as *Simple Spymen* and *One For The Pot*. Here we have lunatic worlds, some almost purely nonsensical, some sharply satiric and disturbing – worlds which are not hermetically sealed off from the real world, but existing at a greater remove from it than is usual, even in farce. Much here depends on the writer's degree of success in rendering a logically self-consistent world, much on his virtuosity, command of pace, and confidence in the medium, and much also on the skills of the performers, which may receive their severest tests in this kind of work.

What Chapman does in *Simple Spymen* is to turn his back on the rather awkward attempts to explain the rationale of the plot that was evident in *Dry Rot*, which had a too leisurely exposition and a muffled climax, and to plunge his audience instead into a vortex of manic activity. He constructs a world of outrageous caricature, governed by a kind of lunatic logic, in which everything is pushed to extremes. Characteristic of *Simple Spymen* is an exuberant inventiveness, a determination to load every rift with comic ore. No attempt is made to hide the absurdity of its disguises and concealed identities. Instead, a playful 'let's pretend' quality, in which speedy improvisation and repetition are of the essence appears, as in this extract:

FOSGROVE. Right. I'm Smith and you're Brown and we're
    staying here for health reasons.
COLONEL. What the devil's our health got to do with it?
FOSGROVE. Well, it all helps to confuse the issue.
COLONEL. Are you sure we want the issue confused?
FOSGROVE. Oh, I think so, sir. Shall we just rehearse it here?
COLONEL. Good idea.
FOSGROVE. I'm Smith.
COLONEL. I'm Brown.
FOSGROVE. I feel rather ill.
COLONEL (*serious*). Yes, you look terrible.
FOSGROVE. No, it's my part, sir.
COLONEL. What part?
FOSGROVE. No, my role.
COLONEL. Oh, I see, yes.
FOSGROVE. Now don't forget you're Brown.
COLONEL. No.

FOSGROVE. And you're dicky too.
COLONEL. Really.
FOSGROVE. Yes.
COLONEL. Oh.
   (*Enter GROBCHICK U.C.*)
GROBCHICK. Where please is Mr Smogs?
FOSGROVE. I don't know, but I'm Smith.
GROBCHICK. Oh.
FOSGROVE. And he's Brown.
COLONEL. Yes, Dicky Brown.
GROBCHICK. Oh.
COLONEL. Yes, and I'm feeling ghastly.
FOSGROVE. I don't feel too good either.
GROBCHICK. That makes three of us.

Here names are juggled, passed around, dropped and picked up again, and the routine, banal on the page, arouses laughter when it is expertly played, and when it is extended beyond the opening gambit quoted above, until neither party is sure which is Brown, and which Smith.

I referred earlier in this chapter to Leo Hughes's suggestion that the chase was the ideal thread on which to hang the 'beads' or 'lazzi' – the pieces of comic business which are the real stuff of farce. For the chase, Hughes argues, involves suspense, without distracting too much attention from discrete episodes; it allows the dramatist to maintain a pace too fast for the leisurely examination which his wildest flights of fancy might not survive; and it allows also for the introduction of many devices basic to farce – concealment, impersonation, repetition, which may be exploited to whatever limits the circumstances warrant, and violent physical action, tumbling, beating and noise. *Simple Spymen* is a fine demonstration of Hughes's thesis. The whole play is virtually an extended chase sequence, with the foreign agent, Max, chasing Grobchick and his secret Atomic Pile Restorer, George and Percy also chasing Grobchick, and George and Percy, in turn, being chased by Colonel Gray-Balding and Lieutenant Fosgrove. The final curtain comes down on a chase sequence involving the entire cast, as George and Percy abscond with Max's £30 000. The chases involve multiple disguises, confusions of identity, and misunderstandings: there are at one point three Grobchicks, two of them phoney, on stage at the same time; George and Percy undergo successive transformations – from street musicians, to secret agents, French waiters and private detectives, ending up with George as first a vicar, then a widow, and Percy as first his organist, then a Colonel. Characters either start with outrageous names which expose them to misunderstanding, as in the case of the following exchange –

> STAND. I'm Forster Stand.
> COLONEL. How very unfortunate for you.
>
> (p. 14)

or they acquire such names in a desperate search to hide their true identity:

> MRS BYNG. Who is this gentleman?
> GEORGE. Er – he is – er – my organist.
> MRS BYNG. Really.
> GEORGE. Yes, he just had a blow out.
> MRS BYNG. Goodness me.
> GEORGE. He is very temperamental, you know.
> MRS BYNG. He must be a great musician. (*Crosses to PERCY.*) What is his name?
> GEORGE. Eh? Oh, Doctor Thumpanbang.
> MRS BYNG. You know I am absolutely positive I have seen him before.
> GEORGE. Really?
> MRS BYNG. I met him this afternoon.
> GEORGE. Are you sure?
> MRS BYNG. But this afternoon his name was Grobchick.
> GEORGE. Oh, yes, well, that's his first name. His full name is Dr. Grobchick Thumpanbang.
> MRS BYNG. That's very hard to believe.
> GEORGE. It's very hard to say.
>
> (pp. 82–3)

Even the invention at the centre of the chase has its part to play in the 'mistaken identity' stakes. For the final joke of the play is that Grobchick's Atomic Pile Restorer is a simple form of carpet cleaner, rather than the nuclear secret weapon that has triggered off such frenzied pursuits. The 'thread' of the chase also allows for a whole series of comic routines involving the physical skills of the actors: some are uncomplicatedly funny: the waiting-at-table mime sequence at the end of Act I (capped, in surrealist fashion, with the loud noise of real breaking crockery); the collapsing piano stool and coat-changing routines at the end of Act II; and Percy's routine with the officer's stick in Act III

> *PERCY then covers up by giving a 'Colonel's laugh', and then proceeds to demonstrate the unique properties of the stick, gabbling away in complete gibberish. He mimes cleaning the stick with a 'pull-through', then slapping a magazine on it and firing it like a tommy-gun. He then changes it into a telescope, peers through it, then holds it out for FORSTER STAND, who by this time is thoroughly out of his depth, and he has a look through. Then PERCY quickly runs through a few more of the stick's varied qualities, i.e., a cricket bat, a violin, a flute, a tennis racket, and finally thrusts it under his arm, salutes and turns his back on them all and looks out of the French windows.*
>
> (p. 105)

Other routines are skilful examples of Chapman's ability to create laughter out of situations of extreme danger and physical risk. The more the tension created by these scenes, the greater the release in laughter when disaster is averted. Such scenes particularly involve George's stooge, the clown figure Percy, (played at the Whitehall by Brian Rix) to whom horrendous misadventures frequently occur. In Act I, terror-struck by the secret agent role forced upon him, he clambers out of the window, and is left hanging several floors up on a window ledge, threatened with electrocution (against the pigeons) and the window slammed on his finger. In Act II, forced up the chimney by George to find the secret packet, soot descends on him, a fire is lit under him, and a poker shoved into a tender part of his anatomy.

But the other notable feature of *Simple Spymen* is Chapman's creation of a successful and effective double act for Brian Rix and Leo Franklyn, as the two street musicians, Percy, *'a nervous lad from up North'*, and George, *'a ripe Cockney'*. Chapman evidently benefited from his partnership with such skilled performers in the run-up to the first night, and certain routines – the 'funny coffee scene', the collapsing piano stool, and the coat-changing episode – were, according to Rix, worked out by him and Franklyn in collaboration with Chapman. In this partnership, Percy is essentially the stooge, fearful and rather simple-minded, but willing to have a go, while George is the more experienced con-man, who manipulates Percy and usually contrives to 'land him in it'. The physical skills of both (though particularly of Rix) are tested to the full in the extensive 'slapstick' passage. And it was these skills, together with the admirably supportive and complementary nature of the partnership, which attracted high praise from both Alan Dent and J. W. Lambert. Dent, in his review, says that,

> Franklyn, with his resourceful and adaptable Cockney, and Rix, with his agreeable and unchanging Yorkshire accent, are a well contrasted pair, agreeing with one another as cordially as sage and onion, and as closely as roast beef and Yorkshire pudding.[15]

J. W. Lambert places the partnership in a more historical context by describing the farce as,

> an excellent framework for two admirable clowns, Brian Rix and Leo Franklyn, the one a whimper, the other a bang, whose mime and mockery – and timing, in Wallace Douglas's expert production – combine to preserve, in a manner truly popular, skills and calculated absurdities at least as old as the Commedia dell'Arte.[16]

The farce which succeeded *Simple Spymen* was *One For The Pot*, by Ray Cooney and Tony Hilton. It was to run for over a thousand performances at the Whitehall, from August 1961 until June 1964; and it carried on the tradition of plays written and performed by members of the company, in this case Ray Cooney, who had joined Rix's company in 1956, during the run of *Dry Rot*, and had played Corporal Flight in *Simple Spymen*. Cooney, sometimes in collaboration with Hilton, sometimes with John Chapman, and sometimes on his own, was to become a prolific farce writer, and a contributor both to Rix's later seasons in the 1970s at the Garrick and the Whitehall, and to the Theatre of Comedy company in the 1980s, based on the Shaftesbury, of which he is the Artistic Director.

The play was a significant landmark for the company in that recognition of their achievement as an acting ensemble now became more widespread among serious critics. *The Times* review declared that,

> Mr Rix, Mr Leo Franklyn, Mr Larry Noble, Mr Basil Lord and

other old faithfuls of the company could give points to any other group in the country for consistency of style, timing, teamwork and perfect command of their audience. Their garden may be small, but they have brought the cultivation of it to a fine art.[17]

Harold Hobson followed suit in his *Sunday Times* review:

> The story, with its chase after money, is less cunning than the farces devised by Feydeau. But the Whitehall company – Terry Scott, Leo Franklyn, Basil Lord, Hazel Douglas, Sheila Mercier and the others – play it with the devotion, the lack of condescension, that the Renaud-Barrault company gives to *Occupe-toi d'Amélie*, or the Comédie Française to *Le Dindon*. There is no feeling here of being occupied with an inferior branch of the drama, a casual charade. The company plays without pretentiousness, but with every nerve stretched, with every talent at its full height.[18]

The key to its success as a farce undoubtedly lies in its inspired use of the repetition motif, the plot depending on the existence of no fewer than four identical Hickory Woods, all of which are played by the main actor, Brian Rix. Much of the enjoyment of the piece lies in admiring the virtuosity, both of the performer undertaking this marathon task, and of the playwrights in juggling exits and entrances (with minimal assistance from one double) so as to allow one actor to impersonate all the Hickory Woods, one after the other, and sometimes it seems, such is the sleight of hand involved, at the same time. *The Times* review describes the effect, and outlines the plot, succinctly:

> The main raison d'être of the piece is to provide the excuse for several intricate pieces of double, triple and even quadruple exposure on the part of Mr Rix himself, who appears first as the familiar nitwit in a cloth cap, then as his hardly brighter twin brother (they were separated at birth, needless to say), who has a posh accent and wears a dinner jacket, rather mysteriously, for casual calls. Soon the first brother is wearing a dinner jacket too, and no one on the stage knows for certain which is which at any given moment, while the audience is transported by the eternal fascination of working out how it is done: how, they keep asking themselves, can we see the back of brother A

disappearing through the french window a split second before brother B comes in from the library door at the other side of the stage?

What brings the brothers from their separate homes to visit a household previously unknown to them can be summed up in one word: money. Old Jonathan Hardcastle has decided to give £10,000 to the son of an early associate who lost all his money through the extravagance of scheming relatives, but he will give it to the lad only if he can prove that he is the sole survivor, so that the same thing cannot happen again. So what more natural? the two brothers have to pretend to be one, in spite of the embarrassing attentions of the dim one's wife, the budding love between the posh one and Hardcastle's daughter, the inept assistance of the dim one's supposed legal adviser and the Hardcastles' mercenary butler, and the arrival of further complications in the form of a third unscrupulous member of the clan from Ireland.

The intricacies of the last act, with three Brian Rixes dashing in and out, and everyone else trying frantically to pretend that nothing out of the ordinary is happening, have to be seen to be disbelieved.[19]

It was this kind of sleight of hand, so cunningly practised, which led Harold Hobson to see something quintessentially theatrical, and magical in the play:

The theatre must always astonish. . . . This is exactly what Brian Rix does in *One For The Pot* . . . Mr Rix astonishes simply by being in a different part of the stage from where you expect him. You know that man in the corner is Mr Rix. You have heard him speak. You have seen his face. You would recognise his clothes anywhere. Well, you are wrong. It isn't Mr Rix. It was Mr Rix once; in fact, only a couple of seconds ago. But it isn't Mr Rix any longer. Mr Rix is indeed at this moment entering through a door at the back of the stage, in a place where you had not the slightest idea he would be.

This is, you say, an elementary effect of prestidigitation. You were taken unawares, because somehow Mr Rix and his company kept you looking in the wring direction. You are pretty sure that they won't catch you a second time. But again you are wrong. You are caught a second time. When this happened, I saw, suddenly, exactly where the third ambush would be laid. I was on the look-out for it. Forewarned. Forearmed. Then, at the crucial moment, Mr Rix made me forget all about it. And, lo and behold, for the third time I fell right into the trap so neatly laid, so swiftly and smoothly sprung.[20]

Though it is in the action that the accelerating insanity of the multiple Hickory Woods is essentially demonstrated, the confusions of identity and role-switching between characters is nicely caught in the script when the posh Hickory Wood, Rupert, tries to explain the situation to Hardcastle's daughter, Cynthia:

RUPERT. I've been trying to explain all evening, darling. I'm not who I said I was.
CYNTHIA. Aren't you?
RUPERT. No. When I first arrived I said I was who I was. When I met you I had to say I was who I wasn't. Then I had to be who I said I was when I wasn't when I really wanted to be who I was when I said I was. Now I want you to know that I'm not who I said I was when I wasn't but who I was when I said I was who I was. (*There is a pause*)
CHARLIE. Say that again.
RUPERT. When I first arrived –
CHARLIE. No! (*MICHAEL – double – is heard singing off – 'Dear Old Donegal'*) There's only one thing for it. Miss Cynthia, come here. (. . . *leads CYNTHIA up to archway and points off towards ballroom. . . . CYNTHIA looks off and double-takes between the ballroom and RUPERT. The singing stops.*) Now look – that's not 'im, is it?
CYNTHIA. I can't believe it. Billy.
RUPERT. Ah, now that's the point, I'm not Billy.
CYNTHIA. Not Billy?
RUPERT. No, Mr Barnet asked me to be, and I didn't know whether to be or not to be.
CHARLIE. Quoting Shakespeare won't help.
CYNTHIA. Well, if you're not Billy, who on earth are you?
RUPERT. I'm – er – (To CHARLIE.) Who am I?
CHARLIE. I've forgotten myself now – two and two?
CYNTHIA. Four.
CHARLIE. You're Rupert.
CYNTHIA. Rupert!

CHARLIE. Billy's twin brother.
RUPERT. And that's Michael. . . . You can't see our family tree
for the Hickory Woods.

(pp. 73–4)

Brian Rix pays a number of tributes in his autobiography to Ben
Travers and the Aldwych company of the 1920s, and it is clear
that he saw his own company as heir to that tradition:

I felt we were the natural heirs to the Aldwych farces. . . . I was
besotted by the 'team' idea, following slavishly in the Aldwych
master's footsteps.

(p. 187)

And, just before the opening of *One For The Pot*, the company
celebrated the fact that they had passed,

the Aldwych Theatre record of ten years, seven months and
four days for one farce team, in one theatre, in consecutive
plays. . . . We invited all the old Aldwych crowd who were still
around and along came Ralph Lynn, Bunny Hare, Winifred
Shotter and, of course, Ben Travers himself.

(p. 187)

It was mainly, of course, in the idea of a team of actors working
together with director and house dramatist(s) on a series of farces
over a period of years in one theatre that the connection rests. But
it is also interesting to note, in *One For The Pot*, how the crusty,
gout-afflicted, brandy-swigging Hardcastle is cast very much in
the Tom Walls mould, how there is something of the put-upon
Robertson Hare victim figure in Billy Hickory Wood, and how,
more particularly, the posh Hickory Wood, Rupert, is conceived
almost as tribute to the Ralph Lynn for whom Travers wrote Ronny
Gamble in *Thark*. The scene in which Rupert confusedly attempts
to propose to Cynthia belongs convincingly to the silly-ass, Bertie
Woosterish world of Ralph Lynn:

RUPERT. Cynthia, may I ask you something? (*She nods.*) Well –
if I wasn't who you thought I was, but somebody who you
don't think I am, would you like me if I was somebody else.
CYNTHIA. Whoever you were I'd like you a lot.

RUPERT. Would you, would you really? (*Rupert goes to kiss her but stops*). Cynthia, I know we haven't known each other long but – I have a proposal to make.
CYNTHIA. Yes?
RUPERT. I – er – need someone –
CYNTHIA. Yes?
RUPERT. To do my ironing.
CYNTHIA (*surprised*): Your ironing?
RUPERT. Yes. Oh – and my cooking, too.
CYNTHIA. Why don't you hire a daily help?
RUPERT. That's no good. What about the nights. I mean – I get terribly lonely.
CYNTHIA. Well. Perhaps you need a dog.
RUPERT. Ah! but a dog needs a mistress – and so do I. (*Pause*) Cynthia, do you like children?
CYNTHIA. Very much.
RUPERT. Well, what I've always thought is – my children must have a mother.
CYNTHIA. That sounds feasible.
RUPERT. Don't you want your children to have a mother?
CYNTHIA. What are you trying to say?
RUPERT. I'm trying to say, I'm me and you're you and that's a big difference. And what with me being me – and you being you – it'll be so handy for the children.
CYNTHIA. With such a large family oughtn't we to get married first.
RUPERT. I don't see why! (*Both rising*). Good Lord, yes. Darling, you mean –

(pp. 53–4)

But other features of the play relate it to the characteristically rumbustious world of the other Whitehall farces, owing much to music-hall, and to the radio and television comedy routines that carried on the music-hall tradition. Here belong scenes of slapstick involving by-play with fire shovels, brass pokers and knock-out drops, and the frequent loud crashes of breaking china and glasses as characters are bundled in and out of a large cocktail cabinet. (A stage direction on page 56 helpfully suggests that '*a small dustbin full of broken bottles and tin cans poured into another dustbin makes an excellent noise*'). Here also belongs the *Charley's Aunt* routine, with Billy dressing up as Aunt Amy and being pursued by a randy suitor, while the real Aunt Amy, mistaken for Billy, is gruffly required to undress by Charlie – 'Nobody's goin' to see your woolly pants.' (p. 83). And here, finally, belong the jokes, many of them, as Hobson noted, old and obvious: the one-line wise-cracks ('I like to know what's what' – 'Well look it up in *Who's Who*'), the nonsense insults ('any more from you and you'll end up in a Glockenspiel to Glyndebourne'), the bad puns ('you must be Cohen' – 'No I've just arrived'), and the non sequiturs which have their own Alice-in-Wonderland logic ('What's he doing in the garden?' 'Planting berries' 'It's pitch black' 'They're black-berries'). But often the badness and the obviousness of the humour are of the essence. Peter Davison's comment on the humour of the music-hall acts is relevant here:

> In the music-hall the audience was always being 'invited to disbelieve', rather than continuously to suspend its disbelief; art and life were never confused. . . . The flavour of a pun would be discussed and all would delight in its badness.[21]

It is also a very English brand of humour, characterised by Pearl Binder, whom Davison quotes, as involving,

> verbal buffoonery, a juggling with the sound and sense of words – a childish delight in mystification, secret meanings, and the appreciation of sound without sense for its own sake.[22]

The last of the Whitehall farces was to be Ray Cooney's *Chase Me Comrade!*, which ran from 15 July 1964 to 21 May 1966. The plot was loosely based on Nureyev's defection to the West. Once again, *The Times* review provides a crisp synopsis:

> The setting is the elegant residence of a naval commander, but once he has taken off for a day's fishing and a Russian ballet dancer (who has chosen freedom) is smuggled in, light comedy gives way to the company's usual routines.
> A pair of girls gets busy shuttling the dancer from room to room in flight from the village policeman, the returned Commander, and a moon-faced security man who is seen tipsily frolicking in the garden with roses in his hair. Leo Franklyn as a long-suffering gardener, looks on in gloating alarm, resignedly surrendering his braces when the time comes; and Larry Noble

makes a nervous last entry only to be instantly clapped into a cupboard.

Mr Rix himself, as the daughter's Civil Service fiancé, goes through a series of increasingly desperate disguises: he makes an obligatory knock-kneed appearance in white tights, but his most arresting transformation is into the head of a recumbent body which grows before one's eyes to fantastic lengths. This moment, in common with the chases, the acrobatic couch work, and the narrowly missed confrontations which make up most of the show, is nicely timed and played at the gallop.[23]

It was this moment which Ronald Bryden, in a *New Statesman* article, singled out to pinpoint what he called 'the mingled idiocy and ingenuity which is the specific pleasure of farce'. His account of his experience of that moment nicely suggests the surrealist, absurdist aspect of Whitehall farce that links it with the world of the music-hall, the Goon show, the films of the Marx Brothers, and ITMA:

Nearing the second curtain of *Chase Me Comrade!* Mr Brian Rix, endeavouring for reasons too numerous to mention, to delude his future father-in-law, an irascible naval commander, by simulating a BBC news bulletin, conceals himself and a microphone beneath a tiger-skin rug by the radio.

The stratagem succeeds up to a point. The frustrated officer, thunderous but preoccupied, has abandoned the gibbering apparatus and is striding back to his study when he encounters the skin crawling furtively toward another door. He stares. The skin halts. Tentatively it rubs its head against his flank. Persuasively, it lays a paw upon his sleeve. Hopefully, long after hope has fled, it rises to gaze into his crimson features, its glass eyes beseeching him to continue as if nothing has happened, to say it has not been found out, that he accepts unquestioningly and casually the presence in his drawing-room of an affectionate Indian man-eater wearing naval trousers.

But as the animated pelt, a bellowing officer at its heels, scrambles off-stage in a whirlwind of slamming doors, the piece achieves that moment for which (Mr Rix explained in a recent *Times* interview) the cast, with fingers crossed, nightly hold back: the 'take-off', the hysterical consummation when actors and audience, throwing off restraint and calculation, mutually surrender to the mingled idiocy and ingenuity which is the specific pleasure of farce.[24]

It also registered with Harold Hobson, who used it and other transformations undergone by Brian Rix, to reflect illuminatingly on the way that farce, with its role-playing, answers to a human need to 'be something other than we are'. I would only add to his point that our pleasure may also be one of recognition: we all play a variety of roles in life, and there is some fellow feeling in our laughter at the more extreme and inept forms of role-playing that the victims of the farcical mechanism are propelled into:

The truth is that farce, with its multiple changes, seems to satisfy some need in Mr Rix's nature, a need which in some measure we share with him. There are moments when we would all like to be something other than we are, and these moments are isolated, enriched and fulfilled for us by Mr Rix.

In his latest venture, Ray Cooney's *Chase Me Comrade!* (Whitehall), Mr Rix, with an extraordinarily suave yet at the same time desperate aplomb, turns himself into a naval commander, a tiger, a ballet dancer, and a man ten feet tall. He is Protean, multiform, plural, and innumerable, free of the limitations of personality and character. Fresh, eager, greatly talented in speed, timing, and exactness and clarity of speech, Mr Rix comes up to each transformation, each new, insuperable difficulty, with the confident enthusiasm of an innocently clever pupil about to receive the headmaster's prize. His joy is communicated, and we go fifty-fifty in the satisfaction of his accomplishment.[25]

But it is not only Rix, as Gerry Buss, who is forced to change identities: Gerry's fiancée Nancy becomes the au pair girl; Alicia, Petrovyan's ballet partner, becomes the Commander's unhappily married wife; and Petrovyan himself, whisked from one hiding place to another, also has identities thrust upon him, now a 'head wood-wormer', now Nancy's fiancé, Yays (based on his pronunciation of the one English word he knows, 'yes'). As the pace of the action increases, Petrovyan's reactions and behaviour become ever more puppet-like. The routine ballet exercises which he has constantly to perform to keep in training produce ever more incongruous bursts of physical activity, leaps and entre-chats. Moreover, as in *One For The Pot*, so here, the surrealist absurdity of events is reflected not only in the physical activities of role-playing, but in the lunatic chop-logic of the script:

> RIMMINGTON. Why are you walking around my house in a state of undress?
> GERRY. Very good question, sir. We are playing charades. I was miming, 'You can take a horse to water but a pencil must be lead'.
> (*RIMMINGTON goes to speak and then stops.*)
> RIMMINGTON. What's that got to do with you having no trousers on?
> GERRY. Nothing. that's why they couldn't guess it.
>
> (p. 63)

Thus Gerry endeavours to explain the inexplicable; and shortly afterwards:

> RIMMINGTON. What's Hoskins doing in my bedroom?
> GERRY (*Quickly*). Very sad. He fell down the well.
> RIMMINGTON. What well?
> GERRY. The well in the garden.
> RIMMINGTON. I didn't know there was a well in the garden.
> GERRY. Neither did Hoskins. That's how he came to fall down it.
>
> (p. 64

Finally the musical chairs role-swapping game ends with Gerry apparently trapped in his last assumed identity – that of Petrovyan, trying to evade capture by the Russians who are intent on projecting him into the starring role in *Swan Lake*, while the real Petrovyan heads back in disgust to Moscow.

Despite the continuing success of the Whitehall farces, events over which Rix had no control were to bring his tenure of the theatre to an end. The owner of the theatre's leasehold, Louis Cooper, had died in 1961, leaving the theatre to his two daughters and his son:

> His widow, Alice, kept a watching brief, but George Jeger (the general manager) was really left in sole charge. Over the years one daughter, Felice, bought out the rest of the family, as and

when they wished to sell, and suddenly there she was at the top of the pile – and the first person to go was George, who had always been at loggerheads with her. After his departure, it was easy to see why. She was, at times, unpredictable, and no amount of patience on my part could cope with the situation as I now found it.

(p. 197)

Rix was to endeavour to continue with the Whitehall tradition in a different form with his repertory season at the Garrick, which I discuss in Chapter 5; but he never quite enjoyed the success that went with his work at the Whitehall. The achievement was a remarkable one, and there is a certain irony, which did not go unremarked by Harold Hobson, in the contrast between what Rix's private enterprise had achieved in forming and maintaining a permanent company, and the immense funds and state support needed to launch a National Theatre company on the other side of the river, in the same year as Rix was relinquishing the Whitehall:

Mr Hall speaks of forming a permanent company as a matter of immense travail, towards which a Treasury grant of £80,000 is derisory. Hearing his eloquent and despairing words, one would imagine that setting up a permanent company was as rare and difficult a crusade as seeking the Holy Grail. Yet for years Mr Brian Rix has had a permanent company at the White-hall Theatre without, so far as I know, any encouragement from the Arts Council. It is a company that has developed its own style of production and acting, and created its own audience.

Why has Mr Rix been able to accomplish, without any fuss, what comes so hard to our leading avant-garde organisation, fortified as it is by journalist approval, Government assistance, the colossal talents of Peter Brook and Michael Saint-Denis, and its quiet sense of performing a social service? One must in justice remark that the scale of the two ventures is quite different; and that creating a style which finds its culmination in the removal of a pair of trousers is not the same thing as reaching out towards Beckett and Pinter and Shakespeare. Nevertheless, the reason for Mr Rix's success is one which more pompous enterprises should ponder.[26]

5

Post-Whitehall Farces

Brian Rix, having failed to secure the lease of the Whitehall, went on tour in 1966 with *Chase Me Comrade!* and another farce by Ray Cooney and Tony Hilton, *Bang, Bang, Beirut*, subsequently re-titled *Stand By Your Bedouin*. Rix starred in *Chase Me Comrade!*, Dickie Henderson in *Bang, Bang, Beirut*. Rix had taken, as he puts it, 'my first tentative steps towards experimenting with a repertoire' (p. 209). Back in London, he arranged with John Hallett, Managing Director of the Garrick, to open a repertory season of farces there in March 1967. He intended to open with *Stand By Your Bedouin*, then alternate this with *Uproar in the House*, by Anthony Marriott and Alastair Foot, and finally add a third play, *Let Sleeping Wives Lie*, by Harold Brooke and Kay Bannerman. He had also arranged for excerpts of the plays to be televised by the BBC. But business was bad, and the season was a failure; the public, according to Rix, seemed to think either that he was 'doing three one-act plays', or that 'the plays were flopping and coming off after one week.' The public associated Rix with the Whitehall, 'and merely wanted to know there was one funny play on in one theatre' (p. 209). As a result, Rix reverted to one play, *Let Sleeping Wives Lie*, transferred *Uproar in the House* to the Whitehall under another management, and took off *Stand by Your Bedouin* altogether.

Rix concludes from this failure that,

> to run a repertoire successfully you have to have fairly unlimited funds – like the National Theatre or the Royal Shakespeare – for frankly it is not a strictly commercial proposition. I had approached the Arts Council on a number of occasions for this altruistic backing, but there was little hope of it ever being forthcoming – hence my attempt to go it alone. I had presented quite a good case. My London productions would have to tour. I would be able to attract a number of artists who were only interested in short runs or a particular play. I would be able

to switch from low comedy, to farce, to high comedy with consummate ease and so on.

(p. 210)

But Arts Council backing was not forthcoming, and,

in the end, lack of funds forced me to present three plays which were identical in concept – with casts who were playing similar parts – for financially I was unable to ring the changes.

(p. 210)

Rix then went back to the Whitehall idea of mounting a single production for, hopefully, a lengthy run, and established in this venture a particularly fruitful association with Michael Pertwee, who wrote three farces for him: *She's Done It Again* (1969), *Don't Just Lie There, Say Something* (1971), and *A Bit Between the Teeth* (1974). The first two were presented at the Garrick, the last at the Cambridge Theatre. Many of the old Whitehall team were still in the company: Leo Franklyn, Sheila Mercier, Helen Jessop, Hazel Douglas, Elspet Gray and Dennis Ramsden. And the plays were directed, as usually at the Whitehall, by Wallace Douglas.

Nonetheless, the old Whitehall formula did not quite work. The plays attracted, on the whole, a more favourable critical press than the Whitehall farces had; they were popular with the public on tour, and to some degree in London, but none had lengthy runs. *She's Done It Again* opened at the Garrick on 15 October 1969, to what Rix called 'some of the best notices I have ever had from *all* the papers,' but did poor business at the box office and closed on 23 May 1970, thus, paradoxically establishing a record for the shortest run Rix had ever had (p. 212). *Don't Just Lie There* did well for eighteen months, from its opening on 18 August 1971 to February 1972, and in this case Rix admits that the play came off 'in error . . . when it was really still full of life' (p. 225); Rix, in fact, decided to take it off in order to give himself a short sabbatical at a time when he was expecting to make a film of the play, and continue a television series of farces in which he was starring – *Men of Affairs*, written by Michael Pertwee. The third play, *A Bit Between the Teeth*, opening on 12 September 1974, was badly affected by the IRA bomb campaign in London over the Christmas season. Rix, then, was disappointed in his attempts to continue a tradition established at the Whitehall. He had an excellent farce

writer in Pertwee, and an experienced team of actors. Why did
the venture limp along as it did? It is possible that Rix, after
fourteen years of energetic involvement in management, acting
and direction, had simply run out of steam; or perhaps he was
spreading his managerial activities too thinly over too many enterprises – television, film, touring, pantomime etc. The Whitehall
farces had built up a particular following, and the loss of the
Whitehall as a centre may have had its effect. Moreover, the
growth in the 1970s of the big subsidised companies like the Royal
Shakespeare and the National on the one hand, and of fringe
theatre on the other, did have an eroding effect, at least for a time,
on the West End commercial theatre.

But had Rix been able to get his repertory idea on a sounder
commercial footing, with more extensive backing and support,
and had he then offered a more varied bill of fare, as he at first
intended, then it is at least likely that he would have had a better
chance of succeeding. For this is precisely what Ray Cooney, a
decade later, in 1982, was to do with his Theatre of Comedy at
the Shaftesbury Theatre. Cooney secured backing from a number
of big names among actors, actresses and directors, completely
refurbished the Shaftesbury so that it was comparable for comfort, ease of access to bars, cloakrooms, etc., and a welcoming
atmosphere, to the big subsidised theatres, and set up a programme, based on the Shaftesbury, and ringing the changes, as
Rix had wanted to do, 'from low comedy to farce, to high comedy'
(p. 210). At the time of writing, this enterprise seems to be
enjoying considerable success, not least because of the lengthy
runs and good notices which Ray Cooney's own farces are
enjoying.

In this chapter, then, I shall look at three examples of post-
Whitehall farce, two by Michael Pertwee, *She's Done It Again* (1969),
and *A Bit Between the Teeth* (1974), and one, written and directed
by Ray Cooney for the Theatre of Comedy, *Run For Your Wife*
(1983).

Harold Hobson's review of *She's Done It Again* affirmed that
Pertwee's farce

is the funniest in which the great Brian Rix has ever appeared.
There are difficulties in the way of communicating a proper
sense of its delicious and delirious qualities. But what looks

feeble and hackneyed on the page glows with glorious life in the Garrick Theatre.

(Hobson, quoted Rix, p. 213)

I would not endorse altogether Hobson's superlatives, but *She's Done It Again* does provide a fine example, to use another Hobson phrase, of 'joyous new wine' in 'old bottles' (p. 218).

Pertwee creates, in the character of the meek and much put-upon parson, Hubert Porter, one of the most successful incarnations for Brian Rix of the 'eternal victim' figure he had played so adeptly in a series of Whitehall farces. Accident-prone from the beginning (mistaking the Bishop's brief-case for his own), Hubert becomes trapped in an increasingly bizarre world of sexual outrageousness, indecent exposure and infidelity, protesting his innocence to no avail, and forced into desperate masquerades and deceptions as he tries to get out of the compromising situations that entangle him. Hubert's brother-in-law, Freddy Gimble, the insolvent hotel manager, acts as the necessary victimiser to Brian Rix's victim; he continues to land Hubert in it, as an unwilling accomplice in a succession of hare-brained schemes to evade the tax man, pay off his gambling debts and strike it rich by pretending his wife has had quintuplets.

The farce also offers a wide range of inventively handled authority figures. At one end of the spectrum, impregnable in his moral authority, and increasingly outraged by what seems to be evidence of extreme depravity, is the Bishop of Opton. At the other end, a sadly decayed authority figure, is the eccentric and senile Professor Hogg, the ex-gynaecologist, who delivers five babies on the trot at the end of Act I, and whose conversation about fishing is shockingly misinterpreted by Hubert, no doubt to the audience's gleeful delight:

HOGG. Somebody has been at my flies.

HUBERT (*shocked dismay*). Oh, good gracious!

HOGG. Why, you may well ask, would anyone want to tamper with an old man's flies.

HUBERT (*most uncomfortable*). There are some very peculiar people about these days.

HOGG. Aha! I know what you're thinking! That I'm getting a bit old for it.

HUBERT. That is entirely your affair, sir . . .

HOGG (*chuckles, nudges him*). Had six little beauties yesterday
 afternoon.
HUBERT. SIX!
HOGG. All in less than an hour!
HUBERT (*rising*). Sir, I will not sit here and listen to this . . .
 this outrageous . . .
                         (*HOGG pulls him down.*)
HOGG. Haha! Jealous, eh?
HUBERT. Certainly not! And frankly, I don't believe a word of
 it.
HOGG. Oh, no! I'm not one of those.
HUBERT (*losing his head*). I didn't suggest you were and I don't
 want to discuss *that* either.
HOGG. If you don't believe me, I have a rather nice picture of
 them laid out on the bank afterwards.
HUBERT (*amazed*). All *together?*
HOGG. Side by side.
HUBERT. This! In Hampshire! But . . . but . . . didn't they
 mind?
HOGG (*laughs*). Mind! they were in no condition to care. Come
 here (*quietly*). You can have one of them yourself tonight.
HUBERT (*rising to D.L., shrilly*). No! Certainly not!
HOGG. We're having them the French way – meunière, with
 just a whisper of garlic.
HUBERT (*beginning to get it*). What exactly are you talking about?
HOGG. Trout, of course, what else?
HUBERT. What else?

                                                    (pp. 27–8)

In between Hogg and the Bishop, we have a feared authority
figure in Rodney Percival, the tax inspector intending a dirty weekend which, as so often in the world of farce, never materialises.

   The female characters in *She's Done It Again* include a number
of familiar stereotypes: dumb blonde, Sylvia the tax-inspector's
girl-friend, Hubert's bossy wife Mary, Hogg's spinster daughter
Ada, plus Faith, the girl-friend of Whisper (the giant 'heavy' and
debt-collector sent to rough up Freddy), and finally, Freddy's off-
stage wife. Pertwee needs the relatively high number of five
women in this farce, for the piece is not only about the financial
entanglements relating to Freddy's tax affairs and the Bishop's
mislaid brief-case, but about pregnancy. And, true to the spirit of

farce, Pertwee creates an increasingly dreamlike and surrealist effect by multiplying pregnancies: Freddy's off-stage wife in labour, then Mary, then Faith, with the Professor propelled from one bedroom to another like a demented automaton, to deliver two pairs of twins and a baby boy. This is capped in Act II by the appearance of another baby – a black one – 'borrowed' from a caravan, and, ultimately, by the successive appearances of Freddy, Hubert and Pop as pregnant mothers, obedient to the necessities of the by now hideously complicated plot. Pertwee is here going back, consciously or unconsciously, to the fertility rituals which lie at the root of dramatic comedy, and he gives us, in *She's Done It Again*, a joyously 'over-the-top' fertility rite. And what makes that rite work so well in performance is Pertwee's ability, acknowledged by Rix,

> to take something fairly recognisable to everyone, establish it firmly as a context people will believe in, and then push the situation to its extreme.
>
> (p. 215)

The situation in *She's Done It Again* becomes progressively more anarchic. The script offers every opportunity for the performers to build on one funny misunderstanding a second even funnier, and a third to crown them all, such that a climax of helpless merriment is produced. This is particularly evident in the successive appearances of the Bishop in Act II, all of them at highly inopportune moments, each of them creating growing panic and consternation among the other characters. The stage-direction for his first appearance gives us the classic Whitehall situation, though, needless to say, Hubert is entirely the innocent party:

> SYLVIA *bursts into tears and flings her arms round (HUBERT's) neck. At this precise moment the BISHOP OF UPTON enters R. unseen. He stops, appalled, at the sight of HUBERT without his trousers, apparently embracing a near-naked girl. He is a grim, pompous man – and hates HUBERT anyway. He carries HUBERT's brief-case, which is similar to his own.*
> SYLVIA (*loudly*). I'm going to have a baby!
> BISHOP (*appalled*). Porter!!

Hubert is surprised a second time, 'acting' his wife, in a rehearsal of what he is going to say to her to persuade her that she has had, not twins, but quintuplets:

HUBERT (*pulls pinafore over knees, adopts a female voice*). What have you to tell me?
FREDDY. It's about our weenies.
HUBERT. Our what?
FREDDY. Weenies.
HUBERT. Don't you think 'Tinies' would sound better?
FREDDY. (*crosses above arm chair to D.R. – irritably*). Oh, all right. (*acting again*) I have something to tell you about our tinies, Mary dear.
HUBERT. What, Pookie Wookie?
FREDDY (*himself*). *Pookie Wookie?*
HUBERT (*ashamed*). That's what Mary calls me sometimes.
FREDDY. Ugh! However. Carry on.
HUBERT (*female*). What, Pookie Wookie?
(*FREDDY kneels D.R. of HUBERT. Unseen by HUBERT or FREDDY, the BISHOP enters Right, carrying brief-case. He stops, appalled by what he sees and hears, above the armchair.*)
FREDDY. Before I say anything, darling, you know I love you, don't you?
HUBERT. I love you, too, Pookie Wookie, with *all* my heart.
BISHOP. PORTER!!

Freddy and Hubert bluff their way out of the situation by pretending they are rehearsing a play, which cues in further disastrous misunderstandings when the Bishop engages Sylvia in a dialogue about the theatre which she entirely misinterprets:

BISHOP (*kindly*). We have been discussing your little secret.
SYLVIA. Oh! He told you?
BISHOP. Yes. Tell me, have you done this kind of thing before?
SYLVIA (*ashamed*). Well, yes. Once or twice.
BISHOP. Ah, so this is not the first time. How long have you been at it?
SYLVIA (*more ashamed than ever*). Well, I was nineteen. This boy gave me a few drinks and –
HUBERT (*rising to BISHOP – desperate yell*) And persuaded her to play!
BISHOP. Don't interrupt, Porter!

(*HUBERT slumps on the R. arm of the sofa*)

(*To SYLVIA*) Have you ever considered turning professional?

SYLVIA (*angrily*). No! I have not! and don't you get the idea I do it all the time.

HUBERT (*dancing about*). She only does it in her spare time.

SYLVIA. If you want to know there's only been three . . .

HUBERT (*rising*). PERFORMANCES!

BISHOP. Will you stop shouting, Porter? I've done quite a bit of it myself, you know.

SYLVIA (*shocked*). Well, reely!

BISHOP. Still would, if my duties would allow. (*chuckles*) But who knows, perhaps we might perform together one of these days.

HUBERT (*another desperate yell*). IN PUBLIC.

BISHOP (*coldly*). Naturally, in public. It would be a pretty dull affair if nobody came to watch.

SYLVIA. You make me *sick!* You're a filthy old man. (*Crosses to door R.*)

BISHOP (*to her a step*). Just a moment, young lady. Will you answer one simple question?

SYLVIA. That depends.

BISHOP. According to the Reverend Porter here, you are a Thespian. Is that true?

SYLVIA. OOH! (*She whacks him across the stomach with her little bag and marches out R. BISHOP slowly turns and treats HUBERT to a long stare*).

HUBERT (*lamely*). Very – temperamental – these – thespians . . .

(pp. 27–9)

The exchanges are a classic example of what Max Miller exploited so well in his music-hall act: innocent material that has a double meaning if the audience cares to supply it. Here the audience savours the full delight of the double meanings, the irony of Sylvia and the Bishop at cross-purposes, and the ever more outrageously suggestive sub-text – 'at it', 'turning professional', 'performing in public', and – the crowning insult – 'you are a Thespian'.

The material in itself is funny, but what enables it to take off so effectively in performance, is its placing as the third and worst of a series of misunderstandings: the audience's resistance is by now low; and the result, given a skilful performance and the appropriate rapport between stage and audience, should be a large degree of unrestrained merriment. Pertwee, however, still has some tricks up his sleeve; and the culminating joke of the piece is primarily a visual one: Freddy, Hubert and Pop, each successively disguised as a pregnant mother, in a final conspiracy to persuade the Bishop that quintuplets really have been born to one lady alone. Unfortunately, all three men have chosen to appear as the same lady, Mrs Grimble. The ultimate 'surrealism' of the plot involves a desperate pretence that the three Mrs Grimbles are wife, mother and grandmother. But invention can go no further; and Pop's despairing cry effectively collapses the precarious 'house of cards' that the intriguers have erected: 'If I'm Granny Grimble, then what the hell am I doing with a bun in the oven?' (p. 42)

Pertwee also makes effective use, in *She's Done It Again*, of two features of the farce world already remarked on in this study. One is the element of ruthlessness in finding material for humour in situations that are painful or sad. As Rix says,

> I think there's a strong vein of cruelty in all humour. People laugh at other people's discomfiture, because they're damn glad not to be in that predicament themselves
>
> (p. 216)

And he points, in Pertwee's play, to

> Derek Royle's brilliantly funny performance as Professor Hogg: old, absent-minded, deaf and dotty. The audiences found him the funniest part of the evening and the critics acclaimed him, without exception. Yet senility, in truth, is sad almost beyond endurance.
>
> (p. 216)

The other, and related, feature, is the close connection between farce and tragedy. Rix develops this point in relation to Pertwee's farce:

> The whole point of good farce is that it teeters on the edge of tragedy. It always threatens ultimate catastrophe, and this is what sustains the dramatic tension. But by a slight twist it makes people roll about with laughter. It is tragedy with its trousers down.

The libidinous, nervous tax inspector; the Reverend Hubert Porter, terrified of being discovered in his contribution to the great quintuplet deception; the crooked hotel proprietor, nervous, too, because all his machinations could go wrong; the dotty old Professor Hogg delivering babies by grace and by God – all these characters, and more, in *She's Done It Again*, were threatened by ultimate catastrophe.

(p. 216)

Laurence Kitchin, in a discussion of the Whitehall farces (and we may include such post-Whitehall ones as those of Pertwee and Cooney), suggests that they should be distinguished from those of Ben Travers:

> The Whitehall team caters for a public less sophisticated than that of Ben Travers. They would be unlikely to understand his line in *A Cuckoo in the Nest* about someone moaning at the bar. Nearer their mark, is the reference in *Chase Me Comrade* to a Jerry born in Poland, for these farces are the pop art of canteens and seaside piers, with no inner logic at all. Brian Rix as a civil servant informs us that someone has busted his braces, and when he impersonates a naval officer he dances the hornpipe. . . . The Whitehall farces draw on the defunct English music-hall and are best seen from that point of view. Those of Ben Travers derive from French boulevard work and Pinero.[1]

But some highly questionable assumptions are made here. There is the usual, rather condescending, assumption that a popular audience is unsophisticated, when Peter Davison, and an earlier critic, S. L. Bethell, have argued most persuasively for a sophistication and an alertness that would surprise some academics.[2] There is, incidentally, a literary joke almost identical to the Travers joke Kitchin quotes in the Pertwee farce. When the Tax-inspector inadvertently refers to the girl-friend who's supposed to be a stranger as Sylvia, Freddy chips in with, 'Who is Sylvia? What is she?' (p. 23). In the discussion of Travers's work in Chapter 3, I refer to his admiration for music-hall stars, and identify certain music-hall elements in his work; it was also his partnership with two actors who were themselves skilled in music-hall techniques, Tom Walls and Ralph Lynn, that essentially created the Aldwych farces. Many of the parts written for Brian Rix cast him very much in the Ralph Lynn or Robertson Hare mould, and it is difficult to believe that such farce writers as Chapman, Cooney and Pertwee were not both aware of and influenced by Travers's work. Moreover, it is simply not true to say, of the best Whitehall farces, that there is 'no inner logic at all'. There is precisely the right degree of inner logic to sustain the farcical mechanism of the plot. We should, then, acknowledge a degree of overlap and connection between the world of Travers's farces, and that of the Whitehall pieces. It is fair to add, though, that the Whitehall farces, unlike those of Travers, are often characterised by a manic extravagance, a pushing things to extremes, evident in the slapstick passages and the wilder comic exchanges. Here, too, is a debt to the more surreal and absurdist aspect of that tradition. (See in this connection, for example, Roger Wilmut's discussion of Flanagan and Allen in *Kindly Leave The Stage*[3].)

In the second Pertwee farce to be considered, *A Bit Between The Teeth*, this mixed inheritance is very evident. As it also post-dates Orton's farces, *Loot* (1967) and *What the Butler Saw* (1969), it is interesting to consider, in addition, whether Orton's more radical and innovatory use of farce had any impact on Pertwee. The farce originated in an idea of Rix's, based on an incident in which a married friend of his had been involved:

> He came out of his girl-friend's flat to find his car had been stolen. The police *had* to be called. My friend had no trouble explaining his predicament to them. . . . But he had hell's own delight explaining to his suspicious missus exactly why he had been parked in North London when he was supposed to be on business in Birmingham.
>
> (p. 231)

Pertwee uses this idea as the starting point for his farce. He gives his adulterer, Reaper, a prim, respectable, rather nervous and inhibited business colleague, Fogg (the Brian Rix part), whose car he borrows for his adulterous escapades, and of whose friendship with his wife he is quite unjustly suspicious. He gives Reaper's wife, Diane, the same Christian name as his mistress's; he also gives the wife occasion to seek Fogg's help (to be of course misinterpreted by the jealous Reaper) over a blackmail attempt relating to some nude photographs she once posed for. And he sets the action in a flat above Reaper and Fogg's jewel firm (it is to be jewel thieves who steal the car), The stage accommodates a tripartite set, revealing three rooms of the flat, kitchen, sitting-room and bedroom.

With these ingredients, Pertwee sets in motion a series of chases on which the beads of comic business and farcical imbroglio are strung. We have Sergeant Ruff chasing the jewel thieves, Reaper's wife, Diane, being chased by her jealous husband, Fogg trying to avoid becoming entangled in these chases, and Reaper being pursued first by one mistress, and then at the end, by another. The chases offer, as ever, excellent opportunities for concealment, confusions of identity, repetitions and violent physical action. Reaper assumes Fogg's name and calls his partner by his own name to cover his tracks; the existence of two Dianes, wife and mistress, who must on no account meet but of course do so, leads to further confusion. The tripartite set has a critical part to play in the farce, allowing as it does for chase sequences, multiple hiding places, simultaneous action, sequences of dramatic irony in which what is going on in one room threatens catastrophe to those in the next room, and the audience can anticipate imminent disaster.

There are passages of slapstick humour and comic business mainly involving Fogg: his trousers fall down, his tin of baked beans explodes, he is driven to devour incriminating photographs and burnt underclothes, he tries ever less successfully to interpret Reaper's signalled mime as to what he should say to the police. In short we see in him that feature of the farce world that Booth characterises as,

> the harassment of the ordinary individual beyond the bounds of reason, his entrapment in an incomprehensible and absurd situation . . . . the farce of the preposterous and desperate predicament.[4]

In this harassment, we are reminded at times of the roles Travers created for Lynn and Hare. Fogg is like the Hare character in being timid, respectable, rather prim, and embarrassed by words like 'breast' and 'extra-marital'; so that in some ways he is the perfect victim for the forces of disorder and amorality personified in Reaper. A review of the first production, indeed, described Brian Rix in terms reminiscent of Robertson Hare, as 'the bespectacled knight of the woeful countenance'. Fogg is also like the Ralph Lynn character in having his 'silly ass' side: there is the conver-

sational accident-proneness – 'I've never looked at another man's
life in all my wife' (p. 5); a similar susceptibility to female charm;
and a similar inaneness in his attempts to cover up the presence
of Reaper's wife. As also in Travers's work, so here, an element
of what might be called seaside postcard or music-hall vulgarity
enters, perhaps of a slightly coarser kind than was present in
Travers – 'I like the way you roll your R's,' says Mrs Barker when
Reaper attempts a French accent. 'I like the way you roll yours
too', is Reaper's rejoinder (p. 42). In Act II, after a struggle between
the two men, *'Fogg's head,'* reads the stage-direction, *'remains glued
in Mrs Barker's cleavage'* (p. 56). And the antics of the chase involve
both Dianes appearing in various stages of undress.

   Where perhaps Pertwee's farce is most clearly distanced from
Travers is in the wildness of some of the improvised deceptions
– the splendid dottiness with which, for example, Reaper in Act
II pretends that his half-dressed girl-friend, discovered by Sergeant
Ruff in a cupboard, is the Contesse de la Touquet:

RUFF. Bridget who, sir?
REAPER (*with French pronunciation*). Brigitt-eu Inspect-eu,
   Brigitte is a bonne amie of old Fo. . . . of my partner. May I
   present the Contesse de la Touquet. Brigitte, je vous presente
   l'Inspecteur Ruff, another bon ami of ours. (*Sotto voce*) She
   speaks very little English.
RUFF (*playing along*). Charmed, Contesse. (*Speaking very
   distinctly*). This may seem a stupid question, but were you
   doing anything terribly important in zee broom cupboard just
   now?
MRS BARKER (*very English*). Pardon?
RUFF. Um – what – were you doing in the cupboard of the
   broom?
REAPER. She's desperately shy – (*sotto voce to RUFF*) – and she's
   married, so fermez la bouche, s'il vous plaît.
RUFF. Bit nippy; perhaps the Countess would like to put on
   some clothes.
REAPER (*quickly*). No, she hasn't any clothes.
RUFF. None at all?
REAPER. She's a nudist.
RUFF. Well, hardly. (*He looks at MRS BARKER as if saying, Well,
   hardly a nudist*)
FOGG. A nearly nudist.

RUFF. Does she live here?
FOGG   )   No. Yes   )
REAPER)   Yes. No   ) *(Speaking together)*
RUFF. Yes and no, eh?
FOGG. On and off.
RUFF. More off than on, by the look of it.
REAPER. Please! Inspector! A petite delicatessen! S'il vous plaît!

In Act I, we have a similarly outrageous series of improvised
explanations, this time by Fogg, when Reaper's series of unexpected returns threaten to reveal the presence of his wife in the
flat. One has the impression here that Pertwee is indirectly influenced by Joe Orton, and the business of the incriminating underclothes in *What the Butler Saw*. In Orton's farce, Dr Prentice, discovered clutching Geraldine's bra and knickers, tries to hide them
by doubling up in pretended pain, kneeling in apparent prayer,
or thrusting them into a vase, the flowers from which he keeps
offering his wife. When the girl's high-heeled shoes are discovered
hidden in the bookshelf, Prentice is suspected of being a transvestite. In similar vein, Fogg is driven to frantic activity to conceal
Diane's underclothes: he puts them in the oven; trying to act at
ease, he burns his hand on one of the elements; he bursts into
lunatic song to cover up his whispered warning to Diane in the
bath; and, cornered by Reaper, who spots women's stockings
hanging out of the wastepaper basket, he's driven to pretend that
he's a transvestite:

REAPER. Foggy, these are women's stockings. Now they
    weren't here before, because I dropped my cigar butt in here.
    Look! Now, they're not yours are they?
FOGG. Yes!
REAPER. Pardon?
FOGG. They are mine.
REAPER. You wear women's stockings?
FOGG. Not all the time.
REAPER. But some of the time?
FOGG. Yes.
REAPER. Why?
FOGG. I'm a trans-vest . . .
REAPER. Tight!
FOGG. Quite.

REAPER. You mean to say you get your kicks out of dressing
   up as a woman?

FOGG. Yes.

REAPER. I knew there was something queer about you!

FOGG. No! Not queer!

REAPER. If dressing up as a woman isn't queer, I don't know
   what is. How did it start?

FOGG. I prefer not to discuss it.

REAPER. Oh come on! I've always been interested in odd balls.

FOGG. If you must know, it was my mother: she wanted a
   daughter and used to call me Sybil.

                                                              (p. 12)

Further excruciating embarrassments dog the unfortunate Fogg.
Reaper returns again to see Diane's painted toe-nails protruding
from the end of the bed; they're assumed to be Fogg's. The underclothes are burned in the oven, and Fogg, once again surprised
by Reaper as he removes them, tries to pass off singed suspender
belt as smoked squid. When he finally has to admit that they are
underclothes he insists that his cooking of them was a symbolic
act of rejecting his transvestite past! Pertwee shows considerable
inventiveness and ingenuity in involving Fogg more and more
deeply in a desperate predicament, just as Orton does with Prentice in *What the Butler Saw*. Consistent, too, with the franker and
more permissive sexual climate of the 70s, and following the
example set by Orton, Pertwee uses so-called sexual 'deviations'
for farcical effect. But it is clear that he does so in significantly
different ways. When Prentice is suspected of transvestism, his
wife coolly and imperturbably comments, 'I'd no idea our marriage
teetered on the edge of fashion' (p. 373). That line, with its
subversive assumption that transvestism is the 'in' thing, would
be quite out of place in Pertwee's farce. His humour presupposes
a norm of conventional heterosexual behaviour; it is notable, too,
that in the passage quoted above, he rather awkwardly has to
signal to the audience the meaning of the word transvestism –
'you mean you get your kicks out of dressing up as a woman' –
and that this cues in a series of jokes about being 'queer', jokes
which equate transvestism in a muddled and inaccurate way with
homosexuality. Orton, on the other hand, uses farce in a most
original way to challenge sexual stereotypes and to present a world
of sexual anarchy in which no conventional assumptions go

unquestioned. In Pertwee's farce no such uncomfortable questioning exists.

There is a connection too between the ending of *A Bit Between the Teeth* and the endings of Orton's farces. Neither in Orton nor in Pertwee is there any return to respectability. In Pertwee's farce the forces of law and order beat a retreat. Sergeant Ruff falls ignominiously downstairs. And Fogg, far from being released from his predicament, finds it indefinitely prolonged, since another of Reaper's girls is in search of him as the father of her child. But the tone of Pertwee's farce is predominantly festive, the mood light-hearted, and the deeper undertones of Orton's farce are lacking.

Ray Cooney's *Run For Your Wife*, like the Pertwee farce, belongs recognisably to a post-Orton world, in which transvestism, homosexuality and bigamy are all grist to the farce-writer's mill, albeit viewed not as alternative and desirable life-styles, but as desperate dilemmas in which to entangle the hapless victim, John Smith, and his well-intentioned friend, Stanley. Appropriate to the double life of the bigamist, John Smith, and to the divided set which reflects that double life, there are, necessarily, two wives, but also two authority figures, in the persons of two detective-sergeants from the neighbouring 'parishes' of Streatham and Wimbledon, and two victims, Smith himself, victim of his own deceptions, and Stanley, who is 'landed in it' by Smith.

As in many of the farces already studied in this book, these two constitute something of a double-act, in which Stanley plays stooge and accomplice to Smith's beguilingly innocent-seeming trickster. The nature of this double act is well caught in one reviewer's response to the actors playing the roles in the opening months of the original production, Richard Briers (Smith) and Bernard Cribbins (Stanley):

Mr Cribbins greets each new label with crumbling resignation, falling flat on his back over a sofa, seeking womb-like solace in a chair, and finally exiting forlornly on hands and knees as another lurid revelation hits him over the back of the head. This performance, a riot of signalled desperation and limpid benevolence, is an effective foil to Mr Briers rapid switches between expressions of hope, inventive energy, and modulated panic.[5]

The farce is unusual and original in that it begins *in medias res*. In most farces involving adultery or illicit sex, the setting up of the situation by the would-be Casanova takes most of the first Act; and it is only gradually that the complications ensue, the nightmare begins. But the Casanova of *Run For Your Wife* has already set up the situation when the play begins. As Milton Shulman's review puts it:

> A taxi-driver called John Smith is a bigamist who has a wife in Wimbledon and another wife five minutes away in Streatham. Because of the uneven hours of his trade and the fact that both wives have jobs, he has managed, through observing a strict time schedule, to keep for three years these two households secret from each other.[6]

The use of bigamy as a mainspring of the farcical action is itself unusual, as Benedict Nightingale noted:

> Farce of concealment, the kind that thrives on character A desperately preventing character B finding out fact X, has been one of the sexual revolutions less noticed victims. It doesn't matter if the husband spots the lover under the bed as much as it did in the days of Feydeau or even Travers. But Ray Cooney offers a solution in *Run For Your Wife*: bigamy, which could land the practitioner in jug, yet somehow doesn't alienate us from him as much as most crimes. So there's genuine tension as Richard Briers, incompetently aided by Bernard Cribbins, tries to keep the secret of his two wives from both them and the police; and from tension comes mirth.[7]

Also, what has been set up is a situation of ingenious and almost mathematical tidiness, depending on split-second timing and the smooth, rational organisation of John Smith's daily routine. Only one intrusion of irregularity or untidiness is needed for the whole elaborately organised fabric of deception to begin to come apart: which is, of course, what happens from the start when the taxi-driver gets involved in a mugging and, mildly concussed, gives separate addresses to police-station and hospital. The police begin asking awkward questions, newspapers give the incident the publicity that Smith at all costs does not want. The result – 'panic sets in early – a test of good farce – and the pace thereafter never slackens'.[8]

As in Ayckbourn's *Bedroom Farce*, Cooney makes use of a divided set for Smith's two households, one in Streatham, one in Wimbledon, with one centre-stage sofa that doubles for both households. That divided set gives the audience a privileged position from which to appreciate the ironies of Smith's double life. It also establishes visually, and wittily, through the device of the shared sofa, which is often sat upon simultaneously by the two wives in their separate households, the dangerous proximity and threatened convergence of John Smith's two worlds. The over-lapping of dialogue and situation gives admirable opportunities not only for dramatic irony, but also for a rapidity of pace highly appropriate to the farce world. The divided set also allows for the device of the telephone calls between the two households, or to one of the households from the outside world (press or police) to make its maximum effect. As Julian Barnes writes in *Flaubert's Parrot* (London, 1984, p. 109):

the telephone in our century has made adultery both simpler and harder (assignations are easier but so is checking up).

Thus the phone in *Run For Your Wife* becomes both an instrument of terror (to the bigamous husband and his accomplice Stanley) and a source of much comic delight (to the audience). Telephone calls induce in John in the second half of Act I a growing hysteria as he feels that his cover is blown (one wife having stumbled on the second wife's phone number). They also involve a whole sequence of role-playing gambits, one of which requires Stanley to cover for John by pretending to be the farmer in whose cottage John waited while his taxi was being repaired after breaking down (his excuse to Barbara for being behind schedule). The ludicrous details of farming life John and Stanley between them invent, both on the phone and off it, are none of them very funny in them-selves; but they take on a comic life of their own through repetition and elaboration. They are like other details in the farce: the incrimi-nating *Standard* newspaper that (like the Figaro in Feydeau's *Un Fil à la Patte*) has somehow to be torn up, or eaten, or otherwise disposed of; the code initials that John Smith uses to remind him of his schedule (CDWB: 'Cuddly day with Barbara', LNBEMM, 'Late night with Barbara, early morning with Mary); the eighty-year-old parents of Mary, one in a wheel-chair, who, according to Stanley, have plunged to their doom while on a hiking holiday on Mount Snowdon – these details become repeated and elaborated 'running jokes', that accumulate a growing momentum of laughter, not to be measured by the impact of single lines taken out of context. For example, John's, 'Keep a very close watch on your bullocks' (p. 30), or Barbara's, 'Has he brought his beetroot with him?' (p. 48) sound only coarsely vulgar, divorced from the dramatic situation. But, coming as they do at moments of escalating confusion or uncertainty about the sexual leanings of the men in the play, they take on a ripely Rabelaisian quality which is wholly delightful.

If the running joke is a staple ingredient of many farces, so too is the chase. And, as the title, *Run for Your Wife*, suggests, the chase is central to Cooney's farce, and is used as the thread to link the 'lazzi' or pieces of comic business. Thus, once John Smith's tidy schedule is disrupted, he has to go into over-drive to catch up on it, in effect chasing his own tail. Once he's been mugged, and given different addresses to police and hospital, he is chased in turn by the press, wanting to photograph him and publicise his life; by the detective sergeants of both Wimbledon and Streatham police stations, puzzled by the two addresses; by his two wives; and by a succession of telephone calls, referred to above.

In this chase, Bergson's 'snowball' principle operates. As the small snowball of convenient lies Smith has constructed to keep his two marriages apart starts to roll downhill and gather speed, its bulk increases, with more and more lies desperately added to explain away the inexplicable. As it gathers speed and bulk, so it engulfs the bystanders almost without exception. Thus, Stanley, Smith's friendly lodger, becomes in turn a farmer with a job lot of beetroot to unload, the husband of one of the wives, a marriage-busting homosexual, and the father of a drug-crazed schoolboy; one wife, Barbara, is passed off as the daily help, and then as Lofty, a transvestite; the other wife becomes Sister Mary, a hysterical nun; and Detective Sergeant Porterhouse finds himself assumed to be a married bisexual who goes dancing with a boy-friend called Gruesome.

The successive transformations, and the ever thickening tangle of misunderstandings are expertly contrived by Cooney, as indeed many of the reviews acknowledged: 'a beautifully constructed piece, so over the top it flies';[9] the play demonstrates 'the ever accelerating momentum essential to farce':[10] 'the evening drives on at such a pace of perlexity as one excuse leads to another misunderstanding that you realise how intellectual the best farces are and what brains the actors need to perform them'.[11]

Cooney is, in fact, particularly successful in building up an accumulation of misunderstandings, such that the hapless Mary seems entrapped at the end of the play in a world where homosexuality and transvestism are the norm.

In the climactic scene in Act II, Detective Sergeant Porterhouse has one mistaken version of events – that there are two Mr Smiths, each called John, each respectably married, one with a child called Stanley; Mary has another more bizarre version, that her husband John has a gay love-nest in Streatham with Stanley, and Porterhouse's interventions strengthen and deepen her suspicions. Each ironically finds the other's responses merely confirming the 'truth' as they see it. Porterhouse's polite offer of tea to 'the other Mrs Smith' lights the train of gunpowder:

MARY. What other Mrs Smith?
PORTERHOUSE. The one who lives here.
JOHN (*quickly*) He means Lofty.
> (*During the ensuing scene PORTERHOUSE pours a cup of tea for STANLEY, JOHN and himself. N.B. The actor playing PORTERHOUSE will find he has plenty of time!*).
MARY. Oh, that's very nice, 'Mrs Smith'!
PORTERHOUSE (*chuckling*). Lofty! (*JOHN and STANLEY look at him.*) (*still chuckling*) I like it!
MARY (*to JOHN*). Has he met Lofty?
JOHN (*with false gaiety*). Yes!
MARY. All dolled up?
JOHN. Yes.
PORTERHOUSE (*chuckling*). Lofty!
> (*JOHN and STANLEY look at him again. PORTERHOUSE gives STANLEY his tea. STANLEY goes to drink.*)
Do you know what I call mine?
> (*MARY looks astonished as she takes in what she thinks is the implication. JOHN and STANLEY react to each other because they realise what MARY must be thinking. JOHN buries his head in his hands as STANLEY bangs his cup down in the saucer.*)
MARY (*finally*). Yours?

PORTERHOUSE (*to Mary*). Mind you, we've been together longer than Mr Smith (*he indicates JOHN*) and his Lofty. (*PORTERHOUSE chuckles at MARY who looks blank. JOHN and STANLEY react to each other. PORTERHOUSE offers STANLEY the sugar. To MARY*). We've had twenty years of it.

STANLEY (*politely*). No sugar for me, thank you.

PORTERHOUSE (*laughing*). I call mine Gruesome. (*JOHN looks up to heaven. PORTERHOUSE pours JOHN's tea*.) It's just a joke of course.

MARY. God, is everybody at it?

PORTERHOUSE. It's only a silly sort of game really.

MARY. A game?

JOHN (*Laughs foolishly*). Yes, a game! No harm! (*Changing the subject, to PORTERHOUSE*). Two lumps for me, please!

PORTERHOUSE (*to MARY*). Actually, I think my wife has grown quite accustomed to Gruesome.

(*STANLEY chokes on his tea and JOHN comes to his assistance. MARY is staggered. PORTERHOUSE, oblivious, puts the sugar in JOHN's tea and hands it to him.*)

....

MARY. This is a real eye-opener! Does your Gruesome dress up like his Lofty?

PORTERHOUSE. Only when we go dancing together.

MARY. Dancing?

(*JOHN chokes on his tea. JOHN and STANLEY quickly rise. During the following lines JOHN gives STANLEY his cup and PORTER-HOUSE's cup and STANLEY puts them and his on the tray behind the settee. JOHN goes to PORTERHOUSE and pulls him up.*)

JOHN (*hastily*). That was a very nice cup of tea.

STANLEY. Yes it was, very nice.

JOHN. Thanks for the chat, too. And all the advice.

(pp. 64–5)

Mary grows more and more angry at these revelations; but Stanley makes things worse when he tries to explain away her abuse of Porterhouse as a 'perverted old poof' as a result of being upset by (non-existent) grandparents, staying with her (non-existent) brother called Sydney. Her response, 'Stanley's potty', is misunderstood by Porterhouse as a reference to her son's toilet-training, and he asks, 'is he still using one of those?' This finally drives Mary into hysteria:

(*She breaks under the strain*)
MARY (*screaming*). Ahhh!
(*JOHN, STANLEY and PORTERHOUSE jump out of their skins.*)
(*Screaming*). Ahhh! (*She stands there and starts to stamp her feet.*)
....
(*JOHN and STANLEY attempt to calm her down.*)
PORTERHOUSE (*Backing away*). It seemed to be Stanley's potty
that set her off.
(*MARY's screams become deep sobs*).

(p. 67)

We have here, once again, a demonstration of Booth's 'harassment of the ordinary individual beyond the bounds of reason . . .
the farce of the preposterous and desperate predicament' (see note
4, this chapter). There is also the sense of danger the audience
experiences as John and Stanley, aghast and awe-struck, watch
and wait for the fantasy worlds they've each invented to collapse
under the weight of their own absurdity. As Bentley puts it, 'there
is something frightening about such worlds, because there is something maniacal about them . . . Danger is omnipresent . . . one
touch, we feel, and we shall be sent spinning in space'.[12] That the
polite banalities of a tea ritual accompany the bizarre revelations
adds a final touch of the surreal to the scene.

The use of homosexuality as a prominent thread in the tangle
of complications certainly owes something to Orton, though it is
treated in a different spirit, and with different effect. Some
reviewers of the London production, in fact, took exception, as
Orton surely would have, to the inclusion in the play of Bobby
Franklyn's 'flamboyant dress-designer':

The one miscalculation is the stereotype of a limp-wristed male
dressmaker who keeps flouncing in on the action. These days,
it would be far more amusing to introduce into a farce a homosexual who was a muscular, heavily moustached sergeant major
or tennis champion.[13]

It might be 'far more amusing', in another perhaps more naturalistic play, but in Cooney's farce the introduction of Bobby Franklyn
is nicely calculated to cue in the role-playing of Stanley and John
as gay lovers, while maximising their embarrassment at the kind
of role-model they have available. It also cues in, neatly enough,

a series of transvestite jokes and suppositions relating to 'Lofty' and 'Gruesome'.

Finally, as in other post-Orton farces (such as Pertwee's *A Bit Between the Teeth*) we have, in *Run For Your Wife*, an ending which far from restoring the situation to normal, leaves the not-so-innocent victim trapped in his role-playing. John Smith attempts to remove the masks he has donned himself and wished on others, in a neat, stylised resumé of all the role-playing gambits attempted (the farceur playfully calling attention through this speech to the joyful inventiveness with which the plot has been successively thickened). But to no avail: the trickster, as in *Entertaining Mr Sloane*, is hoist with his own petard. The dramatic irony is neat, effective and appropriate:

JOHN. O.K. Here we go.
STANLEY. The truth.
JOHN. Of course.
STANLEY. The whole truth.
JOHN. And nothing but.
(*JOHN indicates for STANLEY and TROUGHTON to sit. They do so. During the following speech JOHN circles the stage telling his story.*)
JOHN. Firstly, I would like to dispel the rumour that the blonde young lady who just rushed out in a flood of tears is a nun. This is a concoction entirely of my own making. Nor is she married to Mr Gardner – who does ot have a disturbed schoolboy son called Stanley. And for those who have been led to believe otherwise, Mr Gardner practices neither as a farmer nor as a homosexual. Nor as any combination of the two. Secondly, I wish to go on record that the charming but hysterical red-head through there is neither my daily help nor is she a transvestite. Finally, I would like to say that all the aforementioned little white lies were contrived by me, for the simple purpose of covering up my guilty secret – I am married to the other lady and live somewhere else. Correct Stanley?
STANLEY (*rising, sadly*). Correct, John.
(*STANLEY puts his arm around JOHN in comfort. There is a pause as they look at TROUGHTON.*)
TROUGHTON (*finally*). You lying bastard
(*JOHN takes this in and then slowly looks around blankley at STANLEY who is standing there dumbfounded. JOHN's face breaks*

*into a smile. STANLEY starts to cry. JOHN kisses him.) The music
of 'Love and Marriage' starts as . . . the CURTAIN falls.*

(pp. 77–8)

The Whitehall tradition, then, as this chapter has demonstrated,
continues with undiminished vitality into the present day. What
the Whitehall and post-Whitehall companies have contributed to
farce may be summed up in a variety of ways. They have offered
to the teams of actors involved a most valuable workshop in which
to train and bring to perfection the exceptionally demanding
physical and mental skills that farce performers require. They have
carried on to some degree the fruitful practice exemplified by
Travers, Walls and Lynn, of house dramatist and company
working together on a script when necessary, using improvisation,
re-writing and collaboration to achieve the best results. They have
provided in their repertory, a showcase of themes and techniques,
many of them traditional, but re-invented and 'made new' with
each successive play: the conversation at cross-purposes; the
chase; the double act – often made up of stooge and con-man; the
puns, wisecracks, innuendos and running jokes; the confusions
of identity and role-playing; the mockery of a variety of authority
figures – bishops, officers and sergeants, tax inspectors, doctors
and so on; and a command of accelerating pace, with misunderstandings multiplying and mayhem triumphant. And it is likely,
too, that they have attracted a broader-based, more genuinely
popular audience for farce than Pinero, or even Travers, and may
have so alerted some 'serious' playwrights anxious to reach out to
such audiences to the relevance of farce and its techniques to their
subject-matter.

6

Joe Orton

With Joe Orton, we come to the first of a number of contemporary playwrights who have experimented challengingly and inventively with the genre of farce, and have used the form in more unexpected or provocative ways than is often the case with the Whitehall or post-Whitehall tradition in farce – a tradition which stems partly from Ben Travers, partly from music-hall. None the less, their knowledge of, and debt to, that tradition is often manifest. In this and the concluding two chapters of this book, I shall look at a number of contemporary playwrights whose work, unlike that of Travers, Chapman, Pertwee and Cooney, is seen as 'serious' by the writers of critical studies of modern drama, and discuss their interest in, and experiments with, the genre.

Role-playing; the dialectic of festivity and aggression; the growing entanglement in a nightmare world of characters often reduced to puppet-like responses: all these elements in the world of farce are richly present in the work of Joe Orton. Orton's farces, and in particular *Loot* (1967), and *What the Butler Saw* (1969), embody a mocking response to the contemporary world, a response which, seeing laughter as 'a serious business', uses humour as 'a weapon'.[1] C. W. Bigsby quotes an observation by one of Stoppard's characters, Mrozek, in *Tango*, – 'Don't you see that nowadays tragedy isn't possible any more? . . . Today farce is the only thing possible' – and he comments:

> Orton pressed that conviction to its logical conclusion . . . he became a crucial embodiment of the post-modernist impulse: by means of farce he gives expression to that conviction of a dislocated self, of a reified experience, of a brittle and contingent language, which still seems to define the nature of our private fears, if not always of our public protestations.[2]

This being so, it is perhaps not surprising that there is a strong

120

and clear connection between Orton's life and his art. The element
of the prankster, the joker, the comic role-player was in fact very
strong in Orton's nature. In his casual sexual pick-ups, he would
invent a different identity for himself: 'I make things up,' he
said. 'I call myself a packer, a metal worker, a lithographer, a
hairdresser's assistant. That way I put people off guard. Their
dialogue is natural.'³ He delighted in writing indignant letters to
the press or to respectable authority figures, under the alias of
Miss Edna Welthorpe. To a man who walked out of *Loot*, and
wrote to complain to the manager of the theatre, he responded:

> I must write to tell you that you are not alone in disliking the
> play, *Loot*. I myself consider it to be the most loathsome play in
> London at the present moment. 'Bestial' is how I described it to
> an acquaintance the other day. When I tell you that in the
> second Act (which you had the good fortune to miss) there was
> a discussion upon the raping of children with Mars Bars, with
> other filthy details of a sexual and psychopathic nature, I'm sure
> you'll pardon my writing.⁴

In the theft and ingenious defacing of books from Hampstead
and Islington libraries that he and Kenneth Halliwell went in
for, there was a farcical and subversive zest that was later to be
channelled into the grotesquely inventive criminality of *Loot*:

> I was really occupying myself with those library books . . . used
> to be a full-time job. I would stagger home from libraries with
> books which I'd borrowed and also stolen, and then I used to
> go back with them a couple of times a day . . . I used to stand
> in corners after I'd smuggled the doctored bits back into the
> library and then watch people read them. . . . There was a
> biography of Sir Bernard Spilsbury, the criminologist, with a
> photograph of a rather dreary looking cellar, with the caption,
> 'The remains discovered in the cellar at No. 23 Rosedown Rd'.
> I pasted David's picture of Marat dead in his bath over the
> photograph. . . . One of the interesting things at the trial was
> that the greatest outrage, the one for which I think I was sent
> to prison, was that I had stuck a monkey's face in the middle
> of a rose, on the cover of something called *Collins's Book of Roses*.
> It was a very beautiful yellow rose. What I had done was held

up as the depth of iniquity for which I should probably have been birched.[5]

The prison sentence that resulted from this escapade had its effect, too, on Orton's work. Prison, he claimed, 'brought detachment to my writing. . . . I wasn't involved any more.'[6] It encouraged, in other words, that watchful detachment Feydeau wrote of, when, in 'arranging all that madness. . . . I keep the cool calm poise of the chemist measuring out his medicine'.[7] Even Orton's tragic end, battered to death by his lover, is a kind of distorted reflection of the aggressiveness and brutality examined with irony and comic insight in the plays. Role-playing and role-switching, familiar to Orton the actor and private citizen, sexual confusion and sexual versatility, familiar to Orton the man are used by the dramatist as images for a deeply humorous commentary on human behaviour. The illegality and rebelliousness of Orton's life – partly forced on him by the legal and social penalties attaching to homosexuality – are harnessed in his drama to the subversive and anarchic energies of farce.

Orton as actor needed to be involved in his role, yet be able to measure his effect on an audience and adjust a performance accordingly. Orton as homosexual needed involvement in a steady relationship, but also sought out casual one-night stands with an almost scientific curiosity about human behaviour. He wanted, he is reported to have said, to be 'like a fly on the wall,' observing, eavesdropping.[8] Both paradoxes – of incidental interest in the life – become of central importance in the art. For drama, and in particular the comic drama, require that combination of involvement and detachment, what Yeats called 'cold passion', that Orton so effectively possessed. That Orton was, in fact, keenly aware of the connection between even the wilder imaginings of his farces and real life can be illustrated with particular reference to *Loot*.

There is a particular moment in this play when Hal's dead mother is taken out of her coffin and stuffed in a cupboard, so that the loot from Hal and Dennis's bank robbery can be hidden in the coffin. In the course of the substitution, the dead body is stripped of its clothes and its false teeth, which Hal clicks like a pair of castanets, while fantasising about a Spanish prostitute he'd like to set up in a brothel he wants to buy (pp. 226–7). During the run of the play, Orton's own mother died; he went up to Leicester for the funeral, and, looking through one of the cupboards, 'I found a cup containing a pair of false teeth and threw it in the dustbin. Then I discovered they belonged to my father. I had to rescue them. I found my mother's teeth in a drawer. I kept them to amaze the cast of *Loot*.'[9] Back in London, he took the false teeth round to the theatre:

> I said to Kenneth Cranham (who played Hal), 'Here, I thought you'd like the originals.' He said, 'What?' 'Teeth,' I said. 'Whose?' he said. 'My mum's,' I said. He looked very sick. 'You see,' I said, 'It's obvious that you're not thinking of the events of the play in terms of reality if a thing affects you like that.' Simon Ward (who played Dennis) shook like a jelly when I gave them to him.'[10]

Real life events also played their part in Orton's creation of Inspector Truscott. The dramatist told friends that he had been, as a homosexual, entrapped by the police, and, once in custody, propositioned by them.[11] Moreover, as *Loot* was being revised and rewritten for final production, Orton read with considerable interest of the police enquiry into the behaviour of Detective Sergeant Challoner. Challenor's concern for law and order had apparently turned into a mania which led him to plant evidence on law-abiding citizens:

> Challenor had picked out a demonstrator protesting at the Greek royal visit in 1963 and arrested him, saying, 'You're fucking nicked, my old beauty.' On the way to the police station, riding in the police van, the demonstrator told the enquiry, 'Challenor was leaping about. A girl's voice shouted, 'Will you give us a lift?' And Challenor leaned out and shouted, 'Yes! Round the bleeding chops! . . . Another Challenor victim, whose conviction of seven years' imprisonment for demanding money with menaces and possessing an offensive weapon was finally quashed, testified that Challenor had planted an iron bar on him in his cell and fabricated the charge. He testified that Challenor, looming large in his dark blue raincoat, came into the cell, saying, 'Hello, my little darling, hello my little darling. I don't want you, I want your pals.' When no names were forthcoming, Challenor threw down the iron bar. The prisoner refused to pick it up. Challenor threatened him with it and then punched him in the face.[12]

The beatings up in *Loot*, the exercise of arbitrary authority, the expression, 'You're fucking nicked, my old beauty', all relate to Orton's reading of the Challenor case, and his amused sense of how life was imitating art.

Against this background, it is curious to find some critics attacking Orton's work for unreality or immaturity. J. W. Lambert, reviewing the Joe Orton season at the Royal Court Theatre in 1975, suggested that his appeal was 'to arrested development – to those common among the avant-garde to whom any four letter word will always provoke a frisson'.[13] John Russell Taylor rated his achievement a little higher than this: 'In *Entertaining Mr Sloane*, he managed at the very lowest estimate to write the first solid, well-managed commercial play which belonged, specifically and unmistakably, to the post-Osborne era.' But he refutes 'the very exaggerated claims' made for *What the Butler Saw* as Orton's best play, calls its Act II plot unravellings, 'increasingly spiritless and mechanical', and says of *Loot*, 'It is hard to relate characters or events to any external reality.'[14] While I shall hope to refute these criticisms in the detailed examination of the plays, I suggest that they are at least partly based on that critical snobbery, referred to in Chapter I, that denies to farce the same serious attention that is readily accorded tragedy, comedy or realistic drama. Another relevant factor is that Orton's three full-length plays, and particularly *Entertaining Mr Sloane* (1964), were to enjoy a commercial success denied more obviously 'serious' – and of course no less important – contemporary playwrights like Edward Bond. There is a kind of critical stock reaction, nourished by the highbrow-lowbrow splits in our culture, that equates commercial success with superficiality; and Orton reacted furiously to this when he detected signs of it in John Russell Taylor's Introduction to *Penguin New Dramatists: 8*. Taylor had written, 'Living theatre needs the good commercial dramatist as much as the original artist.'[15] Orton's response, in a letter to his agent, was:

Are they different, then? *Hamlet* was written by a commercial dramatist. So were *Volpone* and *The School for Scandal* and *The Importance of Being Earnest* and *The Cherry Orchard* and *Our Betters*. Two ex-commercial successes of the last thirty years are about to be revived by our non-commercial theatre: *A Cuckoo in the Nest* and *Hay Fever*. . . . I've no ambition to bolster up the commercial theatre, but if my plays go into the West End I don't expect this to be used as a sneer by people who judge artistic success by commercial failure. There is no intrinsic merit in a flop.[16]

In considering Orton's achievement in farce, a convenient starting point is provided by his statement, à propos of *Entertaining Mr Sloane*, that 'What I wanted to do . . . was break down all the sexual compartments that people have.'[17] *Sloane*, admittedly, is less a farce than an ironic comedy of manners, being less frenetic in its action, less complex and inventive in its plotting than *Loot* and *What the Butler Saw*. But it has its farcical elements. On the most elementary level, there are the ridiculous and embarrassing misadventures, characteristic of farce, of Sloane's trousers and Kath's dentures. In Act I, Sloane, stabbed in the calf with a toasting fork, has his trousers eagerly removed by Kath, and her brother Ed at once sees in them evidence for the worst having occurred (p. 82). As for Kath's dentures, they are first left soaking in Stergene in the kitchen on the morning she chooses to announce her pregnancy to Sloane, and then knocked out of her mouth in Act III, so that she is left ludicrously crawling around the floor as events move to their dramatic climax. (p. 146) Moreover, Eric Bentley's definition of the 'dynamic of farce' as 'the interplay between the mask (of actuality) and the real face (of primitive instinct)'[18] is readily apparent in *Sloane*: nothing could better define the comic tension set up between Kath's pseudo-gentility, Ed's military heartiness, and the rapacious sexual hunger that appears every time the mask slips. That conflict between mask and face, the elegant word and the primitive act, Orton was to develop in particularly inventive and original ways in *Loot* and *What the Butler Saw*. Already, in the early play, Orton is anxious not to play safe where farce's conventions are concerned:

> In *Sloane* I wrote a man who was interested in having sex with boys. I wanted him played as if he was the most ordinary man in the world, and not as if the moment you wanted sex with boys you had to put on earrings and scent. . . . I think that the portrait of the queer in Peter Shaffer's *Black Comedy* is very funny but it's an awfully conventional portrait. It's compartmentalisation again. Audiences love it, of course, because they're safe. But one shouldn't pander to audiences.[19]

His protagonists in *Loot*, Hal and Dennis, are equally distanced from stereotypes: they are bank-robbers, but Hal is a compulsive truth-teller, liable at any moment to give the game away under police investigation; they cheerfully sleep together, but don't say 'No' to girls. Their randy and random sexuality is there to assert the dance of life amid funerals and death. Orton was very insistent that directors should not seek to impose any gay stereotyping on a pair of characters he had deliberately presented as quite straightforward in their sexuality:

> I don't want there to be anything queer or camp or odd about the relationship of Hal and Dennis. Americans see homosexuality in terms of fag and drag. This isn't my vision of the universal brotherhood. They must be perfectly ordinary boys who happen to be fucking each other. Nothing could be more natural. I won't have the Great American Queen brought into it.[20]

Orton reinforces his point, both in *Loot* and *What the Butler Saw*, through comic exchanges which subvert and undermine normal sexual assumptions, e.g. from *What the Butler Saw*:

> PRENTICE. Unnatural vice can ruin a man. . . . I'm a heterosexual.
> RANCE. I wish you wouldn't use these Chaucerian words. It's most confusing.
>
> (p. 411)

And from *Loot* –

> DENNIS. I'd like to get married. It's the one thing I haven't tried.
> HAL. I don't like your living for kicks, baby. Put these neurotic ideas out of your mind.
>
> (p. 210)

But what could perhaps be called the 'gay liberation' element in Orton's work is only one part of it. It needs, I think, to be seen as part of a wider celebration of sexuality in all its manifestations.[21] In *Loot*, sexuality is there to assert life in the presence of death, and the farce's originality lies in the way Orton uses the kind of insight Joyce gives to Leopold Bloom at Paddy Dignam's funeral in *Ulysses*:

Whores in Turkish graveyards. Learn anything if taken young. You might pick up a young widow here. Men like that. Love among the tombstones. Romeo. Spice of pleasure. Both ends meet. Tantalising for the poor dead. Smell of grilled beefsteaks to the starving, gnawing their vitals.[22]

Truly, in *Loot*, to reverse the truism in the *Book of Common Prayer*, 'in the midst of death we are in life'. No sooner is the corpse cold in the coffin than Nurse Fay, like Richard III wooing Anne, is briskly coaxing the widower into a new marriage, lining him up as her next victim. Hal fantasises about opening a brothel as he switches the corpse and the bank notes:

> I'd have a French bird, a Dutch bird, a Belgian bird, an Italian bird, and a bird that spoke fluent Spanish and performed the dances of her native country to perfection (*he clicks the teeth like castanets*). I'd call it the Consummatum Est. And it'd be the most famous house of ill-fame in the whole of England.
>
> (p. 227)

Truscott says indignantly of Dennis, 'You scatter your seed along the pavements without regard to age or sex.' He asks Hal, 'Where does he engender these unwanted children?' and Hal replies, 'On crowded dance floors during the rhumba' – a fine comic image for the dance of life. Even the corpse joins in that dance, taking on a crazy life of its own, as it's shoved in and out of coffins and cupboards, made into a tailor's dummy to be used in an exhibition of British needlework, threatened with indecent assault in a garage by a policeman, taken halfway to the graveyard and brought back again. 'Who'd think she'd be back so soon,' says Fay. 'She could never make up her mind in life. Death hasn't changed her', comments McLeavy (p. 239). Certainly, when Orton's inventiveness has submitted the corpse to every possible indignity, most of the false reverence which we give to relics, the morbid worship of mummified remains, the excessive dwelling on death, which Orton associates particularly with the Catholic church – these have been effectively and healthily exploded, along with the viscera of Mrs McLeavy. As John Lahr says of this aspect of the play: 'Like gargoyles in a medieval cathedral, Orton's ghoulish spectacle is meant to scare people into life.'[23]

In *What the Butler Saw*, we have, perhaps, Orton's most extensive celebration of sexuality. From the moment when Dr Prentice unwisely attempts to lay his secretary, and his wife returns from her lesbian club, and her one-night stand with a page boy in the Station Hotel, the pace never slackens. Orton mounts a full-scale comic assault on our customary notions of proper behaviour and ordinary reality, and moves us into a world which is part dream-world, part comic Saturnalia or Bacchic revel. That the two worlds are analogous is in fact suggested by Eric Bentley when he says that, 'like dreams, farces show the disguised fulfilment of repressed wishes'.[24] And Strindberg's influence on Orton, noted in Chapter I, can be seen not only in the matter of the straitjackets and the tormented marital relationship of the Prentices, but also in the way the play reproduces the kind of effect Strindberg wrote about in the Prefatory Note to his own *Dream Play*. He had attempted, he said,

> to reproduce the disconnected but apparently logical form of a dream. Anything can happen, everything is possible and probable. . . . On a slight ground of reality, imagination spins and weaves new patterns made up of memories, experiences, unfettered fantasies, absurdities and improvisations. The characters are split, double and multiply; they evaporate, crystallise, scatter and converge.[25]

An effect very similar to this is achieved in Orton's farce. The characters 'split, double, multiply, evaporate', through the constant removal of clothes, exchange of costumes, multiplicity of disguisings; but they also change identity by becoming the objects of each other's fantasies, until in their bewilderment they can hardly regain a sense of their own proper selves.

Orton also establishes the dream very skilfully in the closing scenes, when a mysterious ladder descends from the skylight, and Sergeant Match, '*in a great blaze of glory*', comes down it like a deus ex machina, a representative of the authority of the daylight world, to preside over the ending. (p. 446) The play concludes as Dr Rance says, 'Let us put our clothes on and face the world', and the characters climb up the ladder back into daylight reality (p. 448). But before this, we have had the comic saturnalia, of which the erect phallus from the shattered statue, held aloft by Sergeant Match, is the appropriate emblem. J. W. Lambert was surprised that Lindsay Anderson restored this episode, previously disallowed by the Lord Chamberlain:

> to end the play by brandishing aloft what purports to be Sir Winston's erect penis seems to me to have nothing to be said for it . . . and much to be said against it on merely artistic grounds.[26]

The criticism is surely misconceived. For the phallus belongs with the other allusions to Dionysiac revel and *The Bacchae* of Euripides: Sergeant Match, a latter day Pentheus in leopard-spotted woman's dress, bleeding from an attack by that frenzied Bacchante, Mrs Prentice, and the deus ex machina effect of the descent from the skylight. As 'the emblem of comedy's ruthless sexual mischievousness and amorality'[27] it sums up perfectly a central theme of the play. And to this theme dream is also relevant. For, like drugs and alcohol (freely dispensed and consumed in *What the Butler Saw*, and also in part belonging to the rites of Dionysus), the dream gives us access to the unconscious mind and to sexual fantasies. Orton's achievement is to take us more deeply into the dreaming areas of the mind than is the case in traditional farce, but to use the tight control of the farcical structure to explore that area. An uninhibited sexuality, then, is central to the play. Orton had always tapped a rich vein of farcical humour in the confusion of sexual roles; but in his last play, fantasies of seduction proliferate as never before, and are upset continually by what appear to be the ever changing sexes of the intended victims. As Sergeant Match helpfully observes to Dr Prentice on one occasion:

> This is a boy, sir, not a girl. If you're baffled by the difference . . . it might be as well to approach both with caution.
> (p. 408)

The anarchic id is very much in evidence: Dr Prentice ordering a variety of characters to undress and lie on his couch; the nymphomaniac Mrs Prentice seeking her sexual satisfaction with a page-boy – 'You were born with your legs apart. They'll send you to the grave in a Y-shaped coffin', comments her husband (p. 371); Nick, Sergeant Match and Geraldine Barclay appearing in partial or total undress, and successively suspected of being the victims of various forms of sexual malpractice. *What the Butler Saw*, in exploring the reality in the dream, demonstrates our dependence on customary roles and costumes, and the alarming but liberating possibilities that exist when these defining areas are removed, when the id escapes from the pursuing ego. As Mrs Prentice says, 'The purpose of my husband's clinic isn't to cure, but to liberate and exploit madness' (p. 388). There is never, of course, a total escape; if that were to occur, the comic tension would be lost, and the play itself would spiral out of control. Orton's skill, finely exercised, is to accelerate the momentum to a point where disintegration threatens, and then, by the narrowest of margins, to steer his characters back to a safe conclusion, which, however, itself remains, in its 'logical illogicality', dream-like.

But if Orton creates, more than most farce writers, an uninhibited 'feast of fools', his work also casts darker shadows than most. Nightmare and revelry are obverse and reverse of the same coin, and the tension between them is crucial to the farce's effect. Indeed, there is a strong connection between them. I have emphasised, so far, that sexuality for Orton was an agent of liberation. But it is also important to note, as C. W. Bigsby does, that in his work, 'sexuality is aggression; it is subversion. It is a challenge to all authority, including, through his emphasis on incest, the authority of the parent, and, beyond that, perhaps of God'. And he goes on to argue that,

> English culture has always been susceptible to the writer who chooses to displace his politics from the political to the sexual sphere, as is evidenced by the gothic novel and the studied eroticism of the Romantic poets. A challenge to sexual norms is, after all, in part a challenge to normative values (viz. the American writers Charles Brockden Brown and Edgar Allen Poe or the English writers Emily Bronte and D. H. Lawrence). . . . British politicians can survive accusations of financial speculation; detected in sexual indiscretion, they are consigned to the outer wilderness.
>
> Orton replaced dialectics with excess. He sought the extreme as though to burn off the prosaic power of the real, the banalities of a bourgeois world for which he had complete contempt. He tried to make transgression itself a value, and in that process unregulated sexuality was an enabling strategy and a central fact rather than simply an image.[28]

This emphasis on the centrality and the wider significance of sexuality in Orton's work is important. But there is also a more directly political attack on the authority principle in the plays, an attack in which the darker, nightmare element is more to the fore, and here we should look at such figures as Nurse Fay, Inspector Truscott and Dr Rance. Such figures have always been important in farce. Rebellion, as I suggested in Chapter I, needs a context, something to rebel against; and, if Orton's rebels and jokers are wilder than most, he similarly raises the stakes where the opposition is concerned, creating grotesque incarnations of authority, related to real life, but having something of the surrealism of Jarry's *Ubu* plays about them. What gives the conflict between the jokers and the authority figures a peculiarly disturbing effect is that the latter are as unpredictable and anarchic as the former. They seem, almost, to be mirror-images of each other, a point made, in fact, by Orton's quotation from Shaw's *Misalliance*, at the beginning of *Loot:* 'Anarchism is a game at which the police can beat you' (p. 193). In the case of Nurse Fay, Orton to some extent plays on our fears of the medical profession, and our relative helplessness in the hands of nurse or doctor. From this viewpoint there is a terrible joke concealed in making the mass-murderer a nurse. And the joke surfaces when Nurse Fay is finally cornered:

> TRUSCOTT. Thirteen fatal accidents. Two cases of suspected fish poisoning. One unexplained disappearance. She's practised her own form of genocide for a decade and called it nursing.
> FAY. I never killed anyone.
> TRUSCOTT. At the George V Hospital in Holyhead eighty-seven people died within a week. How do you explain that?
> FAY. It was the geriatric ward. They were old.
> TRUSCOTT. They had a right to live, same as anybody else.
> FAY. I was in the children's ward.
> TRUSCOTT. How many innocents did you massacre, Phyllis?
>
> (p. 254)

The play has by this time so confused our sense of what is normal and what is lunatic that we hardly know whether to attribute the bizarre catalogue of deaths to the further lethal acts of Nurse Fay, to the hazards of old age, as she resourcefully claims, or to the general malpractice and negligence of the medical profession. But, in the comic extravagance of those references to genocide and the massacre of the innocents, the farce reminds us of some nightmare realities we would prefer to forget.

This is also the case in Orton's presentation of Inspector Truscott who, as he kicks Hal in the crutch, suavely tells Fay, 'You're at liberty to answer your own doorbell, miss. That's how we tell whether or not we live in a free country' (p. 235). Truscott later cross-examines Dennis on his previous experience with the police-force:

TRUSCOTT. And you complain you were beaten?
DENNIS. Yes.
TRUSCOTT. Did you tell anyone?
DENNIS. Yes.
TRUSCOTT. Who?
DENNIS. The officer in charge.
TRUSCOTT. What did he say?
DENNIS. Nothing.
TRUSCOTT. Why not?
DENNIS. He was out of breath with kicking.
TRUSCOTT. If ever I hear you accuse the police of using viol-
    ence on a prisoner in custody again, I'll take you down to the
    station and beat the eyes out of your head.

(pp. 245–6)

In passages like these, Truscott represents that streak of brutal authoritarianism within the law and the establishment that exists as a kind of mirror-image of the criminal violence of those outside the law. In this respect, Truscott and Nurse Fay are made for each other, and there is a ruthless appropriateness in their final ganging up with Hal and Dennis to put the one innocent man in the play, McLeavy, behind bars:

MCLEAVY. What am I charged with?
TRUSCOTT. That needn't concern you for the moment. We'll
    fill in the details later.
MCLEAVY. You can't do this. I've always been a law-abiding
    citizen. The police are for the protection of ordinary people.
TRUSCOTT. I don't know where you pick up these slogans, sir,
    you must read them on hoardings.
MCLEAVY. I want to see someone in authority.

TRUSCOTT. I am in authority. You can see me.

MCLEAVY. Someone higher.

TRUSCOTT. You can see whoever you like, providing you convince me first that you're justified in seeing them.

....

DENNIS. What will you charge him with, Inspector?

TRUSCOTT. Oh, anything will do.

FAY. Can an accidental death be arranged?

TRUSCOTT. Anything can be arranged in prison.

(p. 274)

It is an ending which manages to be in equal parts logical, funny and horrific. The pace of the play, the ferociously funny figures of Fay and Truscott, all push *Loot* further, into more uncomfortable areas of farce than is customary. As Orton himself said, 'the dramatist must have the right to change formal gear at any time. There's supposed to be a healthy shock, for instance, at those moments in *Loot* when an audience suddenly *stops* laughing'.[29]

In *What the Butler Saw* also a very real sense of nightmare co-exists with the festive licence of farce. A harmless secretary is stripped of her clothes, drugged, twice declared insane in one day, courts arrest in boy's clothes as a way of escape, and is forced weeping into a straitjacket. Gradually, the private clinic acquires the overtones of a concentration camp. Dr Rance assumes the role of commandant:

Full security arrangements are in force. No one is to leave the clinic without written permission.

(p. 410)

Dogs are unleashed to patrol the grounds (a spaniel and a minia-ture poodle – nightmare here dissolving into absurdity). Sirens wail, Metal grilles clang down in Act II over all the doors, barring escape. The lights go out, and, as the stage direction reads, '*the room is lit only by the glare of a bloody sunset shining through the trees*' (p. 442). Mrs Prentice, driven frantic by constant sightings of naked men, shoots Nick in the arm; and a manic Dr Rance, seeking fugitives, shoots Sergeant Match in the leg as he sits on the lava-tory in women's clothes (pp. 436–7). The sense of being trapped, not only physically but mentally, becomes increasingly strong, not least because of Dr Rance's Catch 22 logic, used as a weapon against his victims:

> RANCE. Why have you turned your back on the God of your fathers?
> PRENTICE. I'm a rationalist.
> RANCE. You can't be a rationalist in an irrational world. (*Picking up the wig and shoes*) Was it your intention to wear these for auto-erotic excitement?
> PRENTICE. No, I'm a perfectly normal man.
> RANCE. His belief in normality is quite abnormal.
>
> (p. 428)

It is, finally, peculiarly unsettling that Dr Rance, the government inspector figure, with his claim, 'I am a representative of order, you of chaos,' comes to seem the maddest figure in the play, as he ruthlessly certifies people insane and claps them into straitjackets. Indeed, a form of verbal straitjacketing is also very characteristic of him, as he pins his specimens down with 'instant' Freudian analysis, as in his summing-up of Geraldine Barclay:

> It's a text-book case! A man beyond innocence, a girl aching for experience. The beauty, confusion and urgency of their passion driving them on. They embark on a reckless love-affair. He finds it difficult to reconcile his guilty secret with his spiritual conviction. It preys on his mind. Sexual activity ceases. She, who basked in his love, feels anxiety at its loss. She seeks advice from her priest. The Church, true to her ancient traditions, counsels chastity. The result – madness.
>
> (p. 383)

And, just as Sergeant Match is a Pentheus figure who becomes in the end a disciple of Dionysus (joining the forces of disorder by co-operating in keeping the crimes committed out of the paper), so, in Dr Rance's case, we have a more extreme example of the Dionysiac principle built into and entangled with the Pentheus authority principle.

There remains a happy ending – of a sort. Orton, in a high-spirited variation on the far-fetched conclusions characteristic of the comic mode in drama (*The Importance of Being Earnest, Cymbeline, A Winter's Tale* spring to mind) allows his plot to unwind, so that it becomes, in John Lahr's words, 'an elaborate stratagem to allow all the characters to get what they want. The secretary and bell-hop turn out to be Mrs Prentice's children. And Dr Prentice discovers that he's the father – a fact that rejuvenates his sexual desire for his wife. With a tale of double incest under his nose, Dr Rance has another sensational chapter for his book.'[30] And Sergeant Match's investigation into the missing parts of Sir Winston Churchill's statue is crowned with success with the discovery of the phallus in the cardboard box. Yet the final image the play gives us, in its concluding stage direction, is an ambiguous one:

> *They pick up their clothes, and, weary, bleeding, drugged and drunk,*
> *climb the rope ladder into the blazing light.*

(p. 448)

On the one hand, the 'blazing light' and laughter of Orton's comic vision; on the other hand, the darker, more sombre picture of characters *'weary, bleeding, drugged and drunk.'* And Bigsby under-lines that darker picture when he writes that the

> comfortable assurance, so necessary to the enjoyment of bour-geois farce, is destroyed at the end when (the audience) are made to see that what they took to be frivolous sexual games were in fact incestuous trysts in which a mother is raped by her son and a father attempts to rape his daughter. The germ of moral anarchy is suddenly exposed at the centre of the conven-tional confection.

John Russell Taylor asserts that, 'to make comedy out of the extraordinary a play needs a norm, and farce above all needs a straight man'.[31] That norm, in late Victorian or Edwardian farce, was found in the propriety and morality of bourgeois life, its conventional standards of behaviour. When such conventions are no longer accepted, it is sometimes argued, farce's 'kicking over the traces' lacks an appropriate context, and the necessary tension is not there. I have already argued (in Chapter I) that this need not be the case. In a more permissive age, where norms of behav-iour are increasingly questioned, farce has shown no signs of being in decline. Rather the reverse. But it is appropriate in specific cases to enquire why this is so. Thus Taylor uses the generalisation quoted above as a stick to beat *What the Butler Saw* with, denying that the play has a 'norm'. But this is not so. The norm is Geraldine Barclay, the sweetly sympathetic secretary from the Friendly Faces Employment Bureau, whose first response to the lunacy around her is to ask, 'Is it the candid camera?' (p. 383) and whose reaction to Dr Prentice's bizarre confession to attempted murder of a nymphomaniac wife is,

> Poor Dr Prentice. . . . How trying it must be for you. I wish there was something I could do to cheer you up.
>
> (p. 368)

It is also the case that, as events become crazier, Dr Prentice becomes as much the victim and a representative of the norm as Geraldine Barclay; much of the farcical confusion results from his attempts to get back to the relative normality of the opening situation. Equally, in *Loot*, the guileless McLeavy, with his pathetic faith in authority, his deferential behaviour to Truscott, and his staunch Catholic faith, represents a norm of order which is progressively undermined as disorder gains the upper hand.

But Orton creates a more complex irony by building the notion of propriety more intricately into the very fabric of his plots. His rogues and tricksters are sticklers for proper behaviour; they have a passion for keeping up appearances. Ed reads Sloane a lesson in morality, without being aware of how preposterously it fails to fit with his own behaviour:

> Why did I give you a job? Why do thinking men everywhere show young boys the straight and narrow? Flash cheque books when delinquency is mentioned? Support the Scout movement? Principles, boy, bleeding principles.
>
> (p. 134)

The more outrageous Truscott's behaviour in *Loot*, the firmer his moral stance, his pretended rectitude. Nurse Fay answers a charge of murder by referring to her impeccable references; and when McLeavy asserts, of the referees, 'You murdered most of them,' she retorts, 'That doesn't invalidate their signatures.' And it is entirely characteristic that her last line should be, 'People will talk. We must keep up appearances' (p. 275). Furthermore, many of Orton's characters fall back on genteel, stilted or journalistic modes of discourse that belong to an 'old-fashioned' world, as if to escape from or disguise the painful home-truths of their actual behaviour. Kath's tale of her nursing home pregnancy and the boy who couldn't marry her because of his duty to his parents comes straight out of a *Woman's Own* serial (pp. 66–7). Mrs Prentice, at the climax of *What the Butler Saw*, uses the clichés of novelettish fiction: 'I paid for my misdemeanour . . . he made free with me in the same hotel.' (pp. 445–6). In such ways as these, Orton includes in his farces many points of reference to normality, propriety and convention – of a kind. But, whereas in many pre-Orton farces, these are points of reference seemingly acceptable to both dramatist and audience, and existing outside the anarchy, Orton shows the anarchists making use of them for their own purposes. Orton's point is that a great chasm has yawned between the norms people invoke and the lives they lead. The laugh is on us rather than on them. I think this is what Graham Murray meant, commenting in 1966 on his production of *Loot*:

> The final image of *Loot* when Fay, flanked by the two fellahs, says, 'Let's keep up appearances.' That was what Joe was about. . . . Truscott is the old conscience, the old morality; that conscience is dead in our time. It lingers and has become corrupt.[32]

And so in Orton's work there is a significant development of the farce form. Confessing his admiration of Ben Travers, the dramatist none the less insisted that

> the boundaries he set to present day farce are really too narrow. . . . A lot of farces today are still based on the preconceptions of a century ago, particularly the preconceptions about sex. . . . Farce originally was very close to tragedy and differed only in the treatment of its themes. . . . The Greeks were prepared to treat any subject farcically.[33]

The plays, in fact, show Orton very much the master of the traditional techniques of farce. The skill in constructing dizzying edifices of plot, card-castles of intrigue which finally collapse on the builders, the command of accelerating pace, these are abundantly evident; so too is his awareness of the actor's physical skills in relation to props, costumes and set, his building in of comic routines involving, for example, the false eye, the false teeth, the corpse and the coffin in *Loot*, the hiding of Geraldine's underclothes, the business with the vase of flowers, the constant dressings and undressings of *What the Butler Saw*.

But, on the other hand, Orton liberated the genre from some outdated preconceptions; he made it more relevant to contemporary life, more provocative not only in relation to sexuality, but in relation to the police, the church, the law, and the medical profession; he revitalised it, one might say, by going back to the Greeks and to the roots of dramatic comedy. The conventional notion that farces usually end with a return to relative normality has already been questioned in this study. It is often not the case. But it is a matter of degree, and it is certainly possible to argue that order *of a kind* does normally reassert itself, although we may have doubts as to how long. But this is emphatically not the case in Orton's work. In the medieval feast of fools, for a brief carnival period, order was subverted and anarchy ruled; but, in Orton's modern and uncompromising vision, that feast of fools, in all its grotesqueness and licence, offers a permanent image of the human condition, not a temporary one. 'Is the world mad? Tell me it's not,' pleads the anguished McLeavy to Truscott towards the end of *Loot*. And Truscott, perhaps for the moment stepping out of character and speaking for Orton and our sense of the play as a whole, replies, 'I'm not paid to quarrel with accepted facts' (p. 258).

7

Farce and Contemporary
Drama: I

Farce for many people still remains synonymous with the Whitehall and post-Whitehall variety studied in Chapters 4 and 5. That
variety, I've attempted to show, is well worth serious critical attention. But, since Orton, farce has become a much more available
option to the so-called 'serious' dramatist, and the kind of compartmentalisation represented by equating farce with one particular
species of it seems less and less feasible.

The reasons for the reinstatement of farce as an option for so
many of our contemporary dramatists are complex. I would
suggest that the following factors are significant. Firstly, realism
as a dramatic mode had been compromised by the 1950s through
its too long association with the well-made play, which, with its
exposition, complication, denouement and closed ending, and its
rounded, tidily explained, unambiguous characters, seemed to
assume an objective reality increasingly open to question. Even
the injection of new life into the realist tradition by 'new wave'
dramatists like Arnold Wesker or the John Osborne of *Look Back
in Anger* was, in the long term, unsatisfactory; for, despite the
wider social observation and the contemporary relevance, the
plays still seemed rooted in a restrictively naturalistic framework.
Other models were needed. And farce, which is basically a non-
naturalistic mode, was strongly in evidence in a variety of
examples. Earlier dramatists such as J. M. Synge, Sean O'Casey,
and G. B. Shaw had already demonstrated in their very different
ways the potential that farce and its techniques might have to
reinforce serious themes (Synge's *Shadow of the Glen, The Well of
the Saints, The Tinkers' Wedding*, O'Casey's *Juno and the Paycock, The
Plough and the Stars*, Shaw's *You Never Can Tell, Misalliance*, and
Too True to be Good all offer examples). Nearer to the present day,
mid-century European dramatists like Ionesco, Beckett, Adamov

and Genet were using a variety of farcical techniques to explore the irrationality of experience, the absurdity of a seemingly meaningless universe. At approximately the same time, and in this country, the continuing vitality and strength of the popular tradition was manifest in the best of the Whitehall farces, in radio and television shows like *Take It From Here*, *the Goon Show*, *Hancock's Half-Hour*, and in the acts of the stalwarts of music-hall and variety still around in the 1950s – Max Miller, Tommy Trinder, the Crazy Gang. These shows demonstrate a whole battery of refreshingly unnaturalistic techniques and effects, and offer a way out of some of the blind alleys and impasses of mimetic realism. There was, finally, the example of Orton in the 1960s – a playwright who demonstrated very strikingly the ability of farce to adapt and evolve in response to a changing society. Small wonder, then, that many contemporary dramatists have experimented with the genre, and that there is an increasing cross-fertilisation in contemporary drama between the popular or 'illegitimate' tradition, represented by farce, music-hall and pantomime, and the serious 'legitimate' tradition. Peter Davison's recent study, *Contemporary Drama and the Popular Dramatic Tradition in England* (London, 1982), demonstrates admirably the extent and nature of this cross-fertilisation, with particular reference to the music-hall. Katharine Worth, in *Revolutions in Modern English Drama*, has also perceptively discussed the attraction farce has proved to 'present day realists'; she suggests that its 'heartless' techniques offer ways of 'handling harsh physical material' (as in Peter Nichols's *A Day in the Death of Joe Egg* or *The National Health*) and that it also 'offers release from the pressure to analyse and formulate in the over-explicit way that has for so long been the bogie of realism'.[1]

I shall hope, in the remaining two chapters of this book, to give further support to these ideas by discussing some examples of the use of farce by 'serious' contemporary dramatists. In some instances, such dramatists as Shaffer, Ayckbourn, Stoppard and Frayn have shown a renewed interest in the genre and taken it up, as Pinero took it up in the 1890s. Each of these dramatists has written at least one pure farce which demonstrates how open to experiment and relevant to contemporary life the form still is. I shall examine in some detail Shaffer's *Black Comedy* (1965), Ayckbourn's *Bedroom Farce* (1975), Stoppard's *Dirty Linen* (1976), and Frayn's *Noises Off* (1982). In other instances, such dramatists as Pinter, Bond, and Caryl Churchill have experimented indirectly with farce, introducing elements of it into a serious context to create an exciting cross-fertilisation which has different effect with each playwright. Here I shall look at Pinter's *The Birthday Party* (1958), *The Caretaker* (1960) and *The Homecoming* (1965), Bond's *Early Morning* (1968), *Narrow Road to the Deep North* (1968) and *Lear* (1971), and Caryl Churchill's *Cloud Nine* (1979).

Shaffer has written interestingly of how the idea for *Black Comedy* originated in his experience of Chinese classical theatre:

> I went once to the Palace Theatre in London and saw the Peking Opera. They did an excerpt from a play called *Where Three Roads Meet*. The sequence they offered was a scene in a lodging house at night where a warrior lays himself down to sleep – it is wordless this particular scene – and a bandit creeps through a window. It is supposed to be pitch darkness except that it is all done in brilliant light, light so ferocious that it suggests darkness. The warrior gropes for his sword and challenges the intruder. They fight with swords so sharp they seemed, I recall, to cut little bits off the fringes of their clothing. Real swords. The effect on the audience was extraordinary, because it was wildly funny and wildly dangerous as well, so that they were caught between the emotions of alarm and delight.[2]

Fun and danger, alarm and delight: these are experiences which relate very specifically to our reactions to an effective farce. I have already quoted, in Chapter I, Jessica Davis's comment that the pleasure of joking is 'partly festive' and 'partly aggressive'. Aggression fuels the attack on authority, order and morality; the festive impulse celebrates licence, the id winning freee from the ego. It is not surprising that Shaffer, in the same article above quoted, acknowledges 'tremendous pleasure in farce. . . . I would love to do more of it', and he also speaks of a tension in himself between,

> the Apollonian and the Dionysian sides of interpreting life. . . . I feel in myself that there is a constant debate going on between the violence of instinct on the one hand, and the desire in my mind for order and restraint.[3]

In Shaffer's serious plays, the Dionysiac forces are represented by a series of figures – mortal men, touched in some way by the divine or the numinous: Mozart in *Amadeus*, Alan Strong in *Equus*, the Inca God, Atahuallpa in *The Royal Hunt of the Sun*. The forces of order and restraint are represented by a series of very earthbound professional men of good sense and limited talent, who are themselves haunted by a sense of futility, of the meaninglessness of a life without ecstasy in some form or other: Salieri, the court composer in *Amadeus*, Dysart the psychiatrist in *Equus*, Pizarro the professional soldier in *Royal Hunt*. And in each case the Dionysiac figure, though hunted, killed or enslaved, lives on, in *Equus* and *Royal Hunt*, to possess and haunt the man who has entrapped (or killed) him, in *Amadeus*, through Mozart's music, speaking to posterity when Salieri's is disregarded. The conflict in *Black Comedy* takes a very different form, as we might expect, but it is certainly present, and is embodied, not in a potentially tragic conflict between two protagonists, but in an action in which disorder leads all the characters a merry dance, and in which rebelliousness finally wins out over the forces of convention and propriety.

But order also relates, particularly in farce, to the playwright's controlling sense of structure. And Shaffer's feeling for such order can surely be seen in the beautifully structured progression of his farce, and the formal skill he shows in handling the reversed light-darkness convention. But that sense of order, of course, is used to monitor a growing disorder, a gradual disintegration of the situation. Indeed, paradoxically, it is only through the playwright's controlling skill, through his formal dexterity, that disorder and confusion make their proper impact on us. Shaffer's sense of the importance of that technical process, so essential to the whole work, is surely what lies behind his passionate defence of his so-called 'theatricality';

> People who quite like one's work but want to put it down a bit, say, 'Well, it's very theatrical of course'. I always find that very odd. It's almost as if you're making a pejorative remark about a painter by saying of course it's painterly. My quarrel with London is that it's not theatrical enough. I am tired of seeing a one-set play with two people whining at each other all night or delivering a sequence of lectures to the audience. It doesn't seem to me to be what the theatre is for.[4]

Earlier in this study, I quoted the stage direction near the beginning of *Black Comedy*, in which Shaffer describes how, *'as things slide into disaster'*, the look of everything – the room and its owner – changes from elegance to confusion: *'For the place as for its owner, the evening is a progression through disintegration.'* (p. 5) Shaffer's controlling sense of design is very evident in this stage direction, and it is demonstrated in practice.

The opening of the play, up to the point at which light floods the stage and the gramophone runs down, is an object lesson in exposition. Shaffer has to meet two challenges: how to establish the visual convention of the play, reversal of light and darkness, and at the same time how to establish for his audience in a natural manner the extent to which Brindsley's future hangs on what happens in the ensuing action, that at all costs he has to make a good impression on a richly ill-assorted collection of visitors. He has to establish the light-darkness convention firmly, so that the audience won't think an incompetent lights man has gone to sleep; but he mustn't signal it too knowingly and nudgingly so that the illusion of the play world is lost. He does it very naturally through the talk between Brindsley and Carol about the look of the rearranged room, and through the auditory device of the slowed down gramophone record. The rather complicated background information we need – that the furniture has been borrowed, that the millionaire and the fiancée's father are coming to visit, and that there's an ex-girlfriend and a touchy antique-dealer from whom they've borrowed the furniture – all this is conveyed with an elegant economy and naturalness that is quite admirable. Shaffer has said that he likes the idea of a playwright as a workman 'hammering out a solid structure', but that 'I like to bury all my labour and effort so that it appears to be effortless.'⁵ The exposition of *Black Comedy* is certainly an example of that.

What subsequently happens also demonstrates the art that conceals art. The progressive decline into alcoholic stupor of Miss Furnival; the growing apoplexy of the Colonel; the increasingly desperate attempts of Brindsley to cover up; the successive arrivals of Clea, the LEB man, and the millionaire; the successive discoveries – Brindsley of Clea's presence, Clea of Brindsley's fiancée, Harold's of the furniture borrowing: all are handled with an expert sense of timing and a sense of how to build up a series of climaxes, each one greater than the last. One might note in passing that the event which starts the play, the millionaire's expected visit, and the confusion that ends it when the LEB man is mistaken for the millionaire, only for the millionaire to arrive finally when everyone has forgotten him, give the play an ironic structure that owes a great deal to Gogol's *The Government Inspector*.

If, then, the form of *Black Comedy* bears witness to Shaffer's controlling sense of design, the 'Apollonian side' of his nature, the material that the form shapes and mediates to us has its Dionysiac elements; not present in so extreme a form as in Joe Orton's work, but there none the less. That 'violence of instinct', present in Shaffer's nature, and always potentially present in farce, is expressed certainly in the accelerating pace of the action, the accumulation of disasters. But a very real sense of unease, disquiet and alarm is also generated, at particular moments in the play. The Colonel, violently ejected from his rocking chair by the flex of the lamp, may be a figure of fun, but his situation as he '*sits in a strange terror on the floor*', (p. 29) is a frightening one. The hand-guessing game that Clea originates at the penultimate climax of the play, in which everyone guesses wrong, and Carol grows increasingly hysterical, creates a sense of unease more than laughter (p. 57). The confusion has become nightmarish. Clea comes into the play, unseen and unsuspected, like some avenging deity, hurling her thunderbolts, though, as this is a farce, they take the form of jets of vodka and a slap in the face. The fear of being in the dark, of not knowing if you're with a friend or foe is played on. Brindsley, for whom things have got worse and worse, is finally chased and threatened with dire physical violence by an apoplectic Colonel, an enraged Harold, and a furious fiancée; he is only saved in the nick of time from being torn apart like Pentheus in *The Bacchae*. Moreover, though Brindsley is in some respects like the hero of a Feydeau farce, the newly engaged man trying to hide his sexual past, and, as in a Feydeau farce, everything that can go wrong does, there is no return to respectability at the end. On the contrary, the forces of respectability and authority are put conclusively to rout. Brindsley rejects his fiancée and returns to his mistress; the Colonel is enraged; the respectable Miss Furnival succumbs to Bacchus; the man of money who might have made Brindsley a worldly success falls into the cellar. In that respect at least Shaffer's play belongs with Orton. And the routing of the fiancée by the mistress, the stratagems she uses to accomplish her purpose are among the funniest passages in the play.

Shaffer has spoken, with reference to plays like *Equus* and *The*

Royal Hunt of the Sun, of his interest in a theatre of 'ritual and masks', but he goes on to connect this with farce,

> which again is a form of gestural theatre. *Black Comedy* Is almost all gesture. You could almost put plate glass between the audience and the stage and still something comic would emerge from the acted play.'[6]

Black Comedy is in fact a particularly good example of visual effect, and clearly Shaffer's own visual sense is highly developed and expertly employed in choreographing the action of that play. Its initial 'donnée' – that light and darkness were to be reversed – gave great scope to that visual sense. At first Shaffer had considerable difficulty in developing the idea he had got from the Peking Opera. His idea for the play had been enthusiastically welcomed by John Dexter, but progress was slow:

> I was depressed because I couldn't get it going. The problem was that, although funny, it seemed to me to be the kind of idea that would be good for a revue sketch, but it couldn't possibly stretch, couldn't last. First of all, there was no way that situation could obtain realistically for more than a few minutes. They wouldn't just sit there in the dark. Someone would produce candles. If they didn't have candles there would be some other thing, a torch. If it all failed they would simply abandon the evening.
>
> While I was brooding on this and thinking I wish I'd never agreed to do it, someone from the National Theatre rang up and said: 'We've announced your new play and we've already got a terrific response at the box office. You must be very pleased'. I looked down at my desk at what had been advertised and what the public was apparently responding to so nicely, and it was just two pieces of paper, one covered with tomato soup and the other which I had just torn up.
>
> I suddenly thought well, of course, the only way this can work is if there is somebody in that room, preferably the host, who has a reason for keeping those people there and in the dark.
>
> I thought what could it be – obviously he's stolen something. What if he had stolen some furniture from next door, from a neighbour who was away and who unexpectedly returns?

Obviously before he can put the light on or get some help he's got to frustrate everybody else's attempts to light the room until he's got whatever it was out of the room.

Suddenly I had the real farce idea, which is not just one or two objects, but all the furniture in the room and it all has to be moved out without anybody knowing. I remember the idea and just lying there laughing. I think the gods were kind about that one.[7]

The major piece of comic choreography, then, is the central episode of putting the furniture back, at the same time as drinks are dispensed, each to the wrong person. The stage directions for this section detail precisely the harrowingly narrow margins by which disaster is sometimes avoided, sometimes not avoided. At moments, with sublime luck, Brindsley's manoeuvres are successful, though only the audience, not he, can savour the neatness of what has happened, as for example in this passage:

(*BRINDSLEY enters with a broken-down rocking chair of his own. He crosses gingerly to where the COLONEL is sitting and sets down the rocking-chair immediately next to the COLONEL's chair.*)
BRINDSLEY. How are those drinks coming, Dumpling?
CAROL. Fine Daddy. They'll be one minute.
COLONEL. Let me help you.
(*BRINDSLEY, behind the COLONEL, silently prays for him to get up.*)
CAROL. You can take this bitter lemon to Miss Furnival if you want.
COLONEL. Very well. (*He rises.*)
(*BRINDSLEY immediately pulls up his chair and with his other hand pulls the rocker into the identical position. The COLONEL moves slowly across the room, arms outstretched for the bitter lemon. Unknowingly BRINDSLEY follows him carrying the third Regency chair. The COLONEL collides gently with the table. At the same moment BRINDSLEY reaches it up stage of him and searches for the Wedgewood bowl. Their hands narrowly miss. Then BRINDSLEY remembers the bowl is under the table. Deftly he reaches down and retrieves it – and carrying it in one hand and the chair in the other, triumphantly leaves the room through the arch unconsciously provided by the outstretched arms of CAROL and the COLONEL,*)

*giving and receiving a glass of Scotch – which they think is
lemonade.*)

(p. 26)

At other moments, the two emotions of alarm and delight are
created when there is an inadvertent collision or blunder that
threatens disaster or discovery, as, for example, when
'*BRINDSLEY mistakenly lifts the end of the sofa. MISS FURNIVAL
gives a little scream at the jolt*' (p. 28). Throughout the play, Shaffer
takes great pains to choreograph very precisely the movements of
his characters, to specify the exact business he wants. Thus, at the
beginning of the play, we have Carol finding her way up the stairs
in the dark –

(*During the following she gropes her way cautiously up the stairs –
head down, arms up the banisters, silken bottom thrust out with the
effort.*)

(p. 6)

And, a little further on, there is Brindsley's graceful pantomime
as he steers Miss Furnival towards a chair:

(*He finds MISS FURNIVAL's hand and leads her to the chair down
L. Then he sits in it himself first, pulls her gently towards him backwards by the waist, and slides out from under as she sits on him.*)

(p. 8)

Then, after the major exercise of returning the furniture to its
original location, there are further examples of balletic passages
neatly choreographed when, unknown to the others, Clea,
Brindsley's ex-mistress arrives, and finds '*the challenge to create a
dramatic situation out of the darkness . . . ultimately irresistible*' (p. 35).
Clea intercepts Harold's drink, and sits between Brindsley and
Harold on the sofa, the joker in the pack, with each of the men
thinking that she is the other man: (*HAROLD, CLEA and
BRINDSLEY . . . cross their legs in unison*) (p. 36). Brindsley's
subsequent attempts to stop Harold blurting out too much for his
fiancée to overhear about his ex-mistress produce a delightful
series of knock-on nudges: (*BRINDSLEY nudges CLEA warningly –
imagining she is HAROLD, CLEA gently bumps HAROLD*); and, as
the indiscretions multiply, (*BRINDSLEY punches CLEA so hard that*

the rebound knocks HAROLD off the sofa, drinks and all) (pp. 36–7). As Harold and Miss Furnival gang up to make unflattering comments about Clea ('teeth like a picket fence, yellow and spiky. And she had bad skin . . . like new pink wallpaper, with an old grey crumbly paper underneath'), and as 'CLEA *reacts to the exchange of comments about her like a spectator at a tennis match*' (p. 37), so the suspense and 'comic alarm' of the audience is progressively heightened. How will Clea's growing sense of outrage express itself? How will Brindsley, already in dire trouble, be further 'landed in it? Shaffer has him recognise that Clea is present. She slaps him on the face; he thinks at first that it is a jealous reaction from Harold, his gay antique dealer friend (whose furniture has been borrowed and returned), but then, as he feels Clea's bottom, he realises that it is his ex-mistress. This necessitates an extreme reversal of tactics. Far from running Clea down for the benefit of his fiancée, he now insists,

> she was beautiful and tender and considerate and kind and loyal and witty and adorable in every way.
>
> (p. 38)

His urgent whister to Clea, 'Go up to the bedroom, Wait for me there', is received by Harold as an invitation to him, ('Do you think this is quite the moment?') but then, as he realises it isn't, is mistakenly passed on to Carol, the fiancée. So that the culminating piece of comic business in this section in offered by the stage-direction:

> (CAROL *joins the other two on the stairs. We see all three groping blindly up to the bedroom, BRINDSLEY's hands on CLEA's hips, CAROL's on BRINDSLEY's.*)
>
> (p. 40)

Only through the reversed light-darkness convention of the play is it possible for Shaffer to focus for us so exactly in comic visual form the dilemma of the lover caught between mistress and fiancée.

There is something, then, quintessentially farcical about *Black Comedy* because of the predominance of this visual element. Farces traditionally involve frantic cover-ups; but they are more often verbal than physical. In *Black Comedy*, verbal cover-ups exist all right, as Brindsley frantically invents reasons for keeping the company in the dark, or conjures up an imaginary cleaning lady to explain the menacing noises Clea begins to make as she grows angrier. But Brindsley's cover-ups also involve him in desperate efforts to conceal the objects he has borrowed from Harold's room from their owner. The Buddha and the Wedgewood bowl are on separate occasions each wrapped in Harold's raincoat. On another occasion, Brindsley sprawls all over the sofa, feigning lumbago to conceal it from Harold. In farce, accidental encounters multiply to create embarrassing and compromising situations. In *Black Comedy* these are made more bizarre and funnier because, for much of the time, the characters only realise each other's presence when they bump into each other. Thus, *'BRINDSLEY accidentally touches MISS FURNIVAL's breasts. She gives a little scream* (p. 9). Or, 'COLONEL *(roaring in BRINDSLEY's face)*. Here I am Dumpling!' (p. 30) Or *'The COLONEL spits out his lemonade in a fury all over BRINDSLEY who at this very moment is crawling towards him on his knees'* (p. 31). Then again, the victims of farce's elaborate intrigues frequently experience the sensation of being trapped. In *Black Comedy*, they get physically as well as psychologically trapped. Thus, *'BRINDSLEY bumps into CAROL with the chair. CAROL sits on it squashing his foot'* (p. 24); or *'BRINDSLEY moves the box a third time, but this time the COLONEL sits down so quickly he traps BRINDSLEY's hands beneath his own weight'* (p. 50). And, in the final climax of the farce, the millionaire falls through the trap door, which the LEB man, Schuppanzigh, *'slams shut with his foot* (p. 64).

Finally, the revenges and reversals of farce, in which the tables are turned on the trickster by his would-be dupes, often, in *Black Comedy*, take splendidly physical form. Clea, for example, her patience finally exhausted, creates merry mayhem, under cover of darkness, by slapping Brindsley's face and sending a jet of vodka over Carol, Harold and the Colonel. Nemesis here comes upon the victims like, indeed, a bolt from the blue.

There are two further points that are worth making about the reversed light–darkness convention in *Black Comedy*. One is that the aggressive element in farcical humour is strengthened through the fact that darkness releases the characters from some of their customary inhibitions, from the need to preserve the normal politeness of social intercourse. When Brindsley asks Miss Furnival if she has any candles, he mimics her prim reply, 'I'm afraid not, Mr Miller' *(mouthing nastily at her)* (p. 10). Later, he *'makes an obscene gesture at the Colonel'* (p. 17). When Harold explains to Carol, who has referred to a Mrs Michelangelo, that 'he had passionate feelings of a rather different nature', she *'puts out her tongue at him'* (p. 34). Equally, characters unaware of the presence in the same room of the person they are talking about, feel free to vent their feelings, which in turn increases the sense of danger, of skating on thin ice. 'I've your monster father to keep happy,' says Brindsley, as the monster father looms up next to him (p.15).

The second point is that if, as is invariably the case, the accelerating pace of farce, its frenetic and disordered world, have the effect of distancing the audience, not allowing them to become too closely involved with the dilemmas of any one character, the light-darkness reversal of *Black Comedy* strongly reinforces the sense of detachment. We look at something which, in normal circumstances, we wouldn't be able to see. The characters 'see through a glass darkly'. We see in the full blaze of light. We are enabled to look on and savour the human comedy with a kind of Olympian detachment. Particularly is this the case, from the point where the silent Clea enters unobserved by the others, and we enjoy the dramatic irony of watching them compromise themselves, while her progressively inventive exploitation of the situation builds up the comic tension prior to the final explosion.

It is, finally, useful to consider one issue touched on by Joe Orton in the comment quoted in Chapter 6, concerning what he calls 'compartmentalisation'. I quote the relevant passage again:

> I think that the portrait of the queer in Peter Shaffer's *Black Comedy* is very funny, but it's an awfully conventional portrait. It's compartmentalisation again. Audiences love it, of course, because they're safe. But one shouldn't pander to audiences.[8]

Orton is raising here the question of stereotypes. Too great a reliance on them clearly has its dangers, though much depends on how they are handled, whether offensively, innocuously, or inventively. Trevor Griffith's play, *Comedians*, deals with the subject, in the conflict that develops between Challenor, the slick, populist manager who wants comics who 'know what the people want and know how to give it them', and Waters, the retired music-hall performer, striving to persuade his class of would-be comedians that jokes that confirm prejudice and win easy laughs are wrong. Humour based on truth and insight can help to change society:

> Most comics *feed* prejudice and fear and blinkered vision, but the best ones, the best ones . . . illuminate them, make them clearer to see, easier to deal with. We've got to make people laugh till they cry. . . . Comedy is medicine. Not coloured sweeties to rot their teeth with.
>
> (p. 23)

But Griffiths is dealing with the humour of the stand-up comic, and with the series of one-off jokes that are his stock-in-trade, jokes intended to communicate, in *Comedians*, with a bored audience during a brief interval in the bingo. The challenge of such a situation is an acute one, and the temptation correspondingly greater (especially with Challenor as patron) to fall back on glib, facile and ultimately offensive racialist and sexist jokes centering on dumb blondes, miserly Scotsmen, limp-wristed homosexuals, black immigrants, and so on. Yet to suggest, on the basis of this argument, that all sterotypes pander to prejudice would be simplistic.

Tom Stoppard, while admitting that he both hates and loves stereotypes, suggests that they often contain a core of truth:

> I hate the cheapness of cheap television portrayal, where Frenchmen are like Maurice Chevalier and journalists wear trilby hats and drink a lot, but what's fascinating to me is that many Frenchmen are like Maurice Chevalier, and not many journalists go around with rimless glasses saying, 'No thank you, I'll have an orange juice.'[9]

Moreover, the farce writer's focus is on a situation, an accelerating action, rather than on the individuals within it. It is through that action that farce realises its subversive potential and achieves the cathartic release that Waters alludes to when he says, 'Comedy is medicine'. There is much to be said, therefore, for creating character in broad outline, figures who have a representative significance, who will signal immediately by mannerism of speech or behaviour, the kind of function they will have in the play. The farce writer can, if he chooses, create some degree of light and shade in a range of characters, as Ayckbourn does in *Bedroom*

Farce, or in a central characters, as Pinero does with his Magistrate or Dean (though a number of stereotypes are to be found in the supporting cast). Equally, he can challenge an audience's expecations of stereotypical behaviour, as Stoppard does in *Dirty Linen* when he demonstrates that the dumb blonde figure, Maddie Gotobed is far from dumb, or as Orton does in his general onslaught on sexual compartmentalisation (though, even with Orton, authority figures like Truscott or victim figures like McLeavy are inventive reworkings of sterotypes). Or, yet again, he can rely almost entirely on a basis of stereotypes, as Ben Travers and the Whitehall team of writers did, showing their skill in 'making them new', playing variations on old themes. And even here, it is worth noting that Travers prided himself on the 'core of truth' that Stoppard notes in many stereotypes. He observes, as corroborating evidence, that *Rookery Nook*, which was to some extent based on characters he knew in Burnham-on-Sea, Somerset, attracted much local gossip concerning who was who:

> Everybody started to recognise their neighbours in the *Rookery Nook* characters, and the recognisers were duly recognised by the recognisees.[10]

To return to Shaffer. A Joe Orton can legitimately refer to the presentation of the gay antique dealer as 'conventional'. But even he admits to finding it very funny. Moreover, the characterisation is precisely calculated to fit in with the rest of the play. Harold's north-country campness is the best possible foil both to the 'debby' Knightbridge affectations of Carol, and the gruff military heartiness of the Colonel. Similarly, his possessiveness where his male friends are concerned, and his sense of rejection when he learns of Brindsley's engagement raise the emotional temperature exactly when Shaffer wants it to be raised, at the time when other crises of discovery threaten the luckless Brindsley. A cool, liberated, masculine gay of the kind that Orton realistically and challengingly presented in *Loot*, though exactly right for Orton's purposes, would have been quite beside the point for Shaffer's play. Also, where a stereotype will *not* fit the purpose of the play, Shaffer shows himself adept at reflecting the more interestingly a-typical aspect of human nature, by introducing in the person of the LEB man, not a stage Cockney, but a middle-aged German refugee with a cultivated interest in painting, who is of course necessarily mistaken for the expected millionaire.

Ayckbourn has said of *Bedroom Farce*, 'it's a comedy, though it's called a farce, and it's a study of the British in bed, with everything except sex'.[11] His preference for the term comedy may relate to the degree of light and shade in the characterisation: his four couples are exceedingly well observed; it is the oddity and quirkiness of the relationships that interest Ayckbourn, and the mingled pathos and absurdity of them that he hits off. Hayman formulates Ayckbourne's intentions in a number of his plays as 'to put Chekhovian characters into an absurd framework',[12] and one can see the relevance of this to Susannah and Trevor in *Bedroom Farce*. None the less, as I have already suggested, subtlety of characterisation does not in itself disqualify a play from being a farce. And it will hardly do for the playwright having named the play *Bedroom Farce* to disavow the title. It is, indeed, in important respects a farce: there is the accelerating momentum of the action, the steadily increasing havoc wrought by Trevor and Susannah, as they progress from bedroom to bedroom throughout one ill-starred night; there is the ingenious use of the composite set – with its three bedrooms, and the cross-cutting between them; there is the laughter created out of situations that to those involved in them are painful and distressing – Susannah's neurotic break-downs, Nick's physical mishaps, Malcolm's incompetent involvement with assemble-it-yourself furniture kits; and there is throughout Ayckbourn's reliance on the audience's knowledge of conventional farce to play a number of ironic variations on farcical themes.

As in many traditional farces, a marriage is threatened and under attack, but in this case more from internal causes than external. Nor, as in many farces, does the 'eternal triangle' of husband, wife, mistress and/or lover develop. True, Trevor kisses Jan at the party. But what, in a traditional farce, might be a scene of comic jealousy as enraged husband learns of lover kissing wife, in this play is given a new and very funny twist by the determination of both wife and ex boy-friend to come clean about it and tell the husband straightaway (prudently so, since Susannah has caught them in the act, and is likely to make mischief about it). So we have Jan first volunteering the information, in cool matter-of-fact way:

JAN. I had a long talk to Trevor.
NICK. Ah-ha . . .
JAN. Which culminated in Trevor kissing me.
NICK. I see.
JAN. And, to be perfectly honest, with me kissing Trevor.
NICK. Just kissing him?
JAN. Yes. Nothing else.
NICK. Oh, well. Hope you enjoyed it.

(p. 210)

Nick seems to take it in good part, but his man-of-the-world off-handedness doesn't altogether disguise his aggrieved tone. This is capped in Act II by Trevor's ridiculously inarticulate and confused confession which, had Jan not already confessed, would have been quite inexplicable to Nick:

TREVOR. Jan and I – we met at that party and we . . . and Susannah came . . . and we were together and etcetera etcetera and . . . it was nothing at all . . . nothing to it at all . . . but I wanted you to be the first to know about it.
NICK. Thank you

Nick's reaction here is quite perfunctory, since his only preoccupation is how to get rid of Trevor as soon as possible.

Havoc is caused, then, not through attempted adultery, but simply because one couple, Trevor and Susannah, create tension and strain. They are the jokers in the pack, the catalysts that precipitate a series of crises, for each of the three married couples whose bedrooms occupy the stage. Then too, Ayckbourn, like other masters of farce, shows great skill in assembling the particular ingredients that, mixed together, will set off the appropriate fireworks and explosions: in this case, four ill-assorted couples, whose differing life-styles and habits of speech the playwright captures, rather as if he were some anthropologist of contemporary marriage studying the customs of the tribe. We have Ernest and Delia, the staid middle-aged couple exemplifying conventional bourgeois values; Malcolm and Kate, playing adolescent hide-and-seek games in a house where Malcolm's ventures into assemble-it-yourself furniture are always doomed to disaster; Nick and Jan, trendier and more sophisticated; and the infuriatingly self-absorbed, perpetually quarrelling Trevor and

Susannah. Ayckbourn demonstrated in his clever use of the composite three bedroom set, how confusion and anarchy can be carried like an infection from one couple to another, with a kind of knock-on effect as Trevor and Susannah invade each bedroom in turn.

The use of the set poses an interesting technical challenge to the playwright. It was, he says,

> the first time I've made use, to quite such an extent, of the cross-cut device. Jumping the action from bedroom to bedroom gives the play an added rhythm over and above what the dialogue normally provides.[13]

In fact, the ingenuity with which he does this is remarkable. The cross-cuts would obviously not work, or work out clumsily, if, at each darkening of one of the bedrooms, the action had to be frozen, and the characters remain immobile until the lights come on again. Exits and entrances are therefore more than usually important, so that at certain points a bedroom may be left empty. So is forced or natural immobility. Thus, in the opening sequences, the older pair, after their first scene together, go off, she into the bathroom, he to look for a leak in the roof, as the lights come up on Nick and Jan. And, since Nick is an invalid, with a pulled back muscle, who must necessarily remain recumbent and virtually motionless throughout the action, Ayckbourn has rather less in the way of exits and entrances to contrive here. Nick stays, Jan goes to the party. We return to Nick's room for occasional glimpses of his suffering as the Act proceeds. Ernest and Delia's departure for a dinner celebration of their wedding anniversary cues in a party scene at Malcolm and Kate's. Susannah's 'back to the womb' retreat into Kate's bed brings the lights up again on Ernest and Delia's disconsolate return from a disappointing meal. Their exits, she to the bathroom, he to get sardines on toast, brings us back to Malcolm and Kate. And so it continues, the cross-cuts smoothly and elegantly contrived, enabling us to savour the contrasts in life styles of the various couples, and the resulting ironic juxtapositions. Among the particularly effective examples of those juxtapositions is the sequence in Act II, where Malcolm's exasperated insistence that his sexual technique does not induce boredom is cross-cut into Susannah's psychological limbering-up exercises, which are in turn interrupted by Ernest tiptoeing past her to get

his copy of *Tom Brown's Schooldays*, his 'book at bedtime' – the
whole sequence being completed with a cross-fade into another
glimpse of an unsettled night, Nick exasperatedly dealing with *his*
cuckoo in the nest, Trevor:

MALCOLM. . . . .No woman who's been in bed with me has
ever complained of boredom. That was the last thing on their
minds. If I were you, I'd start worrying that there wasn't
something wrong with you.
KATE. That's what I am worrying about.
MALCOLM. You'd do well to. You'd do right to. . . . You ask
Doreen Foster if she was bored with me. She'll tell you. . . .
(*He goes out. Cross fade to ERNEST and DELIA's, SUSANNAH
stands alone.*)
SUSANNAH. I am confident in myself. I have confidence in
myself. I am not unattractive. I am attractive. People still find
me attractive.
(*During this, ERNEST emerges from the bedroom. Seeing her, he
attempts to tiptoe across to fetch his book from the bedside table
without disturbing her.*)
SUSANNAH. I am not afraid of people. People are not fright-
ening. There is noth – (*She sees ERNEST*)
ERNEST (*embarrassed*). Just – fetching a book. Carry on. (He
goes to the door.) Tom Brown's Schooldays. Fearfully good.
Read it, have you? No? Carry on. (*He goes. SUSANNAH
wanders slowly out the other way. Cross fade to NICK and JAN's.
TREVOR suddenly wakes up.*)
TREVOR. No, the point is Nick . . .
NICK. Huh, what?
TREVOR. What? Sorry, did I . . .
NICK. You just startled me.
TREVOR. Have I been asleep?
NICK. Yes.
TREVOR. Sorry.
NICK. Quite all right.

(pp. 225–6)

Moreover, the three-bedroom set is crucial for the central
concept of having the one couple, Trevor and Susannah, occupy
the bedrooms of each of the other couples in turn, leaving chaos
and confusion in their wakes. There is a pleasing symmetry in the

play, such that Trevor and Susannah, having ruined Malcolm and Kate's party, and spread alarm and confusion among the would-be sleepers in the bedrooms to the left and right of the central pair's bedroom, converge again on that bedroom at the end of the play, to create further mayhem – Trevor collapsing the dressing table that Malcolm has painfully assembled through the night. When, together with Susannah, he climbs into Malcolm and Kate's bed, the final image of the play is of the couple as the ultimate cuckoos in the nest, having dispossessed the rightful owners.

A central irony of *Bedroom Farce*, which the title points up, is that, though there are three bedrooms on stage throughout, the last thing any of the beds are used for is making love, or even sleeping in. Much as the characters may long to get a good night's sleep, this is never possible. In one bedroom, Malcolm assembles his do-it-yourself dressing table; in another Nick is wakeful because of a painful back; each pair in turn has to listen to Trevor and Susannah's troubles; when Delia, in the third bedroom, does succeed in dropping off, she is awakened by Susannah moaning and flailing about. So far as any active use of the beds is concerned, audience expectations are amusingly frustrated. Bed for Malcolm and Kate is mainly a place which they can use as a hiding place in their childish game of concealing each other's belongings. For Delia and Ernest, it is somewhere to enjoy a midnight feast of pilchards, and combat the hazards of Delia's cold feet. And for Nick and Jan, the only moment when they are together in bed occurs when Jan, struggling to get Nick back into bed after he has fallen out, crashes with him on it, and is trapped beneath him.

The pursuit of sex and the perilous misadventures along the way – the mainspring of many farcical plots – is conspicuously lacking, then, in *Bedroom Farce*. But, distinctively in this play – and here Ayckbourn makes admirable use of contemporary preoccupations, it is the vocabulary in which people talk about their sexual and emotional relationships rather than the bedding down itself which is at the centre of much of the humour. Trevor and Susannah have a key role in this respect, and, as befits that role, Ayckbourn gives them a careful build up prior to their appearance. For Delia, Trevor is the dear son who's married the wrong woman; for Jan, he's the ex-boy-friend whose faults she knows well enough to make her feel confident she can give the wife advice which may help save the marriage; for Malcolm, Trevor and Susannah mean trouble as guests at his party, because of their public, self-absorbed and self-dramatising bickering. Trevor is the first to arrive at the party, and Malcolm's 'how are you?' triggers off a passage of ponderous self-analysis, in which marriage-counselling clichés are thick on the ground, and the hosts are reduced to a series of monosyllabic supportive noises:

TREVOR. We're still trying to work something out. You know.
MALCOLM. Good.
KATE. Good.
MALCOLM. Good.
TREVOR. I don't know how successful we're being but we're trying. You know . . .
MALCOLM. Yes – well . . .
TREVOR. It's a totally draining experience though. Once you get yourself committed to a – commitment – like Susannah and I have committed ourselves to, you get a situation of a totally outgoing – non-egotistical – giving – ness . . . a total submerging, you know.
MALCOLM. Yes, yes.
KATE. Yes.
TREVOR. You feel yourself – being pushed under . . .
MALCOLM. Yes.
TREVOR. As if on top of you were a great . . . a great . . . (*He tails off.*)
KATE. Yes.
MALCOLM. Yes.
KATE. Yes
    (*A long pause. MALCOLM and KATE wait for Trevor*)
TREVOR (*at length*). Heavy weight. God.
    (*A silence.*)
                                        (pp. 188–9)

There ensues an extremely funny exchange between Trevor, fixed immutably in his own track of gloomy philosophising, and Kate, down-to-earth and sensible, but increasingly exasperated by her inability to get out of bed (where she's taken refuge from her bath when surprised by Trevor's early arrival), and get some clothes on to greet her other guests. The escalating social embarrassment of the scene – Trevor now departs downstairs, only to be succeeded by Susannah, who proceeds to unload *her* private agonies on a still immobile and marooned Kate – provides a fine example of farcical conflict between the social mask and the real face. Susannah and Trevor are unable or unwilling to wear social masks; they bare their souls' agony in public. Those around react with varying degrees of embarrassment, panic, or polite cover-up, but invariably with little success, as in the ensuing exchange between Kate and Susannah:

> SUSANNAH. God, Trevor used to excite me. I was so excited by that man. Do you know what it feels like to be really excited?
> KATE. Yes, yes, I think so.
> SUSANNAH. When we weren't actually physically here in the bed . . . you know making love – I felt empty – utterly incomplete.
> KATE. Yes, it is nice sometimes, isn't it . . .
> SUSANNAH. And now. Now, it's a desert. We hardly touch, you know.
> KATE. Oh.
> SUSANNAH. I think I actually revolt him.
> KATE. Oh, surely not.

(p. 193)

Here, as elsewhere in farce, the playwright uses as material for humour situations or predicaments that for those involved in them are painful or distressing. Viewed in one light, Susannah's tendency to neurotic breakdown and Trevor's desperation could be the staple of a play by Strindberg. Change the angle of vision and you have a farce.

Trevor and Susannah's function as catalysts is seen in the way their anxieties and neuroses begin to infect others and compel them to examine their own sex lives, notably and first, near the beginning of Act II, where Kate puts Malcolm right off his assemble-it-yourself activities with a series of questions about whether she's exciting in bed, and, by implication, whether he is:

> KATE. . . . . I just think perhaps I could be more exciting. For you. I'd hate you to get bored.
> MALCOLM. I'm not bored. I'm just trying to find locking bar C.
> KATE. You will tell me if you get bored with me, won't you?
> MALCOLM. Yes. Sure, sure.

KATE. And I promise to tell you.

MALCOLM. What?

KATE. If I get bored with you.

MALCOLM. You don't get bored with me, do you?

KATE. No. No. Not often.

MALCOLM. What, you mean – when we're – in bed? Here?

KATE. Not often . . .

MALCOLM. Well, that's nice.

KATE. Only once or twice.

MALCOLM. Bored?

KATE. No, not bored. You know, it's just I have my mind on other things.

MALCOLM. You mean, other men.

KATE. No. Ordinary things like, shall we have a carpet in the hall, or shall we stain the floorboards. That sort of thing. They're all to do with us. In a way.

MALCOLM. You mean to tell me while I'm – giving my all – you're lying there thinking about floorboards?

KATE. Only sometimes.

MALCOLM. Bloody hell. (*He snatches up some of the pieces.*) I'm going in the hall.

(pp. 219–20)

But the other couples are drawn in also. Delia has to discuss 'physical relationships' with Susannah as Ernest hovers awkwardly in the background:

SUSANNAH. Delia was saying it's probably the cause of all our problems.

ERNEST. Really?

DELIA I said – something like that, yes.

ERNEST. Did we have any problems? I didn't think we had. I don't think I had any problems. Probably have a problem now but I don't remember having any then. (*He laughs*)

(p. 223)

And Nick is smugly gratified with his own status as Jan's lover after Jan has rather damagingly revealed that Trevor, the ex-boy-friend, thought he was 'awfully good' where bed was concerned (p. 235). Throughout, Ayckbourn shows an accurate and amusing ear for varieties of contemporary speech, and the ways in which sex is talked about: the simple directness of Kate, the staid proprieties of Delia, the trendy casualness of Nick and Jan, the socio-sexual jargon of Trevor, the psychiatric confidence-boosting routines of Susannah.

If *Bedroom Farce*, in its title and tripartite set, heavily underlines bed, if only to disappoint the audience's expectations, the setting of Stoppard's *Dirty Linen* seems at first distinctly unpromising for the world of farce: a committee room in the House of Commons, situated in the tower of Big Ben – a very decorous and formal setting, appropriate to the public lives of the characters. The action of the play consists of the deliberations of a parliamentary committee investigating allegations of promiscuity and immorality among MPs. It is, moreover, a retrospective action, the indiscretions having already occurred, and not, as in most farces, a forward moving action of increasing complication. There is, of course, some development from the opening situation: as the meeting proceeds, the spirit of conspiracy among the members intensifies until they are all united against a lone puritanical latecomer, ironically named French. With some help from Maddie Gotobed, the secretary, he exposes the cover-up; but in the process, he himself falls victim to Maddie's charms, and the committee is finally able to vote unanimously to close its investigations. But such an action is much simpler than the usual involved farce plot; and both setting and action might seem, briefly described, as more appropriate for a witty Shavian discussion play than a farce.

However, Stoppard in fact exploits for maximum comic effect the contrast between the decorous and respectable surroundings, the formalities of committee procedure on the one hand, and the ludicrous and disreputable events the committee are considering on the other. From the beginning the tone is set as Maddie, standing in the committee room, *'takes a pair of silk, lace-trimmed French knickers out of a classy looking bag and puts them on'* (p. 15). An appropriate frisson of expectation is created. More French knickers appear in unexpected places: Cocklebury-Smythe produces a pair from his inside pocket and hands them to Maddie (p. 16), McTeazle produces a further pair from his brief-case and passes them over (p. 21). The repetition of this visual joke moves the play rapidly away from its moorings in the workaday world into the wilder and more anarchic world of farce. Not the least of Stoppard's originality consists in his introduction of as many dropped knickers and underpants as would appear in a Whitehall farce in a play in which there is never a bed or bedroom in sight. Maddie Gotobed is a key figure here. She starts the play wearing very little, though this isn't obvious when she is sitting at her desk. When she gets up, she invariably reveals glimpses of cleavage and thighs. Each time this happens the action freezes, with one member of the committee staring at her while others gaze at a pin-up photo in a newspaper. When she moves around the stage, further garments drop off at the merest touch from a member of the committee. Thus, *'her skirt comes away in McTeazle's hand'* (p. 27), and *'Maddie's slip has come away in McTeazle's hand'* (p. 34). The result is a kind of progressive strip-tease as the play proceeds. However, Maddie Gotobed, despite her name, her scantily clad form, and her proneness to shed clothes at the touch of a hand is no mere dumb blonde stereotype. Stoppard's continuation of his argument concerning stereotypes, previously quoted, is relevant:

> I begin to think that the sophisticated perception is that the naïve generalisation (he has earlier instanced, 'All Italians are voluble') is a useful truth. I'm fascinated by the correspondence between easy stereotypes and the truth. Because there is one. If you think about it, *Dirty Linen* is a play in which a sexy dumb blonde walks on and is utterly patronised, and the play ends with the entire committee adopting the resolution which she said they ought to adopt on page four or whatever it was. She actually is Miss Common Sense rather than Miss Empty Head. Probably she wasn't properly established before she begins to show other sides to herself, but certainly the idea is that she's anybody's plaything, totally empty-headed, with a big bust, and occasionally makes comments which are disquietingly irrefutable, and ends up by controlling the whole committee.[14]

So Maddie's is the voice of rebellious non-conformity in the play, and there is a nice irony in the fact that the most sensible arguments are advanced by the girl whose appearance suggests she is merely a sex object for the predatory male's fantasies.

If, in the presentation of Maddie, Stoppard uses a farcical stereotype with gusto and enthusiasm, but also enjoys, 'dislocating the assumptions about the stereotype',[15] so throughout he delights in using farcical techniques with a great skill and adroitness, but also with a sense of how they may shake up our conventional judgements.

Pushing things to extremes has always been a feature of good farce, and *Dirty Linen* is no exception. The very scale of Maddie's sexual conquests betokens a wild anarchic world. There have not been just a few MPs involved in 'garter-snapping', but one hundred and nineteen, and 'all snapping the same garter.' As McTeazle says,

> We face the possibility that a sexual swathe has passed through Westminster claiming the reputations of, to put no finer point upon it, one hundred and nineteen Members. Someone is going through the ranks like a lawn-mower in knickers.
>
> (p. 20)

There is also the teasing suggestiveness of some of the names – Maddie Gotobed, Cocklebury-Smythe, French, restaurants like the Green Cockatoo and Le Coq d'Or. There is the fact that not one member but all the members of the previous committee have resigned; and that the medical reason given by the Chairman for resigning was not that he broke one, but both his hips. Above all, there is the excessive number of restaurants in which Maddie has been seen with her MPs. The alliterative list of these restaurants she periodically and dutifully recites, initially in order to fix in her mind which ones she has been told to forget. When she does finally come clean about the number and variety of her assignations, the farcical prose-poem that results constitutes the climax of Act I:

> MADDIE. I was in the Coq d'Or, the Golden Ox, Box Hill, Claridges and Crockford's –
> WITHENSHAW. Division bell, Mr French
> MADDIE. – and the Charing Cross, the Dorchester, the Green Cockatoo, Selfridges and the Salt Beef Bar in Rupert Street with Deborah and Douglas and Cockie and Jock . . . and in the Mandarin, the Mirabelle and the Star of Asia in the Goldhawk Road. I was with Freddie and Reggie and Algy and Bongo and Arthur and Cyril and Tom and Ernest and Bob and the other Bob and Pongo at the Ritz and the Red Lion, the Lobster Pot and Simpsons in the Strand – I was at the Poule au Pot and the Coq au Vin and the Côte d'Azur

and Foo Luk Fok and the Grosvenor House and Luigi's and
Lacy's and the Light of India with Johnny and Jackie and
Jerry and Joseph and Jimmy, and in the Berkeley, Biancis,
Blooms and Muldoons with Micky and Michael and Mike
and Michelle – I was in the Connaught with William and
in the Westbury with Corkie and in the Churchill with
Chalky. I was at the Duke of York, the Duke of Clarence
and the Old Duke and the King Charles and the Three
Kings and the Kings Arms and the Army and Navy Salad
Bar with Tony and Derek and Bertie and Plantagenet and
Bingo.

(*During the above speech the Committee all exit through the wrong
door, return and re-exit. The door closes, leaving only FRENCH
with MADDIE.*) (*Yells after them.*)

And I wouldn't have bothered if I'd known it was supposed
to be a secret – who needs it? (*Normal voice*) I sometimes
wonder if it's worthwhile trying to teach people, don't you
Mr. French?

(pp. 51–2)

In its own way this set piece challenges comparison with Molly
Bloom's great prose-poem at the end of Joyce's *Ulysses*. The resemblance is not only stylistic – the breathless, tumbling outpouring
of detail – it is also that Maddie's speech, like Molly's, is an
affirmation, albeit in an absurd and farcical context, of life's multiplicity and its sensual delights. Maddie says 'yes' to life, with the
same conviction as Molly.

If the scale of events, the proposterously excessive number of
sexual conquests, is one characteristic of Stoppard's farce, its visual
and verbal inventiveness is another. Farce, as we have seen
throughout this study, is pre-eminently theatrical, and makes great
play with objects, props, clothes and furniture. Stoppard's play is
no exception, but, characteristically with this playwright, there is
a kind of elegant economy and witty originality displayed in his
visual inventiveness. The freezing of the action and the flashing
of a light at sexually suggestive moments is one example. This is
visually apt, since it suggests a photographer taking pornographic
or sensationalist pictures, and relates to the prurient prying of the
popular press which is the theme of the play. It also functions as
a kind of farcical Brechtian alienation device, calling attention to

the play as a play, reminding us of the playwright as himself a joker, manipulating events for his and our pleasure.

The use of the repeated motif of the knickers and underpants is another example: Cocklebury-Smythe takes a pair of French knickers out of his pocket and gives them to Maddie; McTeazle does likewise with a pair of knickers removed from his brief-case; and Withenshaw takes a pair of Y-front pants out of the sealed envelope in his brief-case. It would be to misunderstand the point, I think, if we saw this as Stoppard heavy-handedly satirising the hypocrisy of the committee members; rather, the knickers and underpants signal the unregenerate natural man who will not be put down, committee on morals or no committee on morals. The effect is that of a flag of defiance. At the end of the play, the knickers motif returns, when the one puritanical member of the committee, French ('that sanctimonious busybody with an Energen roll where his balls ought to be', as Withenshaw describes him – p. 34), produces from his pocket to wipe his forehead, not his usual silk handkerchief, but the pair of knickers put on by Maddie at the beginning. It is a simple but delightfully effective way of showing us the wheel come full circle. The gamekeeper has joined the poachers: Maddie is irresistible.

But, co-existing with and often supporting the visual inventiveness, is a verbal sparkle and wit which is a salutory reminder that 'verbal and literary artifice' is not always, as Jessica Davis asserts, 'simply overwhelmed by physical action in farce'.[16] Stoppard uses a wide range of verbal humour, encompassing puns, innuendo, Freudian slips, malapropisms and simple wisecracks. Cocklebury-Smythe, looking with glazed eyes into Maddie's cleavage, embarks on a disastrously accident-prone conversational gambit:

> McTeazle, why don't you go and see if you can raise those great tits – boobs – those boobies, absolute tits, don't you agree, Malcolm and Douglas – though good men as well, of course, useful chaps, very decent, first rate, two of the best, Malcolm and Douglas, why don't you have a quick poke, peek, in the Members' Bra – or the cafeteria, they're probably guzzling coffee and Swedish panties.
>
> (p. 22)

Or there is Withenshaw, taking his pants out of the envelope and saying, 'the wheres and Y-fronts, the whys and wherefores of the committee are clear to you all', and to Maddie, 'you passed with flying knickers' (p. 28). Thus are conventional clichés enlivened with Freudian slips, and the visual effects and business underpinned by the verbal humour. In fact, words in *Dirty Linen* are as mischievous as objects in many conventional farces. Characters in farce are always accident-prone. But Stoppard's farce victims are as prone to verbal misadventure as physical misadventure. There are a great many verbal falls, slips on verbal banana-skins in the play. And, since Stoppard's characters are professional parliamentarians and have a natural articulateness and fluency, their verbal misadventures are all the funnier.

Another example of verbal humour is provided by the opening passages of the play, in which the first two committee members to arrive communicate via a sustained series of foreign language catch-phrases. These exchanges establish a languid, public-schoolboy tone, a tired sophistication of manner, in comic and extreme contrast to the bedroom behaviour subsequent events reveal. On the one hand, the unregenerate natural man; on the other hand, the mannered artificiality of the public persona. The point is well made when, matching action to words, Cocklebury-Smythe declares, 'Honi soit qui mal y pense', as he produces the French knickers from his pocket. (p.16) And just as this garment returns to be flourished by French at the end of the play, so does the foreign language exhange. The wheel is brought full circle both visually and verbally, as French, living up to his name, breaks into French with, 'vive l'amour', and Maddie concludes the play with Italian – 'finita La Commedia' (p.73).

Stoppard's humour and his manipulation of language occasionally remind one of Orton. Just as Orton used the clichés of popular journalism, of TV soap opera, of commercial advertising, for characters like Kath in *Entertaining Mr Sloane* or Rance in *What the Butler Saw*, so Stoppard shows a similar delight in raiding the rubbish heaps of language. Thus Cocklebury-Smythe, absurdly mixing his metaphors in trying to sustain the role of romantic lover, says to Maddie:

> I think I can say, and say with confidence, that when the smoke has cleared from the Augean stables, the little flame of our love will still be something no one else can hold a candle to as long as we can keep our heads down.
>
> (p. 23)

When McTeazle questions Maddie on her shorthand – 'Do you use Gregg's or do you favour the Pitman method?' – and Maddie replies, 'I'm on the pill' (p. 19), the exchange has very much the absurd tone of Geraldine Barclay being interviewed by Dr Prentice in *Butler*. And, when Cocklebury Smythe, Chamberlain, and McTeazle turn on French and try to implicate him in disreputable events, the effect is very similar to Dr Rance's manic cross-examination of the patients in *Butler*:

FRENCH. I left for my constituency on Friday evening and returned this morning. The only meal I've had this weekend in a London restaurant was tea on Friday at the Golden Egg in Victoria Street.
COCKLEBURY-SMYTHE. L'Oeuf d'Or?
MCTEAZLE. Were you with a woman?
FRENCH. I was with the Dean of St Pauls.
MCTEAZLE. Is she titian-haired?
CHAMBERLAIN. Come off it McTeazle. (*Kindly to FRENCH*) French, can anyone corroborate your story?
FRENCH. The Dean of St Pauls can.
CHAMBERLAIN. Apart from her.
FRENCH. We had Jumbo Chickenburgers Maryland with pickled eggs and a banana milkshake. The waitress will remember me.
CHAMBERLAIN. Why?
FRENCH. I was sick on her shoes.
COCKLEBURY-SMYTHE. Your story smacks of desperation.

(pp. 48–9)

The confusions of sex, the satiric eye for the shoddy contemporary scene, the anarchic zest of the passage all suggest Orton.

And it is, perhaps, finally of Orton's use of laughter to attack public conventions of morality that one thinks in noting the overall effect of Stoppard's farce. Though it is less subversive and less challenging than Orton's work, it does, like that work, affirm people's right to their private lives, and to their sexual natures, however colourful.

When the curtain rises on Michael Frayn's *Noises Off*, Mrs Clackett, 'a housekeeper of character', carrying an imposing plate of sardines, enters a set liberally equipped with exits and entrances – a place, as the stage-direction puts it, 'where the discerning theatregoer will feel instantly at home' – and answers the tele-phone (pp. 1–2). She establishes for us what is, for farce, a prom-ising opening situation: that the owners are abroad, that the house is open to prospective viewers, and that she is about to put her feet up to watch a TV coverage of a royal event. We are about to settle down to watch what seems oddly like a Ben Travers or Whitehall farce, when the actress playing Mrs Clackett, Dotty Otley, falters in her performance, undecided whether to take or leave the sardines as she makes to go off the stage. Whereupon,

> *the disembodied voice of Lloyd Dallas, the director of* Nothing On, *replies from somewhere out in the darkness of the auditorium:* 'You leave the sardines, and you put the receiver back.'

(p. 3)

We move back, then, from the world of one kind of farce that we have momentarily entered, into another world, in which we are to attend first a rehearsal of a farce prior to its first night at the Grand Theatre, Weston-super-Mare, then, in Act II, a performance of part of it a month later at the Theatre Royal, Goole, and finally in Act III, a further performance of part of it some seven weeks later at the Municipal Theatre, Stockton-on-Tees. On each occasion, at rehearsal and on tour, it is the same part of the farce that we witness – Act I of a piece called *Nothing On*, by an author named Robin Housemonger, acted by a touring company consisting of a libellously funny cross-section of the acting profession, each of whom (an incidental pleasure) is given a spoof biography in the programme-within-a-programme, which matches the farce-within-a-farce. Thus, the cleaning lady, Mrs Clackett (variously called Mrs Splotchett, Mrs Crochett, Mrs Cracknell and Mrs Clockett as the true text begins to blur and vanish on tour), is played by a fictional actress called Dorothy Otley, who, the biography tells us, is best known for playing Mrs Hackett, 'Britain's most famous lollipop lady (Ooh I can't 'ardly 'old me lolly up) in over 320 episodes of TV's *On the Zebras.*' There is a jeune premier, Garry Lejeune (who plays Roger Tramplemain in *Nothing On*); and of him we learn that he 'was twice winner of the Rose Bruford Medal for effort' and 'recently made his big screen debut in *Up the Virgin Soldiers*, for which he was nominated as Best Male Newcomer under Forty in any British Low-Budget Comedy Film by readers of the Sun newspaper.' We have a dumb blonde, Brook Ashton, who plays Vicki in *Nothing On*, 'probably best known as the girl wearing nothing but good, honest natural froth in the Hauptbahnhofbrau lager commercial'; and alcoholic old-stager, Selsdon Mowbray, playing Burglar, who 'first trod the boards with the Ben Greet Players', and was a stand-in to Robert Newton during a period in Hollywood; and a director with intellectual pretensions, Lloyd Dallas, who has read English at Cambridge, directed a season for the National Theatre of Sri Lanka, and clearly begrudges time spent away from rehearsing *Richard III*, to get *Nothing On* in a fit state for its provincial tour. The list is completed by a stage-struck, expensively educated Assistant Stage-Manager, Poppy Norton-Taylor, a willing and much put-upon Company Stage Manager, Tim Allgood, and the actor and actress who play the Brents (owners of the house in *Nothing On*), Frederick Fellowes, 'recently seen in the controversial all-male version of *The Trojan Women*,' and Belinda Blair, whose 'first straight parts were in *Good Time Girl*, *Ladies of the Night*, and *Ring Twice for Rita*.

As for Act I of *Nothing On*, with which we become very familiar as the play proceeds, it is a skilful pastiche of a Whitehall farce, with characters popping in and out of bedrooms, suggestive jokes, dropped trousers, a comic burglar and a comic Arab. To quote Katherine Worth's summary:

> Basically, it is a mix-up of two couples, neither of them knowing that the other is in the house. The young man from the Estate Agents, Roger, turns up with the dumb blonde (obscurely connected with the Inland Revenue) for a swift assignation in the supposedly empty house he is passing off as his own. Hardly have they had time to find the right door and get her dress off, when the older couple, the Brents, the real owners, arrive: not abroad, after all, but dodging the Inland Revenue. Stimulated by being secret visitors in their own house, they too seek a bedroom. 'Off to bed, are you?' says Mrs Clackett, with remarkable sang-froid, on being confronted with the employers she thought in Majorca (or was it Sardinia?). And from then on it is a game of hide-and-seek and near misses, as couples race up and down the staircase, opening and shutting doors, finding objects in the wrong places, and becoming even more perturbed by the poltergeist atmosphere in which things move apparently by magic, voices of unknown people are heard from behind

doors, and the television takes off from its stand (with the aid
of a superbly leisurely burglar). Even Dotty loses her aplomb at
this – and her grip on the sardines.[17]

But the farce-within-the farce, entertaining as it is, is there only
as the centre-piece of *Noises Off;* surrounding and accompanying
the illusory mad world that we see on-stage is the real and much
madder world off-stage. What Frayn does is to play a series of
increasingly subtle and dazzling variations on themes of illusion
and reality, mask and face, as the real world and the stage world,
however frantic the efforts to keep them apart, converge, collide,
disintegrate.

Lloyd, the director, is the sardonic god of the stage world, an
exasperated authority figure whose magic is not proof against
gremlins in the set, as we discover at an early point in the technical
rehearsal when one door won't open, and another door won't
shut:

LLOYD. I'm starting to know what God felt like when he sat
    out there in the darkness creating the world.
BELINDA. What did he feel like, Lloyd my love?
LLOYD. Very pleased he'd taken his valium.
BELINDA. He had six days of course. We've only got six hours.
LLOYD. And God said, where the hell is Tim?
    (*Enter from the wings TIM, the Company Stage Manager. He is
                exhausted.*)
And there the hell *was* Tim. And God said, Let there be doors,
    that open when they open, and close when they close, and
    let the doors divide the world which is in front of the set from
    the world which is behind the set.

                                                        (pp. 14–15)

But in the real world, his wandering eye and alternating week-
ends with Poppy and Brooke, each initially unaware of his interest
in the other, are to tarnish his image and undermine his authority.
Similarly with the actors, the little brief authority that mastering
their roles in *Nothing On* gives them is progressively undermined,
first by technical mishaps in the run-through, then by off-stage
jealousies and rivalries, and finally by those rivalries and jealousies
pursuing them on stage to disrupt the performance. In Act I, an
irritated but still confident Lloyd can briskly link illusion and

reality, theatre and life, as equally responsive to no-nonsense discipline and planning:

> LLOYD. . . . That's what it's all about. Doors and sardines.
> Getting on – getting off. Getting the sardines on – getting the
> sardines off. That's farce. That's the theatre. That's life.
> BELINDA. Oh God, Lloyd, you're so deep.
>
> (pp. 15–16)

In Act III, as understudies are all used up in desperate attempts
to keep the play afloat, Lloyd is reduced to coming on as Burglar,
only to find two identical burglars on stage already. Reality is now
totally undermined, anarchy rules:

> LLOYD. I've stepped off the edge of the world . . . I don't know
> where we are. I don't know where we're going.
> FLAVIA. Here is where we are, my sweet. On is where we're
> going.

It is the measure of Frayn's success that this exchange, while
totally appropriate to the shambles of the *Nothing On* performance,
also has a Beckett-like resonance, reminiscent of the
Vladimir/Estragon dialogue that concludes *Waiting for Godot*:

> VLADIMIR. Pull on your trousers.
> ESTRAGON. You want me to pull off my trousers?
> VLADIMIR. Pull *on* your trousers
> ESTRAGON (*realising his trousers are down*). True.
>   (*He pulls up his trousers*)
> VLADIMIR. Well? Shall we go?
> ESTRAGON. Yes, let's go.
>   (*They do not move*)
>
> (p. 94)

Keeping up appearances, preserving the proprieties, retaining
the mask of civilised behaviour, are important aspects of traditional
farce. The source of much of the humorous tension is the conflict
between mask and face. If it is true that the farce writer has some
difficulty in creating this tension in a society which is much less
convention-ridden than it was in the Edwardian or Victorian ages,
what better way to recover that kind of comic tension than to use

the concept of the play-within-the-play? For here, appearance is everything, maintaining the illusion is all important. And, when the illusion begins to crumble, we have a prime source for the actor of embarrassment, confusion and comic tension. As Benedict Nightingale wrote, in a *New Statesman* review of the first performance:

> Frayn obviously knows that the sight of people attempting to behave naturally and nervelessly under unnatural and unnerving circumstances is a prime source of laughter, and one somewhat lost to dramatists in a relatively tolerant, permissive age, like our own. Once the stage was full of young men doggedly keeping smiling over beds beneath which young women were strategically concealed. Now an actor in jeopardy of losing his lines and botching the plot would probably feel more pressure, more threat, more sense of impending disaster – and is therefore potentially much more amusing.[18]

What is also of central importance in a good farce, as we have already noted, is a steadily increasing momentum, albeit stage-managed under the watchful eye and controlling brain of the dramatist. And this Frayn's farce wonderfully achieves. It is an admirably laid out minefield of misadventure, in which the action grows ever more manic and desperate.

In Act I, as Katherine Worth observes,

> troubles are mainly technical – doorhandles stick, props are mislaid, the burglar fails to appear on cue and has to be sought throughout the theatre. The audience is being trained to recognise the danger spots where some of the funniest trouble is to develop later on. . . . the director's interruptions have a double function: funny in themselves, they help to fix the details of the business for the audience with a rather unusual exactness. We get to know almost as well as the actors the exact position of everything on the set: the four doors downstairs, four upstairs, and the places where the characters should be at any particular point.[19]

But, additionally and most importantly, we are alerted, through the gossip of the company know-all, Belinda Blair, to two potential trouble spots in the off-stage lives of the the actors: the youthful

Gary's affair with the 'older woman', Dotty Otley; and Brooke's affair with the director, Lloyd, which provokes an exhibition of temperament from her at the end of the rehearsal.

Act II is to Act I as obverse and reverse of the same coin. This time, Act I of *Nothing On* is played for real, to an imaginary audience of old-age pensioners at Goole. Its cast of actors is sandwiched between two audiences – them and us. For their front of house is our back-stage, our front of house their back-stage. The set is reversed, and we see the stage machinery and flats that are to create the illusion 'out there', while back-stage reality is constantly threatening to undermine it. A series of mishaps before the play starts cues in the ensuing chaos: time accelerates and decelerates, as the public address system gives contradictory estimates of how near, or distant, curtain-up is. Temperament rages, with Dotty the centre of a jealous quarrel between Freddy and Garry. The flowers that Lloyd intends for one of his girls gets passed to the other. Likewise, his whisky becomes detached from its intended recipient, and 'floats free', a constant source of tension, to be hidden at all costs from the alcoholic Selsdon. With curtain up, to quote Katherine Worth's commentary,

> the actors' private drama continues, but – here Frayn is at the top of his invention – always in total silence. A wonderful mime is performed, synchronised with the action of the inner play with staggering dexterity. The tensions between the actors are acted out, as in an early Charlie Chaplin film, through expressive looks, gestures, professional bits of miming, bodily attacks narrowly averted, fiendish practical jokes like tying trouser legs together (Garry Lejeune is the victim of this one.) Actors dash on to the back-stage area, taking their chance to tread on a rival's hand or snatch up a weapon of defence before dashing back on stage to pick up their cues. Eccentric props substitute for the real ones. A hatchet appears (from the fire equipment?) to be ritualistically passed around without any seeming connection with anything. A cactus similarly appears, to be plucked ultimately from the director's posterior. The zaniness takes on a near surrealistic quality, not least in the way the routine of the inner play keeps going despite the anarchy the actors face each time they open a door, to find the wrong prop or person there, or nothing where there should be something.[20]

The problem for Frayn is how to follow a middle act of such inventively manic controlled confusion without anti-climax. What he does is to move us still further along the collision path mapped out in Acts I and II. We now double as provincial audience of *Nothing On*, playing at Stockton-on-Tees in the fourth month of its tour, and London Audience of *Noises Off*. Back-stage rivalries have made much more extensive inroads into on-stage performance. The dividing line between illusion and reality is gone. Props are never in the right place; door handles are missing; the telephone is ripped out of its socket, trailed off the set and brought back with improvised dialogue; there are increasing misunderstandings over who is understudying whom; parts of the text go missing, or are used as a peg to hang bitter off-stage reflections on. Desperate ad-libbing is called for. Brooke, as Vicki, is hopeless at this, and unyieldingly determined not to deviate by a hairsbreadth from the script – so that she remains programmed to say, 'bag, bag, bag,' when there is self-evidently no bag on stage, and 'no bag, no bag,' when it reappears – while her scripted, often repeated 'terrific' becomes ever more inappropriate to the chaos around her. By contrast, the astute Belinda, as Falvia, improvises with aplomb, covering up valiantly when the other characters dry or omit key passages, and finally sends the play off in quite a new direction with her inspired explanation for a third's burglar's appearance – 'he's our social worker' (p. 145). Prompted by her, the cast invent gunshot wedding celebrations for Lloyd and the last-to-appear understudy, his pregnant girl-friend Poppy; then, with a last frantic effort, they steer the sinking ship of *Nothing On* back to harbour with the familiar curtain line to Act I:

> When all around is strife and uncertainty, there's nothing like. . . . a good old-fashioned plate of sardines.
>
> (p. 149)

If one has any reservations about the ending (and Frayn evidently had difficulty with it, since the last Act was revised a number of times before this final version), it is on the score that what has preceded it has been so manic that it seems a little tame to fall back on the conventional 'wedding bells' (albeit play-within-play ones) as a way out of the chaos and disorder. One would have hoped rather for a final conclusive image of anarchy to set the seal on what had gone before.

8
Farce and Contemporary Drama: II

In discussing the work of Ben Travers and the Whitehall and post-Whitehall teams of writers, I suggested an overlap between the farce worlds there created and the world of music-hall as traditionally experienced in such solo performers as George Robey, Harry Tate, Max Miller, and its modern derivatives – radio and television comedy half-hours like 'Take It From Here', 'The Goon Show', and 'Hancock's Half-Hour'. It is an overlap that is of course explicable in terms of the history of drama, since both music-hall and farce have common roots in a comic tradition going back through the *commedia dell'arte* and the medieval *sottie* to Greek and Roman farce. In the farces earlier discussed, such features as the double act, with its cross-talk routines, the physical misadventures of the characters, elaborate pieces of comic business or 'lazzi', the use of catch-phrases and stereotype characters – all are evocative of music-hall entertainment. So too is the occasional breaking of the fourth-wall illusion in moments when the character steps outside his role to comment, or in a form of soliloquy invites the audience to share the plight brought upon him by role-switching. David Thompson, in his study of *Pinter: the Player's Playwright*, comments:

> the element of role-playing is a very important feature of the music-hall comedian's art; the comic plays inside yet outside his role, building an imaginary situation and involving himself in it, switching roles, keeping the audience alert, involved, but able to enjoy the 'gamesmanship' which is a result of the constant referral to audience, the role-changing from actor to commentator. An obvious example relevant here would be Max Miller, whose act mainly consisted of a list of 'sincerely' told outrageous stories about himself or close relations, interspersed

with catch-phrases purporting to comment on the material, and mock serious admonitions to the audience for perceiving sexual innuendo in the material and finding it amusing.[1]

Better to understand the cross-fertilisation that occurs in Pinter's plays between the popular or 'illegitimate' tradition represented by music-hall and farce, and the serious 'legitimate' tradition, it is important to recall Pinter's own work as an actor in the period between 1951 and 1958. Peter Brook, in his book, *The Empty Space*, distinguishes between three kinds of theatre: Holy, Rough and Deadly. Holy theatre is the theatre of ritual and ceremony, theatre that fires the spirit and transcends our everyday experience, as the best of the classical repertory can, in certain conditions and at certain times. Rough theatre is popular, anti-authoritarian, including the Elizabethan drama, music-hall, circus, whatever is vital in the farce tradition. Brook locates it as often outside the conventional theatre set-up:

the theatre that's not in a theatre, the theatre on carts or wagons, on trestles, audiences standing, drinking, sitting round tables, audience joining in, answering back, theatre in back rooms, upstairs rooms, barns.[2]

And he accepts that Rough and Holy theatre can co-exist in the same play, obverse and reverse of the same coin, as they do in Shakespeare's plays. Deadly theatre, Brook suggests, is the form of theatre without its indwelling spirit. It is the commercial theatre with inadequate rehearsal time, the weekly repertory theatre existing on a diet of stale West End successes – the theatre that plays safe but does not satisfy.

Harold Pinter's work as an actor in the period from 1951 to 1958 involved him in all three kinds of theatre. Between 1951 and 1952, he toured Ireland with Anew McMaster's company, bringing Shakespeare to remote country towns and villages. This band of actors with their improvised settings, one-night stands, audiences unfamiliar with any kind of drama were like survivors of an older Elizabethan tradition of travelling players. Here, surely, was rough theatre, and Pinter describes it in terms that suggest Peter Brook's own definition:

Mac travelled by car and sometimes some of us did too. But

other times we went on the lorry with the flats and props, and
going into Bandon or Cloughjordan would find the town empty,
asleep, men sitting upright in dark bars, cowpads, mud, smell
of peat, wood, old clothes. We'd find digs; wash-basin and jug,
tea, black pudding, and off to the hall, set up a stage on trestle
tables, a few rostrum, a few drapes, costumes out of the
hampers, set up shop, and at night play, not always but mostly,
to a packed house.[3]

In 1953 Pinter appeared in Donald Wolfit's Spring season at the
Kings Theatre Hammersmith; the last of the great actor-managers
gave his Shylock, Lear, Macbeth, Malvolio, Wandering Jew, and,
perhaps most notably of all, Oedipus in a double bill, *Oedipus the
King* and *Oedipus in Exile*. It was in this performance that Pinter
recalled a memorable moment when Wolfit stood with his back to
the audience, and with a cloak wrapped round him:

> The man down-stage finished his speech, and we all knew that
> Oedipus was going to speak . . . (Wolfit) held the moment until
> one's stomach was truly trembling, and the cloak came round:
> a tremendous swish that no one else has been able to achieve I
> think. And the savagery and power that emerged from such a
> moment was extraordinary.

And Pinter goes on to say, that though such big theatrical
moments of ritualised gesture do not occur in contemporary
drama, there are

> comparable moments in what I seem to write. The moments are
> very exact and even very small, perhaps even trivial, as when
> a glass is moved from there to there. Now, in my terms, I feel
> that this is a very big moment, a very important moment. You
> haven't got the cloak, but you do have the glass.[4]

The kind of theatre that Wolfit represented undoubtedly
contained, as McMaster's theatre did, a mixture of the 'holy' and
the 'rough'. Wolfit's own provincial touring years are comparable
with McMaster's, though the conditions were less primitive. But
Pinter's anecdote does bring out very clearly a quality in Wolfit
that transcended the everyday, a sense of theatre as ritual – the

element of what Brook calls holy theatre – just as his memories of McMaster evoke predominantly the rough.

From 1954 to 1958, Pinter's acting experience was chiefly in weekly repertory in the provinces, often in south coast seaside resorts like Torquay, Bournemouth and Eastbourne. Ronald Hayman describes the typical repertory situation in 1957 thus:

> For giving twelve performances each week (as well as rehearsing next week's play and learning lines) actors were paid the twice-nightly minimum of £7. 10s. 0d. Some good productions were done in the better reps and even, occasionally, in the weekly ones, but there was too little time and too little money for high standards to be maintained. The plays were mostly well-tried London successes and some directors depended heavily on French's Acting Editions, which often contained detailed stage directions copied from the West End prompt book. What the provincial audiences were seeing were reproductions of stage business that had been effective in London.[5]

A glance at the programme of weekly rep that Pinter (then playing under the stage name of David Baron) was in at the Palace Court, Bournemouth, in June and July 1956, confirms this generalisation (except that he had the good fortune to be involved in only seven performances a week, rather than twelve). The plays are advertised in the *Bournemouth Daily Echo* thus:

> 23 June. Agatha Christie's record breaking comedy-thriller *The Hollow* from the Fortune and Ambassadors Theatres.
> 30 June. *Bell, Book and Candle*, from the Phoenix Theatre, London.
> 7 July. *Tabitha*, the Duchess comedy-thriller hit.
> 21 July. Walter Ellis's hilarious farce, *Almost A Honeymoon*, after two years run at the Apollo and Garrick.
> 28 July. Jack Popplewell's sensational new thriller, *Dead on Nine*, following its triumph at the Westminster.[6]

This sort of set-up recalls Brook's description of the 'deadly' theatre, deadly not necessarily in its results, for it is clear that some good work was done under daunting conditions, but deadly in its parasitical dependence on West End hits, and in the forced one-a-week production-line conditions of weekly rep. But, side by side with this 'legitimate' theatre of the seaside resorts in the 1950s, there went the popular theatre of variety and music-hall – a pale shadow perhaps of the best 'rough' theatre that Brook describes, but vigorous, versatile, drawing on traditional routines of cross-talk act, comic monologue, quick-fire wisecracks. In the Spring and Summer of 1956, for instance, while David Baron was playing at the Palace Court, Arthur Askey, Tommy Trinder, Dave King, Jimmy Edwards, Charlie Chester, Max Bygraves, Sam Costa and Frankie Howerd were some of the variety stars to be found at the Winter Garden and New Royal Theatres in Bournemouth. The mid-1950s were also, of course, vintage years for such radio and television comedies as Hancock's Half-Hour and the Goon Show. Michael Billington refers to the dominance of the music-halls on the theatrical scene in the 1940s and 1950s, and says, 'how understandable it is that the rhythms of the stand-up comic should have implanted themselves in any writer's mind – particularly, one might add, when, like Pinter, he was performing in seaside towns that were a centre, in the summer months, for such entertainment.[7]

Pinter, then, had plenty of contact, not only with the serious, 'legitimate' theatre, but with the popular tradition in its various forms – Shakespeare, music-hall performers appearing in the same provinicial towns, and, not least through his own appreciation of music-hall: he is on record as saying that 'he frequently went to the music-hall as a child, and that among his favourite comedians were Al Read, Max Miller, and the Marx Brothers'.[8] It's relevant here, too, to remember Pinter's interest in writing revue sketches such as Trouble in the Works and The Black and White for the Lyric Revue (Hammersmith, July 1959), and Request Stop, Special Offer and Last To Go, for the revue, Pieces of Eight (Apollo Theatre, 1969); also the fact that radio comedy performers have worked with notable success in Pinter plays, for example, Dandy Nichols (of the TV series Till Death Do Us Part) as Meg in the film of The Birthday Party, and Leonard Rossiter, who achieved popular success in Rising Damp, as Davies in The Caretaker.

I would suggest, then that Pinter's experiences as a performer and a member of the audience, experiencing both 'legitimate' and popular, rough and holy theatre in the 1950s, were the soil from which his own drama grew. An examination of The Birthday, Party, The Caretaker and The Homecoming may suggest his skill in bringing together into a creative relationship elements from these different kinds of theatre.

The Birthday Party at first promises to involve us in the familiar world of the repertory theatre's 'well-made play'. There is an illusion of 'real life' observed through the fourth wall of a realistic set. The play originates in Pinter's real life experience of actors' digs in Eastbourne. The dialogue captures amusingly and accurately the banal, sporadic, and comic exchanges of the breakfast table. Here is the surface of life convincingly rendered, with an eye for its absurdity. We note from the text of the play that it is a three-act, one set piece, with reasonably detailed stage directions. It could quite easily be set up as a Samuel French acting edition. It has strong 'curtains' at the ends of Act I and II, and a use of darkness and menace at the end of the latter act that shows Pinter using for his own purposes the devices of terror, suspense and exciting curtains associated with the thriller or detective play in which he had acted on many occasions (for example, Agatha Christie's *Spiders Web* at the Pavilion, Torquay, in October 1956, or her *Love From A Stranger* at the Palace Court, Bournemouth, in August 1956). But, with the appearance of Goldberg and McCann, there comes a subtle and gradual shift of emphasis. Elements of the music-hall cross-talk act begin to appear:

GOLDBERG. . . . You're a capable man, McCann.
MCCANN. That's a great compliment, Nat, coming from a man in your position.
GOLDBERG. Well, I've got a position, I won't deny it.
MCCANN. You certainly have.
GOLDBERG. I would never deny that I have a position.
MCCANN. And what a position!
GOLDBERG. It's not a thing I would deny.

(p. 39)

It is as if the 'funny man' and his 'stooge' go into a routine, playing with a word or a phrase, passing it backwards and forwards between them. A sense of dislocation and unease is created; the naturalistic world of the well-made play is being threatened by the appearance of two jokers of an unpredictable kind, indulging in a game which may at any moment turn serious, as the blind-man's-buff game literally does. There is, too, a weird appropriateness in making the 'bogeymen' of the play, respectively a Jew and an Irishman. How often have they figured in music-hall comedian's jokes! Now they assume a monstrous life of their own, behaving with the kind of alarming caricature grotesqueness which their stereotype joke situations have often seemed to require. McCann in Act III turns abruptly on Lulu in the role of bigoted Irish priest, though his partner Goldberg upstages him with such withering asides as, 'he's only been unfrocked six months':

> Down on your knees and confess. . . . kneel down woman and tell me the latest. . . . I've seen you hanging about the Rock of Cashel, profaning the soil with your goings-on!
>
> (pp. 90–1)

Goldberg in Act II plays the extravagantly Jewish father figure with relish, all schmaltz and sentiment:

> I had a wife. What a wife. Listen to this. Friday, of an afternoon, I'd take myself for a little constitutional, down over the park. . . . I'd say hullo to the little boys, the little girls – I never made distinctions – and then back I'd go, back to my bungalow with the flat roof. 'Simey,' my wife used to shout, 'quick, before it gets cold!' And there on the table what would I see? The nicest piece of roll-mop and pickled cucumber you could wish to find on a plate.
>
> (p. 69)

And, in a different vein, but in the very accents of another Jewish comedian from vaudeville, Groucho Marx, he plays the sexually knowing, wise-cracking con-man who can run rings round his female victim:

> LULU. He was my first love, Eddie was. And whatever happened, it was pure. With him! He didn't come into my room at night with a briefcase!
> GOLDBERG. Who opened the briefcase, me or you?
> ....
> LULU (*with growing anger*). You used me for a night. A passing fancy.
> GOLDBERG. Who used who?
> LULU. You made use of me by cunning when my defences were down.

GOLDBERG. Who took them down?
LULU. That's what you did. You quenched your ugly thirst. You taught me things a girl shouldn't know before she's been married three times!
GOLDBERG. Now you're a jump ahead! What are you complaining about!

(pp. 89–90)

Pinter achieves a richness of texture in this bringing together of popular and straight drama, and is able to open out the box-set world of the play to accommodate a more alarming, a more poetic view of the world than would be possible within the well-made play. It is interesting to note in this connection that he had acted twice in a play of J. B. Priestley's, *Mr Kettle and Mr Moon* (in September and December 1956, at the Palace Court, Bournemouth, and the Pavilion, Torquay, respectively), and that two incidents are taken over from this play and adapted for use in *The Birthday Party*. In Act I of Priestley's play, the bank manager, weary of his conventional life, refuses to go to the office, buys some children's toys, including a drumstick, puts a record on the gramophone, and beats the coalscuttle in time to the music as an expression of new-found freedom. In Act III of the play, he is visited in his bedroom by a doctor with hypnotic powers, and reappears, apparently brainwashed, and dressed in his conventional bank-manager clothes – bowler hat, black coat and striped trousers (the garb Pinter chose for Stanley's last zombie-like appearance in the first version of *The Birthday Party*). But whereas these images of rebellion and conformity fail to convince within the solidly realistic world of Priestley's play, and seem somewhat hackneyed devices, Pinter creates a genuinely alarming context for them, a dramatic world in which the surreal co-exists with the real. For the two sinister clowns, Goldberg and McCann, have already broken down the fourth wall of illusion, and prepared us for non-naturalistic happenings. And when the moments of drum-beating and brainwashing occur, Pinter is able to handle them with a poetic freedom and effect, precisely because the ground has been prepared. The drum-beating, in particular, is a ritual of astonishing power. Stanley becomes a man possessed, agonisingly trapped in the repetitive compulsions of a childish game, and almost, it seems, summoning up his attackers out of the darkness. Pinter suggests a connection between the big 'larger than life' moment in Wolfit's

performance as Oedipus, and smaller moments in his own plays
– 'You haven't got the cloak, but you do have the glass.' The
beating of the drum in Act I, the breaking of Stanley's glasses in
Act II, McCann blowing into Goldberg's mouth in Act III are all
very good examples of this. Indeed, it is not altogether far-fetched
to see a parallel between *The Birthday Party*, and the play in which
Pinter, as one of the Theban elders, watched Wolfit create his
theatrical moment. The guilt-ridden, blinded victim, in exile,
sought out, questioned and threatened by a succession of visitors,
removed to 'another place' at the end of the play – the description
fits the pathetic Stanley as closely as it does the tragic Oedipus.
'They knew,' says Oedipus, 'they who devised the trap for me,
they knew' (p. 79, *Theban Plays*, Penguin 1972); and Stanley asserts,
'You know what they did. They carved me up. It was all arranged,
it was all worked out' (p. 33). That such a resonance can be felt
even faintly within the play indicates the liberating possibilities
when a playwright of Pinter's skill achieves a cross-fertilisation
between different kinds of theatre.

In *The Caretaker*, there is perhaps rather less cross-fertilisation
than in *The Birthday Party*. The play is concentrated within a smaller
compass; but within that compass Pinter still taps a current of
energy and inventiveness that owes more to music-hall and
popular comedy than to the naturalistic drama. Peter Davison has
already analysed the connection between the music-hall monologue and cross-talk act and certain passages in *The Caretaker*.[9]
Mick's set-piece verbal assaults on Davies in Act II provide particularly good examples. Realistically considered, they are perfectly
appropriate for the context: the tramp is put in his place, demoral-
ised and bewildered by the sharp-tongued, contemptuous Mick,
asserting his territorial rights:

> You're stinking the place out. You're an old robber, there's no
> getting away from it. You're an old skate. You don't belong in
> a nice place like this. . . . You got no business wandering about
> in an unfurnished flat. I could charge seven quid a week for
> this if I wanted to. Get a taker tomorrow. Three hundred and
> fifty a year exclusive. No argument. I mean if that sort of
> money's in your range don't be afraid to say so. . . . Say the
> word and I'll have my solicitor draft you out a contract. Other-
> wise, I've got the van outside, I can run you to the police station
> in five minutes, have you in for trespassing, entering with

intent, daylight robbery, filching, thieving and stinking the place out. What do you say?

(pp. 44–5)

But this and other speeches to some degree frustrate the customary logic of the well-made play, its customary mode of character presentation and plot development. They conjure up, in a vein of semi-comic fantasy, a slightly surreal world in which Mick seems thoroughly at home. It is the familiar world seen through a distorting mirror. We are also very conscious of Mick's skill as 'performer', using verbal aggression to score off one of his fellows, rather as Groucho Marx does in putting down Zeppo in *Horse Feathers*:

GROUCHO. You're a disgrace to our family name of Wagstaff, if such a thing is possible. What's all this talk I hear about you fooling around with the college widow? No wonder you can't get out of college. Twelve years in one college! I went to *three* colleges in twelve years and fooled around with *three* college widows! When I was your age I went to bed every night after supper. Sometimes I went to bed *before* supper. Sometimes I went without my supper and didn't go to bed at all! A college widow stood for something in those days. In fact she stood for plenty!

ZEPPO. There's nothing wrong between me and the college widow.

GROUCHO. There isn't huh? Then you're crazy to fool around with her.[10]

The effect is, of course, much more uncomplicatedly comic, but the technique is similar: the same rapid changes of verbal tack designed to confuse and confound; the same tendency to overwhelm the victim with quick-fire inventiveness, to use language as a weapon.

Davies, too, the tramp with his shabby clothes and shoes that are falling apart, is, realistically considered, a 'natural' whose every turn of phrase carries conviction. But there is more than a touch also of the seedy grandiloquence of Tony Hancock in *Hancock's Half-Hour*. Here, too, was a study in failure, in putting a brave face on a hopeless situation. Hancock too, reached after respectability and status, but never achieved it, was bewildered by the

impedimenta of everyday living, sought in the posher parts of
Cheam (his own address was the Railway Cuttings, East Cheam),
a haven that Davies seeks in Sidcup, backed away from work and
responsibility, complained bitterly of 'foreigners' and paraded his
own 'Britishness' (as in his response in *The Blood Donor* to the
nurse's question, 'Nationality?' – 'British. British. Undiluted for
twelve generations. One hundred per cent Anglo-Saxon, with
perhaps just a dash of Viking, but nothing else has crept in.')[11] It
is not, however, any direct influence I wish to establish. The
Hancock persona has, after all, qualities that are quite distinct
from those possessed by Davies. It is, rather, the verbal inventiveness that Ray Galton and Alan Simpson gave to Hancock and
Pinter to Davies (such that a certain oddity and surrealism appears
in their encounters with everyday life). Pinter shares with Galton
and Simpson an ability to use the shaggy-dog story, the rambling
comic monologue, the music-hall comedian's endless capacity for
self-dramatisation for his own creative purposes. Says Hancock,
in *The Blood Donor*, totting up the list of his good deeds preparatory
to being called to account in the after-life:

When I'm finally called by the Great Architect and he says,
'What did you do?' I shall just bring me book out and say, 'Here
you are, mate, add that lot up.'[12]

The pithy disrespectfulness and unexpected turn of phrase delight
us in the same way as Davies's saga of his quest for a pair of
shoes:

I said to this monk, here, I said, look here mister I said, you
haven't got a pair of shoes, have you, a pair of shoes, I said,
enough to keep me on my way. . . . I heard you got a stock of
shoes here. Piss off, he said to me. Now look here, I said, I'm
an old man, you can't talk to me like that. I don't care who you
are. If you don't piss off, he says, I'll kick you all the way to
the gate.

(p. 23)

Relevant to this is the way an actor plays the role of Davies.
Viewed from one angle, the tramp is a 'natural', and was played
as such by Donald Pleasence in the first production of the play at
the Duchess Theatre in 1960. Viewed from another angle, the role

can be played – as it was by Leonard Rossiter in 1972 at the
Mermaid Theatre – in a style that brings out more effectively the
sense in which Davies too is a performer, standing to lose everything if he fails to find – or sustain – a role in the game of
lifemanship that unfolds in Mick's flat. I quote Michael Billington's
account of the two interpretations:

> Pleasence played the character as a blustering, belligerent,
> selfish impostor. It was a remarkable performance in that he
> seemed to inhabit the role completely. The voice (and physical
> gestures) . . . evoked a lifetime of subservience and
> oppression. . . . Pleasence did not play Davies: he *was* Davies.
> And it came as no surprise to learn that, when the play was
> being filmed in Hackney, Pleasence went out on to the streets
> during breaks in the action and sold matches to passers-by.
>
> Twelve years later Leonard Rossiter played the same role, no
> less brilliantly, in a revival of the play at the Mermaid. It would
> be impossible, however, to imagine Mr Rossiter standing out in
> Puddle Dock and selling matches; or at least, if he had done so,
> he would not have fooled many of the customers. For on this
> occasion the role was *presented* to us and the actor's identification
> was somewhat less than total. From the first one was acutely
> aware of Mr Rossiter's assumption of mock-gentility and
> refinement. . . . of the way the mouth formed a repulsive
> rectangle rather like the aperture in a letter-box with the tongue
> protruding against the lower lip; and of the deferential gestures
> with two fingers raised to the brow in mock salute. Above all,
> Rossiter indicated to us that this was a man for whom work was
> the dirtiest four-letter word in the English language. . . . This
> man was, above all, a skiver, a work-shy drop-out, a born
> malingerer. But whereas Pleasence seemed to be working from
> the inside out, Rossiter worked from the outside in presenting
> the character to us through an accumulation of external detail.[13]

Billington then suggests that this is an indication of the way 'actors
have, over the last decade, slowly moved away from a total Stanis-
lavskian realism towards a greater degree of Brechtian presentation'.[14] But he could also have noted that Brechtian presentation
has a great deal in common with the techniques required in music-
hall, the need to be inside yet outside the role, and that Rossiter's
performance must have fitted well with what Almansi and Hend-

erson describe as the games of hide-and-seek that occur in *The Caretaker*, games in which Davies gives 'a series of unconvincing performances in his various identifying roles ("honourable tramp", "honest friend", "well-travelled man of experience", potential "caretaker" and "interior decorater")' while 'actually fighting a battle for his life'.[15]

In the third play to be considered, *The Homecoming*, Lenny's role-playing and manipulation of language show Pinter, as with Mick in *The Caretaker*, creating effects similar to those of the music-hall monologue, and, as in *The Birthday Party*, there is a tension set up between conventional realistic drama, the surface level of the play, and a more surrealistic world existing below the surface. Thus Pinter to some extent uses and plays upon audience expectation of those conventional family dramas, with which he was wearisomely familiar in his repertory acting days – well-made plays within a box-set, in which meals, pouring of drinks, guests arriving, small-talk, such situations as the bride brought home to meet the family play a large, and largely predictable, part. He teases us at times with echoes in language or situation of such plays, only to pull the rug out from under our feet, creating effects which are mocking, funny, frightening, or a mixture of all three. He says to us in effect, 'You may have thought you could relax in the secure world of the well-made play, thought perhaps lazily that that world approximated to the real one. But you can't and it isn't. Co-existing with its refinements, its small-talk, its conventional gestures, is a world that is much less predictable, much odder, much crueller, and in which there are no tidy patterns. A good example is the Ruth and Lenny sequence in Act I that leads from the offer of a glass of water to small-talk about Italy, and on through Lenny's attempts to put down Ruth with his tales of macho-male aggressiveness against women, to Ruth's final victory over Lenny in the matter of drinking the water. Throughout the sequence, conversational gambits from conventional drama act as points of reference: the offer of a drink, a polite enquiry about family holidays, an attempt to flirt which is rebuffed. But, as the talk develops, so the familiar landmarks disappear. We find ourselves in a stranger, partly comic, partly frightening territory. Banal exchanges about 'dear old Venice' take on an Alice-in-Wonderland quality as Lenny improvises an Italian experience that never was; then, with one hand offers to authenticate the 'true' story of a woman propositioning him with appropriate circumstan-

tial detail, while with the other, he plays such tricks with language
as tilt the tale rowards the absurd:

> . . . one night down by the docks, I was standing alone under
> an arch, watching all the men jibbing the boom, out in the
> harbour, and playing about with a yardarm . . . standing under-
> neath this arch, watching all the steamers steaming up.

(p. 46)

There is a strong echo here of a Flanagan and Allen double-act
which also created surrealistic humour out of dockland sights:

> BUD. I went down to the docks.
> CHES. Oh, you saw the ships?
> BUD. Yes, I saw all the ships coming into whisky.
> CHES. Coming into port.
> BUD. Coming into port – oh, a marvellous sight . . . see all the
> labradors at work.
> CHES. The what?
> BUD. The labradors.
> CHES. The labradors – the salvadors!
> BUD. The stevedores, you fool – Oi!
> ....
> Marvellous sight, see them getting all the sargo off the
> ships. . . . what they make the sargo pudding with. . . .[16]

And, in the Pinter, Lenny's repeated 'underneath the arch' again
points to Flanagan and Allen, with their famous song, 'Underneath the Arches'. Lenny's second story, involving in this case
aggression against a mother-figure rather than a sex symbol, starts
with the fussy repetitiveness, the anecdotal detail of some Frankie
Howerd or Max Miller monologue:

> An old lady approached me and asked me if I would give her
> a hand with her iron mangle. Her brother-in-law, she said, had
> left it for her, but he'd left it in the wrong room, he'd left it in
> the front room. Well, naturally, she wanted it in the back room.
> It was a present he'd given her, you see, a mangle, to iron out
> the washing. But he'd left it in the wrong room, he'd left it in
> the front room, well that was a silly place to leave it, it couldn't
> stay there. . .

(p. 48)

As the story builds to its climax – a punch-line of coarse aggressiveness, capped with an impudent piece of 'helpful' advice which adds insult to injury, we see Pinter, through Lenny, using the ruthlessly comic world of the music-hall monologue for his own purposes:

> So there I was, . . . risking a rupture, and this old lady just standing there, waving me on, not even lifting a little finger to give me a helping hand. So after a few minutes I said to her, now look here, why don't you stuff this iron mangle up your arse? Anyway, I said, they're out of date, you want to get a spin-drier . . .

(p. 49)

Here is Lenny the shrewd role-player, whose gamesmanship is deadly earnest, who plays the audience expertly, only to put the boot in, as he literally does at the end of both these stories. Ruth, however, coolly refuses to be disconcerted or put down by Lenny's tactics. The struggle between the two generates considerable dramatic tension. She successfully counter-attacks, first as mother-figure (she angers Lenny by calling him Leonard, 'the name my mother gave me') then as sexual predator in her use of the glass of water:

> RUTH. Have a sip. Go on. Have a sip from my glass. (*He is still*) Sit on my lap. Take a long cool sip. (*She pats her lap. Pause. She stands, moves to him with the glass.*) Put your head back and open your mouth.
> LENNY. Take that glass away from me.
> RUTH. Lie on the floor. Go on. I'll pour it down your throat.
> LENNY. What are you doing, making me some kind of proposal? (*She laughs shortly, drains the glass.*)
> RUTH. Oh, I was thirsty.

(p. 50)

The slow-motion, surreal concentration on the ritual of the drinking invests the incident with a powerful erotic significance. We realise how Pinter's technique indeed achieves effects comparable with Wolfit's moment in *Oedipus in Exile* – 'You haven't got the cloak but you do have the glass.' At the same time, the investing of the innocent object with a sexual significance is a technique familiar in the world of farce, and the dark humour of the exchanges depends upon that kind of incongruity.

I quoted earlier in this study Eric Bentley's observation that the dynamic of farce depended upon the interplay between the mask (of social decorum) and the real face (of primitive instinct). The struggle that develops over the glass of water provides one example of such an interplay, in which, characteristically for Pinter, the farcical element is only part of a subtle mix of the serious and the comic. An even more striking example from Act II is the moment when Teddy comes in with the suitcase to take leave, Lenny puts a record on the gramophone, requests the pleasure of a dance with Ruth before she leaves, and slowly Ruth responds sexually, first to Lenny, and then to Joe, who lies on top of her while Lenny caresses her hair. While this mime of sexuality is going on, Max plays the welcoming father, forgiving his son for concealing the marriage and evoking the beauties of motherhood and family life:

> We're talking about a woman of quality. We're talking about a woman of feeling. (*Joey and Ruth roll off the sofa on to the floor.*)
>
> (p. 76)

The moment builds on and arises out of previous ones, when Pinter at first plays on our expectations of the conventional family play, and then 'breaks the mould', creating a disturbing tension between the surface and what lies beneath it, between mask and face.

In Pinter, then, role-playing, the relationship of mask to face and elements of music-hall monologue and double-act show his indebtedness to farce and the popular tradition.

The way that Bond draws on that tradition is very different. Katharine Worth has written, in relation to Sean O'Casey's plays, of how O'Casey's use 'of sad farce to control painful material struck out a line which was to become one of the main lines of modern drama'.[17] The comment has a direct relevance to Bond, and, in particular, to certain of his earlier plays, such as *Early Morning, Narrow Road to the Deep North* and *Lear*. which explore the social and moralised violence and aggression that Bond sees as endemic to our civilisation:

I write about violence as naturally as Jane Austen wrote about manners. . . . Aggression has become moralised and morality has become a form of violence. . . . It is as if an animal was locked in a cage then fed with the key. It shakes the bars but can never get out.[18]

With such a subject, it is important to Bond to create the right context. In such plays as the three mentioned, he invents dramatic parables and semi-mythical worlds, at a distance from, yet firmly related to, the modern world. And in these plays elements of farce are used mainly to 'control painful material', to keep an audience critically alert, and to relate the mythical world to the modern world. That he does this so skilfully may be in some measure due to the interest in music-hall techniques he shares with many other farce writers in this study. As Tony Coult writes:

The intimate audience-performer relationship of the music-hall, and the place that variety shows held in working-class culture remain as strong influences in Bond's analysis of his own job as an artist: 'I don't see the plays I write as being intellectual in the sense of being cut off from popular expression. I grew up at a time when the theatre was still part of popular experience in the music-hall. When I saw my first play, which was *Macbeth*, I saw it in terms of the music-hall.[19]

Bond has attacked actors trained in the Stanislavsky method, 'hugging feelings to themselves', and displaying 'irrelevant subjectivity', when rehearsing one of his plays; and he has insisted instead on a 'presentational' Brechtian style of playing, since 'telling a story is an essential part of epic theatre'.[20] Here too, it should be noted, he finds a model in the popular music-hall tradition:

I do consciously write for people who *behave* on the stage. When I write a part for Shakespeare, I do have in a certain sense the techniques of someone like Frankie Howerd in mind . . . (With) Frankie Howerd, the extraordinary thing was, one realised in a sense one was performing a dance with him. You weren't sitting there listening, he was reacting to you all the time. You knew what the climax was, he knew what the climax was, but you worked together for it.[21]

Bond's *Early Morning* is a phantasmagoric, surrealist play, that uses a fantasy Victorian world to comment on our own world. Bond sees the Victorian age and its values as the dead past, which, because it is so recent, is still cripplingly attached to our shoulders until we cut it loose, just as, in the play, the Siamese twin, George, is attached to Arthur's shoulder. We have seen already, in Orton's farces, how he raises the stakes by creating authority figures like Truscott and Rance who are grotesque mirror-images of the anarchic forces they seek to control, and how he creates a complex irony by putting into the mouths of these figures appeals to that morality and propriety which their every action confounds. We also noted in his work the element of the surreal and the nightmarish, the way in which Orton uses laughter not only to achieve a comic catharsis, but also to make us uneasy as his farce lights up areas of violence and ruthlessness in contemporary life.

Bond, in *Early Morning*, works in a very similar way, using farce to disturb and disorient us, to raise uncomfortable questions even as we laugh. He sees an uneasily repressed violence always threatening to break free, as related to a repressed sexuality channelled into perverse forms of expression, and he comments:

> Violence is the big problem of our society – in the way that sex was the problem that haunted the Victorians. And what we must not do is make violence pornographic. . . . The Victorians made sex pornographic, which meant that they could then use it for political ends. Sex became not a natural function, but something to use.[22]

Specifically, in *Early Morning* we have the grotesque sexual entanglements and role-playing of Florence Nightingale, who, in Scene 5 comes on to announce:

> I'm changed. Queen Victoria raped me. I never dreamed that would happen. George will know. I'll disgust him. . . . I've started to have evil thoughts. Her legs are covered in black shiny hairs.
>
> (p. 155)

Farcical indeed, but the rape, as David Hirst points out, is 'a metaphor for the corrupting force of Victorian ethics'.[23] And Florence's subsequent farcical misadventures convey the progressive prostitution of women in the cause of a repressive political system. The angel of mercy sexually services the war wounded of the Crimean campaign as she does the rounds of the wards. She opens a brothel, but dies when Disraeli and Gladstone both make love to her together, become overexcited at the news of the relief of Mafeking, and strangle her:

> There I was in bed with Disraeli and Gladstone. They always shared a booking. They got very excited as usual and just then Gladys (a nom d'amour) said 'Listen'. There was a newsboy shouting in the street. Mafeking had been relieved. That on top of the rest was too much. They got over-excited – and here I am.
>
> (p. 201)

David Hirst aptly comments:

> This has all the sharpness and satirical force of a political cartoon. Gillray's celebrated picture of Napoleon and Pitt carving up the world, for example. It conveys with economy and wit the fact that, in lending her support to a corrupt system, Florence has in the end been sacrificed: screwed by opposing political interests.[24]

Farcical distortions are used, then, in *Early Morning* to make political comments. Another of Florence Nightingale's roles is that of public hangwoman, coyly flirting with Prince Arthur among the corpses. Gladstone appears as a kind of mad shop-steward figure instructing a lynch mob how to inflict maximum damage on their victim. Throughout, the point is made that repressive, authoritarian figures can invoke morality, democracy, decency, to their own ends, that indeed, as Bond argues in *Lear*, our civilisation is founded on 'moralised aggression': 'Your law always does more harm than crime, and your morality is a form of violence' (p. 99). Thus Queen Victoria, presiding over the trial of Len and Joyce, declares with great moral concern: 'Put him on oath, but don't let him touch the Bible, King James would turn in his grave.' (p. 148) Gladstone, addressing the lynch mob, insists: 'We don't tolerate no totalitarian larkins 'ere . . . yer 'ave t'ave yer trial to make it legal. . . . Rules are made to abide by,' (p. 170) and he applies the same methodical know-how to instruct the mob in kicking Len to death:

> The secret is to move from the thigh and let the weight of the tool do the work. That economises yer effort so yer can keep it up longer. . . . The other way looks good but it's all on the surface . . . yer don't do yer internal damage.

(p. 172)

And when Florence Nightingale and Queen Victoria discuss the details of the hanging, the cosy domestic small talk about knitting the hoods that are put over the victims' heads adds to the horror: 'I use a new hood each time,' says Florence Nightingale, 'it adds that little touch of feminine sensibility. That's very precious in war' (p. 188).

At the other end of the social spectrum of the play are the stereotyped working-class characters, Len and Joyce. The stereotyping serves to distance us from them as much as is the case with the caricatured historical characters. We see in them an aggressiveness and blood-lust that echoes that of government, but in a more primitive and mindless form. And, as with the governors, that blood-lust is accompanied by unexceptionable moral sentiments. They may murder and eat a queue-jumper outside the Kilburn State Empire while waiting to see *Policemen in Black Nylons* (anachronism being one of the ways in which Bond relates past to present), but they are kindly souls; they offer parts of the dismembered body to fellow-queuers, since as Len explains, 'yer can't nosh 'an not offer round;' and when they strip the body, Joyce draws the line at taking off the victim's underclothes – 'I don't 'old with this rudery yer get' (p. 150). This scene is of particular importance, coming as it does early in the play. *Early Morning*'s dominant image is that of cannibalism, the eat-or-be-eaten mentality that Bond dramatises in the extraordinary final section of the play where the characters, having succeeded in destroying each other early on, are transported to a Heaven where they continue to dismember and devour each other. And Bond balances the Goya-esque savagery of these images with a final image of Arthur's bodily resurrection, even as Queen Victoria and her companions finish off eating the dead body. Bond, even at his most Swiftian and despairing, retains a faith in man's ability to learn from and outgrow his society. But, by introducing the theme

on an almost purely farcical level, before returning to it at a deeper
and more serious level, Bond prepares the audience psychologically. So both cannibalism and resurrection are presented at the
beginning of the play in an outrageously humorous manner: first
the devouring of the queue-jumper; then, when Len and Joyce
have their appeals dismissed and are sentenced to death, the
theme of resurrection is introduced in a farcical manner – they
burst into a song-and-dance act which exemplifies their refusal to
die:

> Lord George hanged my father
> Dad fell through the trap
> But he started bouncing
> Dad's neck wouldn't snap
> Lord George said to father
> Play the game, my lad
> But he kept on bouncing
> You can't hang my dad.

(p. 152)

As the play proceeds, images of death and resurrection, of life cut
off and life returning, move beyond the initial farcical level, and
as they recur become stronger and richer in their power to throw
light on the themes of the play. This is, of course, a technique
that goes as far back in British drama as the medieval miracle
plays, as, for example, in the Towneley *Secunda Pastorum*, where
the farcical sheep-stealing and mock nativity precede and
strengthen the serious and real nativity.

Narrow Road to the Deep North is described by Martin Esslin as 'a
beautiful parable play, very Brechtian in its mixture of orientalism
and moral didacticism, Brechtian also in the sparseness and
economy of its writing'.[25] The parable recounts how the gentle
protagonist, Kiro, seeks enlightenment from three authority
figures in turn, as revolution and counter-revolution affect his
country. There is Basho, the poet-priest, who venerates traditional
religion but becomes an apologist for a tyrannical government;
Shogo, the tyrant, who kills and imprisons to create firm and
efficient government; and Georgina, the bible-bashing missionary
following the Imperialist flag, who shares with Shogo a belief in
firm government, but would impose it from within by manipul-

ating the people's moral code. Kiro, despairing of enlightenment from any of these, finally commits suicide, though Bond places the suicide critically, as a private, self-indulgent act, by coinciding it with the cries for help of a swimmer in danger of drowning – cries ignored by Kiro, intent on his private drama. The swimmer saves himself by his own unaided efforts, and the concluding image of the play is not, therefore, that of a protagonist's tragic defeat, but of the necessity for life to go on.

As this brief account suggests, the play does not have the surrealist, nightmare quality of *Early Morning*; farce techniques are less in evidence and less needed. They are, however, appropriately introduced in Scenes Five and Six, in which the Victorian colonising figures of Georgina, the Commodore, and his Jack Tar gunmen are launching an attack on Shogo's kingdom to make it an outpost of empire, and Basho is being enlisted as a puppet of the Imperialists:

> COMMODORE (*to BASHO*). . . . You must come to England some day – for a short visit. They'd love you. You'll learn a lot. The English countryside, calm, peaceful, green, orderly, civilised, the distant cry of ladies riding to hounds and digging out old Tom Badger. Georgina's firing the opening shot.
> (*The TARS are loading the cannon with a ramrod*)
> ....
> GEORGINA. Isn't it ready yet?
> GUNNER TAR. Got a do it right.
> GUNNER TAR'S MATE. As the mathematician said to 'is girl friend.
> GUNNER TAR. Don't want it comin' out the wrong way.
> GUNNER TAR'S MATE. As the girl friend said to the mathematician.
> GEORGINA. Fortunately that's my deaf ear.
> GUNNER TAR (*stepping back from the cannon*).
> That'll put a curl in the end of their pigtail.
> COMMODORE. I'm glad that's settled – whiff of what's-it up their thingummy, haw?
> GEORGINA. Two lines of Abide With Me. (*Sings*) Abide with me, fast falls the eveing light. Three cheers for Jesus! Hip hip! (*Shouts and tambourine:* 'Hoorah!') Hip hip! (*Shouts and tambourine:* 'Hoorah!') Hip hip! (*Shouts and tambourine:* 'Hoorah!' *She drops a light on the cannon. There is a flash and a*

roar. The men cheer.) I saw an angel hovering over it with a
Union Jack!

(pp. 220–1)

The appropriateness of rendering these scenes in terms of farce is
two fold. It is partly that the speed with which farce can move
suits the way that Bond perceives the sequence of events in the
play and his emphasis on action:

> The essential thing. . . to explain the structure in *Narrow Road*
> is, you see Shogo in complete control and all the rest of it, and
> then the next minute someone says that was last week and it's
> all over, it's changed. You see it's like that, and the careful
> arguing what, what, why, why was not very relevant. . . . I
> mean I wanted to say, look it's happening.[26]

This brisk, speeded-up effect makes its own ironic comment on
events, as for example in Scene five, in which the decision to
attack Shogo's city is made:

> COMMODORE. This city thingummy, is it prosperous?
> BASHO. Yes, very.
> GEORGINA (*her tambourine trembles*). I beg your pardon.
> COMMODORE. Any manufactures?
> BASHO (*shrugs*). No.
> COMMODORE. Good! (*He taps GEORGINA's tambourine excit-
> edly*). I'll wire Birmingham – we march tomorrow.
> ....
> GEORGINA. Hallelujah! (*She bangs her tambourine*)

(p. 198)

Secondly, the customary exaggerations of farce give an additional
cutting edge to Bond's view of the moralised aggression of the
colonisers. This is particularly evident in the naked absurdity of
Georgina's enlisting of Jesus as righteous warrior in the Imperialist
cause; but it is also evident in the sexual innuendos of the Gunner
Tars' double-act as they load the cannon: the sex-drive harnessed
to the death-dealing guns.

Briefly to conclude these observations on Bond. I would instance
a similar use of farcical techniques near the beginning of *Lear*,
Bond's reworking of the Shakespeare play. In this, Goneril and

Regan, renamed Bodice and Fonatanelle, exist in a kind of parodic relation to their formidable and venomous prototypes. They are, for Bond, figures of black farce, childishly indulging their cruelties and sexual appetites. They initiate a revolution to overthrow Lear by contracting marriages with his enemies, the Dukes of North and Cornwall, and then complain in bitter asides to the audience of their husband's sexual incompetence. 'When he gets on top of me,' says Fontanelle, 'I'm so angry I have to count to ten. That's long enough. Then I wait till he's asleep and work myself off. I'm not making do with that for long.' 'Virility,' says Bodice, 'It'd be easier to get blood out of a stone, and far more probable. I've bribed a major on his staff to shoot him in the battle' (p. 24). Bond's variation on the blinding of Gloucester has Warrington (the Gloucester figure) subjected, like a puppet figure in an evil Punch-and-Judy show, to every kind of monstrous cruelty. His tongue already cut out, he is methodically beaten up, while Bodice calmly knits, and Fontanelle jumps up and down with perverse, infantile glee:

> FONTANELLE. Christ, why did I cut his tongue out? I want to hear him scream. . . . Kill his hands! Kill his feet! Kill him inside! Make him dead! Father, father! I want to sit on his lungs!
> BODICE (*knits*). Plain, pearl, plain. She was just the same at school.

These caricature figures belong well enough to the semi-mythical world that Bond wishes to create as the starting point of his play; albeit that world has its contemporary reference, and we can glimpse something of twentieth-century cruelties and obscenities in the distorting mirror of farce. The horrible fun that Bond gets from these grotesque figures also serves some very useful purposes. Bond knows many in the audience will be familiar with the Shakespeare original. He wants in Act I to confront directly and in caricature form the extremities of cruelty and violence in *King Lear*, and, as it were, to exorcise some Shakespearian ghosts. In so doing, he prepares the ground for his own exploration of violence and oppression in Acts II and III. Moreover, as David Hirst points out, the breaking of the illusion (through Bodice's direct address to the audience), and the exaggerations of farce that accompany the terrifying scene put the audience 'on the spot', exactly as Bond intends:

> We are not allowed the relatively comfortable experience of emotional catharsis nor allowed to reject the cruelty. The laughter Bodice elicits from us both makes us accomplices and yet shocks us into a more considered response.[27]

Caryl Churchill's *Cloud Nine* provides a final example in this chapter of a play which draws most inventively and ingeniously on farce techniques, in order to link sexual politics with British Imperialism, and establish a critically alert response in the audience to these topics. C. W. Thomsen suggests an indebtedness to Joe Orton's 'polished, exuberant farce', and comments on the usefulness to Churchill of using techniques 'which may seem experimental but are in fact firmly rooted in the tradition of farce'.[28] Thus, both the laughter involved and the familiarity of the convention create a receptive climate for the radical attack she then mounts on sexual, social and racial oppression. For a convenient summary of *Cloud Nine's* opening action, I quote Hugh Rotrison, who headlined his review (again alluding to Orton) *What the Boy Saw, a Victorian colonial farce:*

> It starts in Africa where the local commissioner's family, complete with resident mother-in-law, is visited by Harry Bagley, explorer and bounder, and Mrs Saunders, a widow of amazing spirit. The cast of *Boy's Own Paper* caricatures is then permutated in pairs to show what a variety of passions throbbed behind the Imperial facade. Clive's wife, Betty melts into the arms of Harry, who has already bestowed his favours on her adolescent son, Edward, and on Clive's African boy, Joshua, though he ends up, for decency's sake, marrying the governess, Ellen, who for her part loves Betty. Cross-casting of Jim Hooper as Betty and Julie Covington as Edward underlines the artificiality of the characters who are crisply sent up by their own clichés.[29]

As with Bond's *Early Morning, Cloud Nine* uses the Victorian age as a reflecting glass to show us the attitudes of our own society; as with Stoppard's *Dirty Linen, Cloud Nine* uses stereotypes, but in such a way as to question all our assumptions about them; as

with Orton's *Loot* and *What the Butler Saw*, *Cloud Nine* uses role
reversals, men and women in drag (though in a different way) to
drive home the repressiveness of our socially conditioned roles;
and, as also in Orton's farces, this one takes delight in exploiting
cliché to call attention to the way its use perpetuates our imprisonment in out-moded and reactionary attitudes. The play's opening
immediately dispenses with any assumptions that this is to be a
straightforward naturalistic play; and it also establishes a critically
alert response in the audience. The characters, assembled under
a Union Jack on an African verandah at sundown, step forward
to address the audience in rhymed couplets as they are formally
'presented' by Clive, the white commissioner, who is, as he says,

> . . . father to the natives here
> And father to my family so dear.

First comes Clive's wife, Betty, played by a man:

> I am a man's creation as you see,
> And what men want is what I want to be;

then the native 'boy' Joshua, played by a white:

> My skin is black but oh my soul is white.
> I hate my tribe. . . . As you can see
> What white men want is what I want to be;

next, Clive's son, Edward, played by a woman, who, despite
Clive's efforts to 'teach him to grow up to be a man', declares,

> I find it rather hard as you can see;

and, finally, Clive's baby daughter, Victoria, who is merely a
dummy (pp. 7–8).

One could not imagine a more immediately effective, a more
strikingly dramatic way of establishing the socially and sexually
oppressive nature of the roles imposed on the characters than this
formalised, very funny, yet thought-provoking opening, in which
the bodies of the actors reflect the struggle between mask and face
in a white, Anglo-Saxon, male-dominated society. The farcical
action that develops arises from the increasing difficulty of the

characters in conforming to their roles. In this farcical action, Churchill's use of cliché, of the conventional phraseology associated with the stereotypes, is particularly apt. Thus Betty is the frail flower of Victorian womanhood, to whom Clive can say such things as, 'you're so delicate and sensitive,' (p. 8) and, 'so today has been all right. No fainting? No hysteria?' (p. 9) The assumed purity and innocence of women to whom sex is a dirty word is foregrounded similarly in the exchanges between Ellen and Betty in Scene five:

> ELLEN. Betty, what happens with a man? I don't know what
>   to do.
> BETTY. You just keep still.
> ELLEN. And what does he do?
> BETTY. Harry will know what to do.
> ELLEN. And is it enjoyable?
> BETTY. Ellen, you're not getting married to enjoy yourself.
>
> > (p. 36)

With a man playing Betty's role, the ludicrousness of these sentiments is made doubly obvious, as is the view of women that they reveal. We see that they are not 'natural', that for men to maintain their superiority, it is necessary to denigrate women as the weak and useless sex. Significantly, in the ball game episode (p. 18), each successful catch by Betty or Ellen provokes applause. Little is to be expected of women. Yet Edward is mocked when he slips up. That the roles are oppressive to women themselves is seen in Betty's response to Harry when he says, 'and you are safety and light and peace and home'. 'But I want to be dangerous', is her reaction (p. 15). More obviously, it is seen in the widowed Mrs Saunders, who will not conform to her expected role of bereaved gentlewoman. She shocks the company by going to see the stable boys beaten, and when Joshua is sent to see how the 'little women' are faring, she replies, 'We're very well, thank you Joshua, and how are you?' (p. 27) denying that women are any more in need of pampering than the men. The clichés that threaten to imprison others, she puts into reverse. Thus she says,

> I could never be a wife again. There is only one thing about
> marriage that I like.
>
> > (p. 34)

And to Clive, when he starts *'caressing her feet and legs'* and *'disappears completely under her skirt'*, she says, with refreshing honesty:

> I wish I didn't enjoy the sensation because I don't like you Clive. . . . I don't like you at all. But I do like the sensation.
>
> (p. 17)

Caryl Churchill further highlights the absurdity of the socially-conditioned, stereotype roles as they reveal themselves through cliché, by having Clive, as face thrusts out behind mask, utter the semi-pornographic clichés which indulge his fantasies of men as studs, ravishers or stallions. Thus he warns Mrs Saunders, when she gallops off into the bush, 'You will be raped by cannibals. . . . if you were shot with poisoned arrows. . . . I'd fuck your dead body and poison myself' (p. 16). While to his wife he later says, 'We must resist this dark female lust, Betty, or it will swallow us up' (p. 29). The split mentality whereby women are either plaster saints to be sentimentally coddled, or abandoned harlots to serve the fantasies of their men, could not be more clearly – or amusingly – indicated.

If women have to be conditioned to certain ways of behaving, so do the men, with farcical results in the case of Edward, with his interest in dolls and necklaces, and of Harry Bagley, the gay explorer who is forced to conform outwardly to the expected role of romantic bachelor. The ludicrous and oppressive nature of the role forced upon him is highlighted by Churchill in three ways. There is the slightly over-the-top use of cliché in his playing of the role, as when he says to Betty, on his return from the jungle, 'You have been thought of where no white woman has ever been thought of before' (p. 15). Or, to Clive:

> A chap can only go on so long alone. I can climb mountains and go down rivers, but what's it for? For Christmas and England and games and women singing. This is the empire, Clive. It's not me putting a flag in new lands. It's you. The empire is one big family. I'm one of its black sheep, Clive. And I know you think my life is rather dashing. But I want you to know I admire you. This is the empire, Clive, and I serve it. With all my heart.
>
> (pp. 19–20)

There are the ironic and startling volte-faces, when suddenly the mask is dispensed with, and brutal frankness replaces cliché: thus, after the opening scene with Betty, in which Harry expresses his 'worship' of her, he nonchantly turns to Joshua and says, 'Shall we go in a barn and fuck? It's not an order' (p. 16). This is all the funnier, since it is the first indication the audience have had of his real sexual preference. And there is, finally, the fact that Churchill dramatises in the action of the play the full repressiveness of the sexual pigeon-hole Harry is forced into, when he and Ellen (who has a lesbian attachment to Betty) are compelled to marry each other to cover up their real inclinations. This 'closing of the trap' is set in motion in an extremely funny sequence, in Scene four, where the farcical ingredients of role-playing, social embarrass-ment, misunderstanding, and the conflict between mask and face all play their part. Clive's extolling of the comradeship of men and his distrust of women lead Harry to think he shares his sexual orientation. Whereupon he makes a pass. Clive reacts with horror, and Harry's hasty retreat, self-condemnation, and readiness to contemplate marriage point up the way social oppression can create self-oppression and self-hatred:

CLIVE. My God, Harry, how disgusting.
HARRY. You will not betray my confidence.
CLIVE. I feel contaminated.
HARRY. I struggle against it. You cannot imagine the shame. I have tried everything to save myself.
CLIVE. The most revolting perversion. Rome fell, Harry, and this sin can destroy an empire.
HARRY. It is not a sin, it is a disease.
CLIVE. A disease more dangerous than diptheria. Effeminacy is contagious. How I have been deceived. Your face does not look degenerate. Oh Harry, how did you sink to this?
HARRY. Clive, help me, what am I to do?
CLIVE. You have been away from England too long.
HARRY. Where can I go except into the jungle to hide?
CLIVE. You don't do it with the natives, Harry? My God, what a betrayal of the Queen.
HARRY. Clive, I am like a man born crippled. Please help me.
CLIVE. You must repent.
HARRY. I have thought of killing myself.
CLIVE. That is a sin too.

HARRY. There is no way out. Clive, I beg of you do not betray my confidence.

CLIVE. I cannot keep a secret like this. Rivers will be named after you, it's unthinkable. You must save yourself from depravity. You must get married. You are not unattractive to women. What a relief that you and Betty were not after all – good God, how disgusting. Now Mrs Saunders. She's a woman of spirit, she could go with you on your expeditions.

HARRY. I suppose getting married wouldn't be any worse than killing myself.

(pp. 33–4)

Sexual oppression relates very directly to colonial oppression. Clive's opening address to the audience links the native population and his own family, as alike subject to his paternalist authority:

I am a father to the natives here
And father to my family so dear.

(p. 7)

Later, when Maud is anxious about Betty's health, the link is again apparent in Clive's reproof, 'I look after Her Majesty's domains, I think you can trust me to look after my wife' (p. 11). That Joshua is played by a white man establishes visually, of course, that Clive and his family see him as white, reject his environment, and refuse to acknowledge any of the natives' rights and values. Joshua himself is almost completely brainwashed into accepting this artificial role as inferior white. However, there is a significant moment when Joshua tells Edward (in Scene four) a tribal creation myth that belongs to his own people, despite rejecting it in the next breath for the 'truth' of missionary accounts of Adam and Eve. And, when his parents are killed by British soldiers putting down a tribal uprising, Churchill uses the concluding tableau of Act I (as Clive delivers an asinine speech celebrating the pious fraud of Harry's marriage to Ellen) to suggest the impending crack-up of colonialism. The stage direction reads,

While he is speaking JOSHUA raises his gun to shoot CLIVE. Only

*EDWARD sees. He does nothing to warn the others. He puts his hands
over his ears. BLACK.*

(p. 38)

It is, also and more immediately, an effective signal that points
forward to Act II of the play, in which Churchill changes the
dramatic technique for a more naturalistic presentation of life in
contemporary London. Churchill explains the contrast between
the two Acts in her Introduction to the play:

> The second act is set in London in 1979 – this is where I wanted
> the play to end up, in the changing sexuality of our own time.
> Betty is middle-aged, Edward and Victoria have grown up. A
> hundred years have passed, but for the characters only twenty-
> five years. There were two reasons for this. I felt the first act
> would be stronger set in Victorian times, at the height of colon-
> ialism, rather than in Africa during the 1950s. And when the
> company talked about their childhoods and the attitudes to sex
> and marriage that they had been given when they were young,
> everyone felt that they had received very conventional, almost
> Victorian expectations and that they had made great changes
> and discoveries in their lifetimes.

The contrasting techniques of the two acts relate in part to Churchill's feeling for the difference between past and present; as she
goes on to say:

> The first act, like the society it shows, is male-dominated and
> firmly structured. In the second act, more energy comes from
> the women and the gays. The uncertainties and changes of
> society, and a more feminine and less authoritarian feeling, are
> reflected in the looser structure of the act. Betty, Edward and
> Victoria all change from the rigid positions they had been left
> in by the first act, partly because of their encounters with Gerry
> and Lin.

But there is a more important reason why the tight structure and
laughter-provoking techniques of farce are necessary to Act I, but
are replaced by a looser, more naturalistic approach in Act II. The
farcical techniques, as I suggested earlier, win the audience over
by their familiarity, but in doing so, encourage a questioning,

sceptical view of conventional authority and accepted codes of behaviour. That response hopefully established, the naturalism of the second act does not represent a complete change of tack by the dramatist. If it did, there would be a danger that the antithetical structure of the play would be lost, and the active involvement of the audience in comparing and contrasting, and following through the questions raised in Act I would not occur. So Churchill maintains alertness and 'distance' in two ways: there is the hundred year time-jump which only ages the characters twenty-five years. And there is a continuation of role swopping and cross-sexual role casting in Act II. Thus, in the original Joint Stock production, the actress who played Edward in Act I, played Betty in Act II, and the actor playing Clive in Act I played Lin's four year old daughter in Act II. As in Act I, there is a rationale and purpose behind this kind of role switch. To quote Caryl Churchill again:

> Betty is now played by a woman as she gradually becomes real to herself. Cathy is played by a man, partly as a simple reversal of Edward being played by a woman, partly because the size and presence of a man on stage seemed appropriate to the emotional force of young children.

The structure and dramatic techniques of *Cloud Nine*, then, actively invite the audience to compare and contrast past and present, to note what is like and unlike. In the second act, we are shown a society in process of change, becoming more self-aware, less easily conditioned by gender roles, class barriers and stereotypes. Churchill doesn't suggest for a moment that coming to terms with the new freedoms is easy. There is much humour and pathos in, for example, Betty's painful progress towards self-understanding; or in the co-existence in Martin of enlightened support for women's liberation and self-centred male chauvinism; or in Edward's gradual realisation that a wifely role-model in his gay relationship with Gerry is not the most appropriate one. Progress, albeit slow and painful, is made, and that progress is appropriately reflected in the dramatic mode Churchill adopts. The characters, no longer imprisoned like puppets in the tight structure of farce, are diverse and unpredictable, with the diversity and unpredictability of life in a changing society, where the individual must seek his own identity, rather than accept an 'off-the-peg' role-model.

9
Conclusion

Having examined a representative selection of farces, we are now in a better position to consider what seem to be the recurrent characteristics of the genre.

Simon Callow uses the image of a spinning top to define that stage in rehearsing a play when the separate parts begin to come together: 'a spinning top which doesn't hum until it reaches a particular speed'.[1] That image seems to me to be particularly relevant to farce, to the writing of it as well as to the playing of it. If a farce is to hum like a spinning top, the writer must take a delight in pushing things to extremes. This will be evident in the accelerating pace of the action, the multiplication of misunderstandings, reversals, and confusions of identity, and often also in the inventive prodigality of the playwright, a juggler's ability to keep a great many balls in the air at once.

Thus we have the multiple pregnancies in *She's Done It Again*, the four identical brothers in *One for the Pot*, three men identically disguised as stage Turks in *Simple Spymen*, the seeming revelation that all the world is gay in *Run for Your Wife*, the removal in *Black Comedy*, not just of one or two objects, but of all the furniture in the room, the scale of Maddie Gotobed's reported sexual conquests in *Dirty Linen*, and Orton's use of all the varieties of sexuality in *What the Butler Saw*: buggery, necrophilia, lesbianism, hermaphroditism, rape, sado-masochism, fetishism, transvestism, nymphomania, and incest as well as 'straight' sexual intercourse.

'Taking things to the limit' will also be apparent in that plots and stratagems will invariably go wrong, misadventures, unfortunate coincidences and ruinous encounters will multiply; and the worst that can happen in a given situation will be guaranteed to happen. As Brian Rix puts it, 'a good farce . . . always threatens ultimate catastrophe, and this is what sustains the dramatic tension'.[2] The statement echoes Orton's observation that 'a sense of persistent danger' is crucial to farce,[3] Shaffer's comment on the Peking Opera sword fight which gave him the idea for *Black Comedy*, 'wildly funny and wildly dangerous' (see Chapter 7, note 1) and Bentley's 'danger is omnipresent' (see Chapter 1, note 37). One thinks of the desperate attempts the actors make to salvage the sinking ship of 'Nothing On' during its provinical tour in *Noises Off*, risking every kind of humiliation and physical damage; the tension created as disaster is fractionally averted again and again in moving the furniture out of the darkened room in *Black Comedy*, the hairsbreadth margin between giving the game away, and maintaining the deception when D'Arcy is cross-examined at Scotland Yard in *Plunder*.

However, commonplace, credible surroundings are important as the starting point in farce; in which, typically, ordinary people will be caught up in extraordinary goings-on. Again, to quote Brian Rix:

> The play must begin very firmly on the ground. So many bad farces start off with a ridiculous situation and flop because they fail to establish a contrast between farcical development and stable background.[4]

If that recognisable world is one in which authority figures loom large, and/or settled and regular routines are firmly laid down, so much the better for the disruptive effect when the routines come unstuck and the authority figures are flouted, put at risk or go on the rampage. One has only to think here of the army in *Reluctant Heroes*, the law in *The Magistrate*, the church in *Dandy Dick* and *One for the Pot*, school in *The Schoolmistress*, doctors, psychiatrists, nurses and policemen in *Loot* and *What the Butler Saw*, MPs in *Dirty Linen*, theatre directors in *Noises Off*, and MI5 in *Simple Spymen*.

On such groundwork, the farce-writer can effectively build. The background and initial premises established, he will increase the pace and complicate the action, entangling the victims in humiliating or desperate situations, creating an anarchic world in which authority, order and morality are all under threat. In this world a degree of manic activity will be evident, induced by the accelerating momentum of the action, and involving frequently the harassment of those caught up in it almost beyond the bounds of reason.

The simplest, classic expression of this manic activity is some kind of chase sequence. Chases from room to room, in and out of cupboards, and up and down stairs occur variously in *A Bit Between the Teeth*, *One for the Pot*, and *Noises Off*, *Simple Spymen* is virtually an extended chase sequence, involving foreign agents, army officers, and the inventor of a supposed secret weapon; the titles of Ray Cooney's two farces, *Chase Me Comrade* and *Run For Your Wife* indicate the primacy of the chase in the actions of the plays; in Pinero's *The Magistrate* the convergence of all the characters who should under no circumstances meet each other, on a single room in the Hôtel des Princes is a form of 'chase', or 'follow my leader'; and in a more leisurely way, but still providing the momentum of the action, is the knock-on effect of the wrecking progress of Susannah and Trevor from one bedroom to another in *Bedroom Farce*.

More generally, there is involved in the action of most farces a necessity to maintain appearances, to preserve a respectable facade as events spiral out of control. In trying to contain the uncontainable, explain the inexplicable, thrust the genie of misrule back into the bottle from which it's been released, disguises and role-playing are often forced upon the actors: In Pinero, Miss Dyott's double life as the schoolmistress and a musical comedy singer presupposes that from the start; in *Dandy Dick*, more gradually, the real face of the compulsive gambler appears through the dean's mask of churchly rectitude; Brian Rix's Protean disguises in *One For the Pot*, and his successive appearances in *Chase Me Comrade* as naval commander, a tiger, a man ten foot tall and a ballet dancer, are more extreme versions of the role-playing demanded by the exigencies of the plot. Then, too, as the action accelerates, quick-witted improvisations of dialogue or action become essential, and the characters are propelled into frantic activity to keep one step ahead of disaster. (One thinks, for example, of Queckett in *The Schoolmistress* trying to pretend that Miss Dyott's pupils are his nieces, Gerald and Clive's attempts to conceal the presence of an attractive girl in the house in *Rookery Nook*, Fred and Alf parrying the cross-examination of Colonel Wagstaff in *Dry Rot*.) As Gassner and Quin observe:

> The cast (of a typical farce) is in continual flux with new arrivals and sudden departures. The precipitous entrance and exit are the most common stage directions in farce. They enhance the instability of the action; they intensify the bustle; they foster a

feeling in the on-lookers of uncertainty. Anything can happen next and probably will.[5]

Representative examples here might be Reaper's embarrassing re-appearances when least expected in Act 1 of *A Bit Between the Teeth*; the successive appearances of the Bishop in Act II of *She's Done it Again*, all at highly inopportune moments; the manic exits and entrances of Nick, Geraldine, Mrs Prentice, Sergeant Match and the two psychiatrists in the climactic moments of Act II of *What the Butler Saw*.

The activity generated also clearly involves a variety of comic routines and business (or 'lazzi') using the physical skills of the actors. There is the choreography of removing the furniture in *Black Comedy*; the assemble-it-yourself dressing table business *Bedroom Farce*; the collapsing piano-stool and coat-changing routines of *Simple Spymen*; Dr. Prentices' attempts in *What The Butler Saw* to hide incriminating underclothes and high-heeled shoes in a variety of incongruous places; the routines Travers and Lynn between them thought up for the Aldwych farces; the expertly managed business of the dinner scene in *The Magistrate:* and so on.

It is worth reiterating at this point, that the helpless merriment a good farce can generate at certain moments usually depends on the principles of repetition and accumulation, which in turn weaken the resistance of the audience, and make their laughter easier to trigger off. On one funny misunderstanding, a second is built that is funnier, and a third funnier still. As I suggested in relation to *Run For Your Wife*, there can be a growing volume of laughter, not to be measured by the impact of single lines taken in isolation, but very much a product of the momentum and pace of the action (see Chapter 5).

Pace is also a factor in not allowing the audience to examine too closely the 'probable improbabilities' of the plot, or to identify too closely with any one character. The primacy of action in farce requires the playwright to create, as a general rule, character in broad outline, figures, as I suggest in Chapter 7, 'who have a representative significance, who will signal immediately, the mannerism of speech or behaviour, what they are like'. Geraldine McEwan, interviewed by Simon Trussler concerning her roles in Orton's *Loot* and Feydeau's *La Puce à l'Oreille (A Flea in Her Ear)*, compares the characterisation to 'a good caricature, which catches the essentials of personality but hasn't the complexity of the true portrait';⁶ and Sybil Thorndike in the same interview, corroborates this view: 'In a farce, characters are never *quite* real people.'⁷

The farces I have discussed contain, in fact, many examples of stereotypes: the comic charlady, the fiery Prussian, in Travers's *Rookery Nook*, the horsey Georgiana Tidman, and the military suitors in *Dandy Dick*, the gay antique dealer in *Black Comedy*. But this does not mean that they cannot be used inventively and amusingly, nor that they are not precisely calculated for their contribution to the overall action. Moreover, where a working association exists between a 'house' dramatist and team of actors, an opportunity occurs to use a particular actor's 'persona' or 'stereotype' in a creative way. Thus Travers offers successive incarnations of the 'silly ass' figure for Ralph Lynn, the meek-and-mild victim for Robertson Hare, the man-about-town type for Tom Walls. And the Whitehall dramatists use Brian Rix in a succession of parts in which he is the well-meaning, sometimes rather gormless innocent valiantly trying to cope with successive disasters or humiliations.

Moreover, a number of contemporary dramatists experimenting with the genre, have taken delight in using stereotypes only to subvert them, as occurs in Stoppard's *Dirty Linen* and Churchill's *Cloud Nine;* or, in the case of Orton, firmly substituting for a stereotype (in this case a gay one) characters who resist pigeon-holing and abide by no rules (as is the case with Hal and Dennis in *Loot*).

At first glance, Pinero, in his central characters, and Ayckbourn, with his couples in *Bedroom Farce*, adopt a more naturalistic approach to character. But closer examination indicates that, in Pinero, the concept of mask and face, or role-playing, is what creates the light and shade in the Dean, the Magistrate and the Schoolmistress. And, In Ayckbourn, an element of exaggeration points up the childish games of Malcolm and Kate, the intensity of Trevor and Susannah, the old-fashioned conservatism of Ernest and Delia and the trendy sophistication of Nick and Jan. Ayckbourn examines his couples, like a social anthropologist quizzically noting the strangeness of marriage tribal habits in Great Britain.

Farce, as I stated earlier, is essentially a non-naturalistic mode, though an element of paradox is involved here; for the strategy of most farce writers is to use at least some of the trappings of realism, and to beguile an audience with the familiar and the

ordinary, before introducing the extraordinary. There is the recognisable world and characters with which the farce conventionally
begins; there are the detailed furnishings and everyday props of
a domestic interior, set cosily in the frame of the proscenium arch;
there is also the indebtedness of the genre in this century to the
familiar mechanics of the well-made play. But what is then offered
in the action of the play is an undermining of this recognisable
world, a shaking of it to its foundations. The genre works from
within, as it were, to subvert and question what is conventionally
accepted or known; at its best, it confounds and disrupts, it makes
the ordinary into the extraordinary.

It is not surprising, then, that farce often draws attention to its
artifice in a variety of ways: there is the farce-within-a-farce of
Noises Off, requiring the audience of that play to double as the
audience of *Nothing On;* there is the use of melodramatic conventions within the farce in *Dandy Dick* and *The Schoolmistress* and the
direct address to the audience that Pinero employs at the end of
his farce; the stylised choreography of many stage directions (in
Pinero, Shaffer and others); a deliberate calling of the audience's
attention to the nonsense element in a situation or a spoken exchange (in many of the Whitehall farces). There is also the recurrent
way in which farce makes use of the double act, the pairing of two
'comedians' who set each other off. Darbey and Tanver provide an
early example in *Dandy Dick*. The Lynn/Wall partnership in the
Travers farces provides an obvious example. So do Brian Rix's
pairings with John Slater in *Dry Rot*, with Leo Franklyn in *Simple
Spymen*, and with Jimmy Logan in *A Bit Between The Teeth*. The
tradition is maintained with the pairings of John Smith and Stanley
Gardner in *Run for Your Wife* (played in the first performances by
Richard Briers and Bernard Cribbins, subsequently by Terry Scott
and Eric Sykes). Even in Orton, as Maurice Charney says of *Loot*,

> the whole play is delightfully self-conscious about its own means
> of expression. The actors are always performers. . . . The play
> is divided into jokers and straight men without regard to other
> character functions.[8]

Allied to this are other forms of debt to the music hall tradition:
the use of double entendre (*She's Done It Again*), catch-phrases
(*Rookery Nook*), a badness or obviousness in the humour itself,
with the audience tacitly invited to savour the depths to which

the script can descend (*Simple Spymen*), the conversation at cross-purposes, and a playfulness with language itself, what Pearl Binder describes as 'verbal buffoonery, a juggling with the sound and sense of words' (see Chapter 4, note 33) which we see employed in simple form in the Ben Travers and Whitehall farces, and in more sophisticated forms in Stoppard, Pinero and Orton.

Earlier in this study, I quoted Shaffer's comment on the tension 'between the Apollonian and the Dionysian sides of life . . . the violence of instinct . . . the desire for order and restraint' (see Chapter 7, note 2). And I related this to the hilariously anarchic disorder which gradually prevails in *Black Comedy*, on the one hand, and to Shaffer's controlling sense of design on the other. It is interesting to find Orton, too, using these terms:

> I always say to myself that the theatre is the Temple of Dionysus, and not Apollo. You do the Dionysus thing on your typewriter, and then you allow a little Apollo in, just a little to shape and guide it along certain lines you may want to go along. But you can't allow Apollo in completely.[9]

Clearly there is an irony that Orton is alert to in the paradox that farce involves – the disciplined expression of anarchy; the logical presentation of a crazy world; but, significantly, he indicates a wish to remain, as far as possible, true to chaos; and he is thinking particularly, I suggest, of the overall effect of farce. His sense of the right kind of balance (with the scales weighted in favour or Dionysus) is relevant not only to his own work, but to farce generally. The prevalent assumption that farce, is on the whole, a conventional form, and that the typical farce, after its holiday from normality, ends with a restoration of the status quo, has, throughout this study, been held up to question and often found wanting. Pinero's sharp critical eye for hypocrisy in high places, and for the repressive roles endured by women in Victorian society, show the farceur as social critic. The end of *The Schoolmistress* strikes a blow against convention. The anarchic notes on which Travers's farces end are disruptive, not supportive, of the status quo. In the Whitehall and post-Whitehall farces, we have the trickster trapped in his trickery at the ends of *Chase Me Comrade* and *Run For Your Wife*, and the whole process of victimising Fogg about to start again at the end of *A Bit Between the Teeth*. The forces of respectability and morality are put to rout at the ends of *Black*

Comedy and Dirty Linen. Orton, of course, is pre-eminent, as Maurice Charney says, as the critic and satirist of 'all the values that straight middle-class society most cherishes'.[10] Caryl Churchill, in *Cloud Nine*, uses farce in an Ortonesque way to question and subvert conventional sexual roles, and Bond in *Early Morning*, as well as Churchill in *Cloud Nine*, relate sexual repression to political oppression. Certainly Orton, Churchill and Bond are more subversive and questioning of their societies than Pinero, Travers or the Whitehall dramatists of theirs. But the difference is one of degree, not of kind. The good farceur does indeed 'allow a little Apollo in', but his real allegiance is to Dionysus and the lessons he can teach.

As to the curious idea, quoted in Chapter 1, that 'the situations in farce do not mean anything', it is clear, I think, from the above, how wide of the mark that statement is; even where there is no overt satirical edge, no ambiguous or disturbing ending, farce explores and dramatises a universal conflict between id and ego, the rational and the animal, the social mask and the real face, authority or convention and freedom. It acts out and gives expression to our wilder and more anarchic imaginings and impulses, though it does so under the watchful and controlling eye of the playwright, who must exercise all his structural skill and technique to orchestrate the anarchy. Moreover, it is a genre to which the modern age is peculiarly responsive. As L. C. Pronko acutely observes in his study of Eugène Labiche and Georges Feydeau,

> After two world wars, Existentialism, the Absurd, we are particularly sensitive now to dimensions of farce which the nineteenth century could not have recognised. In his . . . *Laughter* . . . Bergson declares that the purpose of comedy is to correct mankind. Since comedies of character and manners accomplish this, they are unmistakably superior to farce, which only shows the mechanism of things, of life itself, and obviously cannot correct anything. Today we feel that this very mechanism of things has become such a terrifying reality that farce suddenly turns out to be the most metaphysical of comic forms, leaving far behind it the more prestigious classical modes which are merely social.[11]

Briefly now to sum up what have been some of the aims of this study. In examining a selection of farces from the 1880s to the 1980s, I have traced a number of influences, connections and relationships: Pinero's indebtedness to French farce; the extent to which Travers drew on Pinero, and the Whitehall farce writers on Travers; the impact of Orton's work; music-hall influences generally; and the adaptation by 'serious' dramatists of farce techniques to their own purposes. I have tried to analyse the humour, theatricality and meaningfulness of farce in this period, and to rescue it from some of the false assumptions still made about the genre. And what I hope, finally, may have emerged, is the continuing vitality of farce, the inventiveness of its practitioners, and the extent to which they have been able to 'make it new'. That applies to all the dramatists here discussed. For them, as for Meyerhold – to repeat the words quoted at the beginning of this study – 'the idea of the actor's art, based on a worship of mask, gesture and movement, is indissolubly linked with the idea of the farce. The farce is eternal'.

Appendix: a Chronological List of Plays

1885	A. W. Pinero, *The Magistrate*
1886	A. W. Pinero, *The Schoolmistress*
1887	A. W. Pinero, *Dandy Dick*
1926	Ben Travers, *Rookery Nook*
1927	Ben Travers, *Thark*
1928	Ben Travers, *Plunder*
1950	Colin Morris, *Reluctant Heroes*
1954	John Chapman, *Dry Rot*
1958	John Chapman, *Simple Spymen*
1958	Harold Pinter, *The Birthday Party*
1960	Harold Pinter, *The Caretaker*
1961	Ray Cooney, Tony Hilton, *One For the Pot*
1964	Ray Cooney, *Chase Me Comrade*
1964	Joe Orton, *Entertaining Mr Sloane*
1965	Harold Pinter, *The Homecoming*
1965	Peter Shaffer, *Black Comedy*
1967	Joe Orton, *Loot*
1968	Edward Bond, *Narrow Road to the Deep North*
1968	Edward Bond, *Early Morning*
1969	Joe Orton, *What the Butler Saw*
1969	Michael Pertwee, *She's Done It Again*
1971	Edward Bond, *Lear*
1974	Michael Pertwee, *A Bit Between the Teeth*
1975	Alan Ayckbourn, *Bedroom Farce*
1976	Tom Stoppard, *Dirty Linen*
1979	Caryl Churchill, *Cloud Nine*
1982	Michael Frayn, *Noises Off*
1983	Ray Cooney, *Run For Your Wife*

Notes

CHAPTER 1: THE NATURE OF FARCE

1. Jonathan Culler, Structuralist Poetics (New York, 1975) p. 116.
2. Heather Dubrow, Genre (London and New York, 1982) p. 37.
3. Ibid., pp. 28–9.
4. David Hirst, Comedy of Manners (London, 1979) pp. 96–109.
5. L. J. Potts, Comedy (London, 1948) p. 151.
6. Allardyce Nicoll, The Theatre and Dramatic Theory (Connecticut, 1962) p. 88.
7. Cleanth Brooks and R. B. Heilman (eds), Understanding Drama: Twelve Plays (New York, 1945) pp. 138–9.
8. V. Meyerhold, 'Farce' in R. W. Corrigan (ed.), Theater in the Twentieth Century (New York, 1963) pp. 205–6.
9. G. B. Shaw, Our Theatre in the Nineties (London, 1932), vol. II, p. 120.
10. Jessica Milner Davies, Farce (London, 1978) pp. 2–7.
11. Ibid., p. 6.
12. Ibid., p. 1.
13. Oxford Companian to the Theatre, quoted in Eric Bentley, The Life of the Drama (London, 1965) p. 227.
14. Encyclopedia Britannica, 11th ed., c.v. Farce.
15. J. M. Brown in Saturday Review of Literature, 24 Mar. 1951, p. 26, quoted Leo Hughes, A Century of English Farce, p. 20.
16. Davis, p. 22.
17. N. R. Shapiro (introd.) Feydeau, Four Farces (Chicago, 1972) p. xi.
18. Quoted in J. Adamson, Groucho, Harpo, Chico and sometimes Zeppo (London, 1973) p. 165.
19. Walter Kerr, Tragedy and Comedy (New York 1967) p. 182.
20. Simon Trussler (introd.) New English Dramatists 13 (London, 1969) p. 11.
21. Morton Guewitch, Comedy: the Irrational Vision (Cornel, 1975) p. 234.
22. Eric Bentley, 'The Psychology of Farce (introd.) Let's Get a Divorce, and Other Plays (New York, 1958) p. x.
23. Adamson, Groucho etc., p. 156.
24. Davis, p. 27.
25. Eric Bentley, The Life of the Drama (London, 1965) p. 240.
26. Ibid., pp. 240–1.
27. Kerr, p. 16.
28. Davis, p. 85.

29. Ibid., p. 17.
30. Leo Hughes, *A Century of English Farce* (Princeton, 1956) p. vi.
31. Peter Shaffer, 'A Times Profile', *The Times*, 28 Apr. 1980, p. 7.
32. Ben Travers, *A-sitting on a Gate* (London, 1978) p. 94.
33. Quoted in Shapiro, *Four Farces*, p. xvii.
34. Henri Bergson, 'Le Rire', in Wylie Sypher (ed.), *Comedy* (New York, 1956) p. 112.
35. Bentley, 'Psychology of Farce', p. xx.
36. Quoted in Martin Esslin, *The Theatre of the Absurd* (Penguin, 1968) p. 184.
37. Quoted in Shapiro, *Four Farces*, p. xxxiv.
38. M. R. Booth (ed.), *English Plays of the 19th Century*, vol. IV (London, 1973) p. 13.
39. John Russell Taylor, *The Rise and Fall of the Well-Made Play* (London, 1967) p. 17.
40. Quoted in Shapiro, *Four Farces*, p. xxiii.
41. Ibid., p. xix.
42. Shaffer interview, *Sunday Times*, 29 July 1973.
43. R. W. Corrigan (ed.) *Roman Drama* (New York, 1966) pp. 11–12.
44. Bentley, 'Psychology of Farce', p. xiv., p. ix.
45. Quoted in John Lahr, *Prick Up Your Ears* (London, 1978) p. 272.

CHAPTER 2: A. W. PINERO AND THE COURT FARCES

1. W. D. Dunkel, *Sir Arthur Pinero* (Chicago, 1941) p. 42.
2. Quoted Michael Billington, programme note, Chichester Festival production of *Dandy Dick*, Oct. 1973.
3. Michael Coveney, *Financial Times*, from *London Theatre Record*, vol. 6, no. 20, p. 1074.
4. Michael Billington, programme note, *Dandy Dick*.
5. Leo Hughes, p. vi.
6. Quoted Dunkel, p. 95.
7. Dunkel, p. 28.
8. Hesketh Pearson, *The Last Actor-Managers* (London, 1950) p. 30.
9. Dunkel, p. 4.
10. Booth, p. 14.
11. Ibid., p. 34.
12. G. B. Shaw, *Our Theatre in the Nineties* (London, 1932) vol. II, p. 121.
13. John Russell Taylor, *The Rise and Fall of the Well-Made Play* (London, 1967) p. 56.
14. Martin Meisel, *Shaw and the Nineteenth Century Theatre* (London, 1963) p. 252.
15. Bentley, *The Life of the Drama*, pp. 242–3.
16. Ibid., p. 242.
17. Hamilton Fyfe, *Sir Arthur Pinero's Plays and Players* (London, 1930) p. 35.
18. Bergson, quoted in Kerr, *Tragedy and Comedy*, p. 243.
19. Booth, p. 36.

20. Walter Lazenby, *Arthur Wing Pinero* (New York, 1972) p. 50.
21. Fyfe, p. 46.
22. Ben Travers, *A-Sitting on a Gate* (London, 1978) p. 63.

CHAPTER 3: BEN TRAVERS AND THE ALDWYCH FARCES

1. Ben Travers, *A-Sitting on a Gate* (London, 1978) p. 64. (For subsequent quotation from this work in Chapter 3, page references are inserted in the text.)
2. Kerr, *Tragedy and Comedy*, p. 176.
3. Ben Travers, *Vale of Laughter* (London, 1957) p. 152.
4. Ibid., p. 152.
5. Kerr, p. 177.
6. G. S. Fraser, 'Travers, Ben; in James Vinson (ed.), *Great Writers of the English Language: Dramatists* (London, 1979) pp. 579–80.
7. Macqueen Pope, *An Indiscreet Guide to TheatreLand* (Muse Arts Ltd, London, 1947) pp. 35–6.
8. Ibid., p. 36.
9. Ibid., p. 36.
10. *The Times*, Review, 23 Dec. 1933, p. 86.
11. Browning, *Poetical Works 1833–1864* (Oxford, 1970) p. 656.
12. *The Times* review, 23 Dec. 1933, p. 86.
13. George Orwell, 'The Art of Donald McGill' in *Collected Essays, Journalism and Letters of George Orwell* (London, 1968) vol. II, p. 164.
14. Travers, *Vale of Laughter*, pp. 35–6.

CHAPTER 4: BRIAN RIX AND THE WHITEHALL FARCES

1. *The Times*, Review, 20 Mar. 1958, p. 3.
2. Quoted in Brian Rix, *My Farce From My Elbow* (London, 1975) p. 136.
3. Bamber Gascoigne, *The Observer*, 19 July 1964, p. 20.
4. Ronald Bryden, *New Statesman*, 24 July 2964, p. 126.
5. Brian Rix, *My Farce From My Elbow* (London, 1975) p. 70.
6. Jessica M. Davies, *Farce* (London, 1978) p. 25.
7. Beverley Baxter, *Evening Standard*, quoted Rix, p. 92.
8. Colin Morris, quoted Rix, p. 90.
9. Ivor Brown, *The Observer*, quoted Rix, p. 93.
10. Rix, *My Farce From My Elbow*, p. 75. (For subsequent quotation from this work in Chapters 4 and 5, page references are inserted in the text.)
11. Leo Hughes, *A Century of English Farce*, p. 25.
12. *The Stage*, 27 Mar. 1958, p. 13.
13. Kenneth Tynan, *The Observer*, 23 Mar. 1958, p. 15.
14. J. W. Lambert, *Sunday Times*, 23 Mar. 1958, p. 11.
15. Alan Dent, *News Chronicle*, 20 Mar. 1958, p. 3.
16. J. W. Lambert, *Sunday Times*, 23 Mar. 1958, p. 11.
17. *The Times*, 3 Aug. 1961, p. 5.

18. Harold Hobson, *Sunday Times*, 6 Aug. 1961, p. 25.
19. *The Times*, 3 Aug. 1961, p. 5.
20. Harold Hobson, *Sunday Times*, 6 Aug. 1961, p. 25.
21. Peter Davison, *Contemporary Drama and the Popular Dramatic Tradition in England* (London, 1982) p. 52.
22. Pearl Binder, *The English Inside Out* (London, 1961) pp. 180–1.
23. *The Times*, 16 July 1964, p. 9.
24. Ronald Bryden, *New Statesman*, 24 July 1964, p. 126.
25. Harold Hobson, *Sunday Times*, 19 July 1964, p. 27.
26. Ibid., p. 27.

CHAPTER 5: POST-WHITEHALL FARCES

1. Laurence Kitchin, *Drama in the Sixties* (London 1966) pp. 194–5.
2. See S. L. Bethell, *Shakespeare and the Popular Dramatic Tradition*, reprinted in vol. 8 of *Literary Taste and Mass Communication: Theatre and Song*, ed. P. Davison, R. Meyersohn, E. Shils (Cambridge, 1978); and Peter Davison, *Contemporary Drama and the Popular Dramatic Tradition in England* (London, 1982).
3. Roger Wilmut, *Kindly Leave the Stage* (London, 1985) pp. 60–2.
4. M. R. Booth (ed.), *English Plays of the 19th Century*, p. 23.
5. Michael Coveney, *Financial Times* review, in *London Theatre Record*, vol. III, issue 7 (26 Mar.–8 Apr. 1983) p. 234.
6. Milton Shulman, *Evening Standard* review, *London Theatre Record*, p. 233.
7. Benedict Nightingale, *New Statesman* review, *London Theatre Record*, p. 234.
8. David Benedictus, *Plays and Players*, June 1983, p. 27.
9. Sue Jameson, *London Broadcasting* review, *London Theatre Record*, p. 233.
10. Francis King, *Sunday Telegraph* review, *London Theatre Record*, p. 233.
11. Eric Shorter, *Daily Telegraph* review, *London Theatre Record*, p. 232.
12. Eric Bentley, 'The Psychology of Farce', p. xx.
13. Francis King, *Sunday Telegraph* review, *London Theatre Record*, p. 233.

CHAPTER 6: JOE ORTON

1. Joe Orton, quoted in John Lahr, *Prick Up Your Ears* (London, 1978) p. 160.
2. C. W. E. Bigsby, *Joe Orton* (London, 1982) p. 60.
3. Orton, quoted Lahr, p. 32.
4. Ibid., pp. 274–5.
5. Joe Orton, *Transatlantic Review*, 24, spring 1967, p. 96.
6. Quoted by James Fox. 'Joe Orton', *Sunday Times Magazine*, 22 Nov. 1970, p. 49.
7. See Chapter 1, note 33.
8. Orton, quoted Lahr, p. 31.

9. Ibid., p. 64.
10. Ibid., p. 232.
11. Ibid., p. 238.
12. Ibid., p. 237.
13. J. W. Lambert, *Drama: the Quarterly Theatre Review*, autumn 1975, p. 49.
14. John Russell Taylor, *The Second Wave* (London, 1971) pp. 139–40.
15. Taylor, quoted Lahr, p. 206.
16. Orton, quoted Lahr, p. 206.
17. Orton, *Transatlantic Review*, spring 1967, p. 94.
18. Bentley, 'The Psychology of Farce', op. cit., p. viii.
19. Orton, *Transatlantic Review*, p. 95.
20. Orton, quoted Lahr, p. 248.
21. Though see in this connection C. W. E. Bigsby's interesting discussion of Orton's sexual identity as 'crucial to his art' (*Joe Orton*, pp. 67–9).
22. James Joyce, *Ulysses* (London, 1967) p. 136.
23. John Lahr, Review of *Loot*, *Plays and Players*, Aug. 1975, p. 30.
24. Bentley, p. x.
25. Strindberg, *Six Plays*, trans. Elizabeth Spriggs (New York 1955) p. 193.
26. J. W. Lambert, *Drama*, autumn 1975.
27. John Lahr, Review of *What the Butler Saw*, *Plays and Players*, Sept. 1975, p. 21.
28. Bigsby, pp. 67–8.
29. Orton, quoted Simon Trussler, 'Farce', *Plays and Players*, June 1966, p. 72.
30. Lahr, *Plays and Players*, Sept. 1975, p. 23.
31. Taylor, *The Second Wave*, p. 138.
32. Lahr, p. 254.
33. Orton, quoted Trussler, *Plays and Players*, June 1966, p. 72.

CHAPTER 7: FARCE AND CONTEMPORARY DRAMA: I

1. Katharine Worth, *Revolutions in Modern English Drama* (London, 1972) p. 39.
2. Peter Shaffer, 'A Times Profile', *The Times*, 28 Apr. 1980, p. 7.
3. Ibid., p. 7.
4. Ibid., p. 7.
5. Ibid., p. 7.
6. Ibid., p. 7.
7. Ibid., p. 7.
8. Joe Orton, *Transatlantic Review*, spring 1967, p. 95.
9. Ronald Hayman, *Tom Stoppard* (London, 1977) p. 144.
10. Travers, *A-Sitting on a Gate*, p. 85.
11. Ayckbourn, quoted by Oleg Kerensky, *The New British Drama* (London, 1977) p. 1.
12. Ronald Hayman, *British Theatre since 1955* (Oxford 1979) p. 69.

13. Alan Ayckbourn, Preface, *Three Plays* (London, 1977) p. 9.
14. Hayman, *Tom Stoppard*, pp. 143–4.
15. Ibid., p. 143.
16. Jessica M. Davis, *Farce* (London, 1978) p. 17.
17. Katharine Worth, 'Farce and Michael Frayn', Modern Drama, Mar. 1983, pp. 49–50.
18. Benedict Nightingale, *New Statesman* review, *London Theatre Record* (11 Feb.–24 Feb. 1982) p. 94.
19. Worth, *Modern Drama*, p. 49.
20. Ibid., p. 50.

CHAPTER 8: FARCE AND CONTEMPORARY DRAMA: II

1. David T. Thompson, *Pinter: the Player's Playwright* (London, 1985) p. 72.
2. Peter Brook, *The Empty Space* (London, 1968) p. 73.
3. Harold Pinter, *Mac in Plays: Three* (London, 1978) p. 17.
4. Harold Pinter, 'The Knight Has Been Unruly – Memories of Sir Donald Wolfit', *The Listener* (18 Apr. 1968) p. 501.
5. Ronald Hayman, *The Set-Up* (London, 1973) p. 186.
6. For a complete list of plays in which Pinter acted from 1951 to 1959, and the roles he played in them, see Thompson, *Pinter: the Player's Playwright*.
7. Michael Billington, *The Modern Actor* (London, 1973) p. 173.
8. Thompson, *Pinter*, p. 24.
9. Peter Davison, 'Contemporary Drama and Popular Forms' in A. K. Stout (ed.), *Aspects of Drama and the Theatre* (Sydney, 1965) pp. 184–6.
10. Joe Adamson, *Groucho, Harpo, Chico and Sometimes Zeppo* (London, 1973) p. 186.
11. Ray Galton, Alan Simpson, *Hancock's Half Hour* (London, 1974) p. 101.
12. Ibid., p. 105.
13. Michael Billington, *The Modern Actor*, pp. 201–2.
14. Ibid., p. 202.
15. Guido Almansi and Simon Henderson, *Harold Pinter* (London and New York 1983) p. 56.
16. Quoted in Roger Wilmut, *Kindly Leave the Stage* (London 1985) p. 61.
17. Katharine Worth, *Revolutions in Modern English Drama*, p. 116.
18. Edward Bond, Preface, *Lear*, in *Plays Two* (London, 1978) pp. 3–7.
19. Tony Coult, *The Plays of Edward Bond* (London, 1979) p. 13.
20. Edward Bond, 'Us, Our Drama and the National Theatre', *Plays and Players*, Oct. 1978, p. 8.
21. Coult, *The Plays of Edward Bond*, p. 85.
22. Quoted in R. Hudson, C. Itzin, S. Trussler, 'Drama and the Dialectics of Violence', *Theatre Quarterly*, 2 (Jan.–Mar. 1972) p. 9.
23. David Hirst, *Edward Bond* (London, 1985) p. 106.
24. Ibid., p. 107.
25. Martin Esslin, *Brief Chronicles* (London, 1970) p. 177.

26. Quoted in 'A Discussion with Edward Bond,' *Gambit*, vol. 5, no.17, pp. 28–9.
27. Hirst, pp. 138–9.
28. C. W. Thomsen, 'Three Socialist Playwrights' in C. W. E. Bigsby (ed.) *Contemporary English Drama*, (Stratford-upon-Avon Studies 19, 1981) p. 168.
29. Hugh Rorrison, *Plays and Players*, May 1979, p. 23.

CHAPTER 9: CONCLUSION

1. Simon Callow, *Being An Actor* (London, 1985) p. 180.
2. Brian Rix, *My Farce From My Elbow* (London, 1975) p. 216.
3. Orton, quoted Simon Trussler, 'Farce', *Plays and Players*, June 1966, p. 72.
4. Rix, quoted Trussler, ibid., p. 58.
5. J. Gassner, E. Quin, *Readers Encyclopedia of World Drama* (London, 1970) p. 265.
6. Geraldine McEwan, quoted Trussler, 'Farce', p. 58.
7. Sybil Thorndike, quoted Trussler, ibid., p. 53.
8. Maurice Charney, *Joe Orton* (London, 1984) p. 87.
9. John Lahr, *Prick Up Your Ears* (London, 1978) p. 15.
10. Charney, *Joe Orton*, p. 85.
11. Leonard C. Pronko, *Eugène Labiche and Georges Feydeau*, (London, 1982) p. 167.

Bibliography

EDITIONS OF PLAYS

All page references to plays discussed are taken from the following editions:

Chapter 2

A. W. Pinero, *The Magistrate* (Samuel French, 1936).
A. W. Pinero, *The Schoolmistress*, in *Plays by A. W. Pinero*, ed. G. Rowell (Cambridge University Press, 1986).
A. W. Pinero, *Dandy Dick* (Heinemann Educational Books, 1959).

Chapter 3

Ben Travers, *Rookery Nook* (Samuel French, 1927).
Ben Travers, *Thark* (Samuel French, 1931).
Ben Travers, *Plunder* (Rex Collings, 1976).

Chapter 4

Colin Morris, *Reluctant Heroes* (English Theatre Guild, 1951).
John Chapman, *Dry Rot* (English Theatre Guild, 1956).
John Chapman, *Simple Spymen* (English Theatre Guild, 1960).
Ray Cooney, Tony Hilton, *One For The Pot* (English Theatre Guild, 1963).
Ray Cooney, *Chase Me Comrade* (English Theatre Guild, 1966).

Chapter 5

Michael Pertwee, *She's Done It Again* (English Theatre Guild, 1970).
Michael Pertwee, *A Bit Between The Teeth* (Samuel French, 1976).
Ray Cooney, *Run For Your Wife* (Samuel French, 1984).

Chapter 6

Joe Orton, *The Complete Plays* (Methuen, 1976).

Chapter 7

Peter Shaffer, *Black Comedy* (Samuel French, 1967).
Alan Ayckbourn, *Three Plays* (Penguin Books, 1979).
Tom Stoppard, *Dirty Linen & New-Found-Land* (Faber, 1976).
Michael Frayn, *Noises Off* (Methuen, 1976) (Brief references to Griffith's *Comedians* and Beckett's *Waiting for Godot* are taken from the Faber editions, 1976 and 1965 respectively.)

Chapter 8

Harold Pinter, *Plays: One* (Eyre Methuen, 1976).
Harold Pinter, *Plays: Two* (Eyre Methuen, 1978).
Edward Bond, *Plays: One* (Eyre Methuen, 1977).
Edward Bond, *Plays: Two* (Eyre Methuen, 1978).
Caryl Churchill, *Cloud Nine* (Pluto Press, London, 1979).

SELECTED CRITICISM

Almansi, G. & S. Henderson, *Harold Pinter* (London, 1983).
Bentley, Eric, *The Life of the Drama* (London, 1965).
Bigsby, C. W. E. *Joe Orton* (London, 1982).
Bigsby, C. W. E., ed., *Contemporary English Drama*, Stratford-on-Avon Studies, vol.19 (London, 1981).
Billington, Michael, *The Modern Actor* (London, 1973).
Booth, M. R. (ed.), *English Plays of the 19th Century*: vol. IV, Farce (London, 1973).
Brook, Peter, *The Empty Space* (London, 1968).
Charney, Maurice, *Joe Orton* (London, 1984).
Coult, Tony, *The Plays of Edward Bond* (London, 1978).
Davis, Jessica M., *Farce* (London, 1978).
Davison, Peter, *Contemporary Drama and the Popular Dramatic Tradition in England* (London, 1982).
Dubrow, Heather, *Genre* (London and New York, 1982).
Hayman, Ronald, *British Theatre Since 1955* (Oxford, 1979).
Hayman, Ronald, *Tom Stoppard* (London, 1977).
Hayman, Ronald, *The Set-Up* (London, 1973).
Hirst, David, *Edward Bond* (London, 1985).
Hirst, David, *Comedy of Manners* (London, 1979).
Hughes, Leo, *A Century of English Farce* (Princeton, 1956).
Kerensky, Oleg, *The New British Drama* (London, 1977).
Kerr, Walter, *Tragedy and Comedy* (New York, 1967).
Kitchin, Laurence, *Drama in the Sixties* (London, 1966).
Lahr, John, *Prick Up Your Ears* (London, 1978).
Lazenby, Walter, *A. W. Pinero* (New York, 1972).
Orton, Joe, *The Diaries* (London, 1986).
Rix, Brian, *My Farce From My Elbow* (London, 1975).
Shapiro, N. R., (introd.) *Feydeau, Four Farces* (Chicago, 1972).

Stout, A. K., ed., *Aspects of Drama and the Theatre* (Sydney, 1965).
Sypher, W., ed., *Comedy* (New York).
Taylor, John Russell, *The Rise and Fall of the Well-Made Play* (London, 1967).
Taylor, John Russell, *The Second Wave* (London, 1971).
Thompson, David T., *Pinter: the Player's Playwright* (London, 1985).
Travers, Ben, *A-Sitting on a Gate* (London, 1978).
Travers, Ben, *Vale of Laughter* (London, 1957).
Wilmut, Roger, *Kindly Leave the Stage* (London, 1985).
Worth, Katharine, *Revolutions in Modern English Drama* (London, 1972).

Index

227